quentin
tarantino

ALSO BY JAMI BERNARD

First Films: Illustrious, Obscure and
Embarrassing Movie Debuts

Total Exposure: The Movie Buff's Guide
to Celebrity Nude Scenes

quentin tarantino
the man and his movies

JAMI BERNARD

HarperPerennial
A Division of HarperCollins*Publishers*

HarperCollins books may be purchased for educational, business, or sales promotional use. For information please write: Special Markets Department, HarperCollins Publishers, Inc., 10 East 53rd Street, New York, NY 10022.

FIRST U.S. EDITION

Designed by Nancy Singer

Library of Congress Cataloging-in-Publication Data

Bernard, Jami.
   Quentin Tarantino : the man and his movies / by Jami Bernard. — 1st ed.
      p.   cm.
   ISBN 0-06-095161-3
   1. Tarantino, Quentin.   2. Motion picture producers and direc-tors—United States—Biography.   I. Title.
   PN1998.3. T358B47   1995
   791.43'0233'092—dc20   95-39167
   [B]

95 96 97 98 99 ❖/RRD 10 9 8 7 6 5 4 3 2 1

*To my mother, Gloria Bernard,
an uncommonly strong woman
who passed along her qualities,
for better or worse,
to her children*

contents

Photographs follow page 138.

acknowledgments

I owe a special debt of gratitude to Stephen Schaefer, who helped research this book and who drove around Los Angeles for hours trying to find houses Quentin lived in and video stores that no longer existed. Also, to my friends and agents, Scott and Barbara Siegel, whose constant support and enthusiasm cannot be overestimated. Dorrie Crockett had the thankless task of transcribing most of the eighty-odd interviews conducted for this book—one of them was five and a half hours long—including figuring out how to render the specifics of Quentin's different laughs.

While writing this book, I was constantly amazed by the generosity of the actors, filmmakers and behind-the-scenes people who gave so willingly of their time to talk about Quentin. Harvey Weinstein opened the files and resources of Miramax to me. Bumble Ward and her staff, plus the staff of the William Morris Agency, seemed to be on twenty-four-hour call for whatever materials I needed, from phone numbers to scripts. Connie Zastoupil was always ready to talk endlessly about her son, even though her own life story proves just as interesting. Eric Stoltz did his interview while on vacation in the Caribbean; John Travolta gave up time while he was supposed to be memorizing lines for a morning shoot. An impeccably gracious

Oliver Stone flew to New York so that we could meet face-to-face, despite that review I wrote of *Heaven and Earth*. A heartfelt thanks to the following people who gave or arranged interviews, or who provided some form of research, including the guy who downloaded eight hundred pages of Quentin gossip from the Internet:

Interviews:

Allison Anders, Patricia Arquette, Rosanna Arquette, Roger Avary, Lawrence Bender, Jan Bohusch, Terence Chang, Mike Fleming, Allen Garfield, Richard Gladstein, Carlin Glynn, Carlos Goodman, Craig Hamman, Piers Handling, Jeff Hill, Dennis Hopper, Samuel L. Jackson, Cathryn Jaymes, Harvey Keitel, Catalaine Knell, Robert Kurtzman, Craig Ledbetter, James Le Gros, Victoria Lucai, Bill Lustig, Michael Madsen, Liz Manne, Stanley Margolis, Jerry Martinez, Steve Martinez, Peter McAlevey, Dylan McDermott, Don Murphy, Richard Peña, Bronson Pinchot, Stevo Polyi, Ving Rhames, Alexandre Rockwell, Robert Rodriguez, Tim Roth, Michelle Satter, Barbara Scharres, Tony Scott, Stacey Sher, Mike Simpson, Christian Slater, Scott Spiegel, Erica Steinberg, Eric Stoltz, Oliver Stone, Cynthia Swartz, Ella Taylor, Uma Thurman, Tony Timpone, Nancy Travis, John Travolta, Rand Vossler, Russell Vossler, Rowland Wafford, Jeremy Walker, Bumble Ward, Bob Weinstein, Harvey Weinstein, Michael Weldon, Mike White, David E. Williams, Bruce Willis, John Woo, Connie Zastoupil, Paul Zimmerman.

Research:

Michelle Bega, David Bianculli, Marion Billings, Larry Blaustein, Paul Bloch, Chris Bowen, Dwight Brown, Doug Buffo, Dorrie Crockett, Susan Cully, Ralph Donnelly, Marianne Goldstein, Steve Gravestock, Gilly Halpairn, Meg Heenahan, Stacey Jackson, Michèle Maheux, Joanna Molloy, Cynthia

Parsons, Jim Pascoe, Seth Poppel, Mark Reina, Rich Romano, George Rush, Randi Schmelzer, Diane Stefani, George M. Stevenson, Tony Timpone, Doris Toumarkine, Jason Weinberg.

Photos:

David McGough, Scooter, Albert Ferreira, David Allocca, all of DMI; Miramax; Alan Weissman; Rowland Wafford; Jerry Martinez; Rand Vossler.

Moral Support:

Diane, Gloria and Sam Bernard; Norman Bey; Eliot Cohen; Russell Calabrese; Tom Della Corte; Barbara Garson; Ben, Esther and Ora Geshensky; Milton Goldstein; Mark Hamilton; Jonathan Horne; Amanda Kissin; Batton Lash; Frank Leonardo; Mike Mooney; Scott and Barbara Siegel; Terry Smolar; Jerry Tallmer; Claudia Tindall; Lisa Tindall; JoAnne Wasserman; Mason Wiley.

And a special thanks to Quentin Tarantino, who generously cooperated with this book, opening even those doors that might lead to bad places, and whose choice of title for this biography was either "Cute Boy Director," "Sexy Young Director" or "Pretty-Boy Wunderkind."

introduction

The first time I met Quentin Tarantino, I found him irritating—a reaction many people share when first meeting him. He was at the Cannes Film Festival for *Reservoir Dogs*, a movie that began as a guerrilla production and ended up a phenomenon, and he was jumping around like a puppy newly off its leash, vibrating with excitement, talking so fast the words had to elbow each other out of the way to be heard.

But like his movies—and like any puppy that licks your face—Quentin grows on you. In subsequent encounters at film festivals, interviews and parties over the next three years, I came to enjoy him for the same energy and rat-a-tat delivery that initially seemed so odd. His enthusiasm is genuine, his movie knowledge vast and unexpected, and there is something appealing about this brash newcomer saying what's on his mind and making exactly the movies he wants to make. His success may be due to his talent, but his popularity is due to the way he taps effortlessly into the pop-culture stew that nourished him. This former video-store clerk, now dubbed "the new Martin Scorsese," gives hope to all those who toil in minimum-wage jobs that don't quite match the size of their dreams.

The moment I knew that I really enjoyed Quentin not only as a filmmaker but as a person was aboard the Miramax yacht in the Cannes harbor several days before *Pulp Fiction* was splashed in the face of an unsuspecting public. I hadn't seen Quentin since he was bopping around the Toronto Film Festival a year and a half before, but the first thing he did was to pick up our previous conversation as if not a day had gone by. He remembered me, he remembered my tastes, he knew my work as a critic for the New York *Daily News* and before that the *New York Post*, and most of all, he was sensitive to what was on my mind. Unlike those who claim Quentin lives his life through movies—which is to say that he doesn't "live" his life at all—I find him thoroughly connected and engaged with the world. A snob would have forgotten or rejected our long-ago conversation, a social climber would have filed it on an index card, but Quentin had actually chewed over the subject and was ready and eager to broach it again. (That subject, by the way, was his ability to depict female characters, and his comeback to that was *Pulp Fiction*'s Mia Wallace, a "pierce-them-and-suck-out-the-juice kinda woman.")

Like any unseasonably famous newcomer, Quentin is already surrounded by controversy—disgruntled former friends and colleagues, investigations into the sources and depth of his talent, questions about his character. I got a personal taste of Quentin's self-involvement when he stood me up on two occasions. Quentin has a way of apologizing without apologizing:

"No, actually I didn't stand you up on Monday, all right. I ended up standing you up on Sunday—this is really funny, 'cause I was thinking about it all fucking day, and then I just like forgot, it just went out of my mind, and then I totally remembered on Monday." Being Quentin, evidently, means never having to say you're sorry.

In my interviews with Quentin I did not shy away from controversies that surround him, and neither did he. Still, interviewing Quentin on any subject is more fun than interviewing almost anyone else. What other director will debate you until the sun rises, with utter seriousness, about the difference between using the word "penis" or "clitoris" as a metaphor? As with any artist, his slowly building body of work will eventually do the talking for him.

Which is not to say the loquacious Quentin will ever shut up. Like the quirky, mesmerizing diatribes and discourses of his movies, chatting with Quentin Tarantino—with all his obsessions, paradoxes and contradictions—is one of life's pleasures.

Jami Bernard
New York, 1995

quentin tarantino curriculum vitae

My Best Friend's Birthday. . . . .
Director, co-screenwriter (with Craig Hamann), actor; written and added to from late 1984 through 1986; shot in pieces during 1985 and 1986; abandoned 1986 when a few rolls of film were ruined during processing. Certain scenes are finished and were transferred to video; raw footage still exists.

The Golden Girls. . . . .
Cameo on TV show as Elvis impersonator; aired November 19, 1988.

True Romance. . . . .
Screenwriter; completed in 1987; released 1993 with Tony Scott directing.

Natural Born Killers. . . . .
Screenwriter; first draft completed in 1989; released August 1994 with Oliver Stone directing.

From Dusk Till Dawn. . . . .
Screenwriter from story by Robert Kurtzman and John Esposito; also actor, executive producer; written late 1990 to early 1991; rewritten 1995; tentative release late 1995 with Robert Rodriguez directing.

Past Midnight. . . . .
Rewrote script (but credited only as associate producer) in late 1990 to
early 1991; released 1991.

Reservoir Dogs. . . . .
Director, screenwriter, actor; written late 1990 with revisions into mid-
1991; shot five weeks in 1991; premiered Sundance Film Festival
January 1992; released late 1992.

Killing Zoe. . . . .
Executive producer; released 1994 (written and directed by Roger
Avary).

The Coriolus Effect. . . . .
Released 1993; played voice of Panhandle Slim.

Pulp Fiction. . . . .
Director, screenwriter (from stories by Tarantino and Roger Avary),
actor; written 1992–93; premiere Cannes Film Festival 1994 (winner
Palme d'Or); released October 1994.

Sleep with Me. . . . .
Actor (cameo as "Sid"), premiere Cannes Film Festival 1994; released
September 1994.

It's Pat. . . . .
Uncredited rewrite; released 1995.

All-American Girl. . . . .
Featured role on TV show; telecast March 22, 1995.

Destiny Turns On the Radio. . . . .
Actor (plays Johnny Destiny); released April 1995.

Somebody to Love. . . . .
Cameo as bartender; tentative release 1995; written and directed by
Alexandre Rockwell.

Crimson Tide. . . . .
Uncredited rewrite; released May 1995.

Desperado. . . . .
Actor; tentative release 1995; directed by Robert Rodriguez.

Four Rooms. . . . .
Director, screenwriter, actor in one of four segments (others directed
by Allison Anders, Alexandre Rockwell, Robert Rodriguez); written mid-
1994; shot late 1994; tentative release November 1995.

Reservoir Dogs
color chart

Harvey Keitel—Mr. White/Larry

Tim Roth—Mr. Orange/Freddy

Michael Madsen—Mr. Blonde/Vic

Christopher Penn—Nice Guy Eddie

Steve Buscemi—Mr. Pink

Lawrence Tierney—Joe Cabot

Eddie Bunker—Mr. Blue

Quentin Tarantino—Mr. Brown

CHAPTER 1
The Big Faint

Mr. Pink: *Holy shit, did he fuckin' die on us? So, is*
            he dead or what?
Mr. White: *He ain't dead.*
Mr. Pink: *So what is it?*
Mr. White: *I think he's just passed out.*
Mr. Pink: *He scared the fuckin' shit outta me. I thought*
            he was dead for sure.

                              —Reservoir Dogs, *1992*

On the night of September 23, 1994, *Pulp Fiction* opened the
32nd New York Film Festival. The opening night is a coveted
spot for a movie; it has the highest profile of any selection and
it can set the tone for the rest of the prestigious two-week
event.

Although the big party is traditionally held later that night
at Tavern on the Green, those with tickets to *Pulp Fiction* milled
around Lincoln Center's Avery Fisher Hall for more than an

hour before the movie, schmoozing, drinking, getting into the mood for a movie that was not for the faint of heart.

By the time the lights went down, the audience was keyed up—if not largely drunk. *Pulp Fiction* had won the Palme d'Or at Cannes to great acclaim but had remained a tantalizing mystery in the U.S. Director and screenwriter Quentin Tarantino was brought onstage to introduce his film and cast, and trooped them upstairs to the second-tier box seats traditionally reserved for the opening-night filmmakers. Along with Quentin and the cast was Harvey Weinstein, head with his brother Bob of Miramax Pictures, the company that had taken an $8 million chance on *Pulp Fiction* when every major studio passed. Harvey watched over Quentin like a proud if anxious father; he had grown fond of saying that "Miramax is in the Quentin Tarantino business."

The movie unspooled, and then it was time for The Scene: John Travolta, fearing Uma Thurman will die from an accidental overdose of heroin, is about to plunge a hypodermic needle of adrenaline into her heart. The camera shifts from the sweat on John's brow to the froth trickling from Uma's mouth to the glistening drop on the tip of a very, very long needle. Just as in Cannes, the audience went wild from the sheer audacity of the scene. They splayed their fingers before their eyes, feeling both sick and euphoric with anticipation. Eric Stoltz gave the countdown: "One . . . two . . . *three!*"

At the very moment Travolta plunged the needle, a man in the orchestra keeled over onto the carpet in a dead faint. There were screams and calls for a doctor. No one knew which was more exciting, Quentin's world or the real world.

"I thought that someone had had a heart attack or something, and I was quite anxious," Eric Stoltz recalls. "I was sitting next to Quentin and I said, 'What if this guy dies from seeing this scene? I feel kind of responsible.' And Quentin leaned over and said, 'You know, Eric, when they screened *Jaws*, a man had a heart attack and died, and they told that to Steven Spielberg and he said, good, that means the movie works.' I wasn't exactly reassured."

The movie stopped. The lights came up. Two of the first people on the scene were Miramax honcho Harvey Weinstein and *Pulp Fiction* producer Lawrence Bender.

Ten minutes later, an announcer's voice was heard over the public-address system. *"The victim is okay!"* His choice of words made everyone queasier. The implication was not only that Tarantino was an exciting new filmmaker, but a dangerous one too. Perhaps his movies could kill.

The "victim," a diabetic, had either gone into insulin shock or had simply fainted from the familiar sight of a needle writ large. He sat out in the lobby to catch his breath, then came back into the theater to finish the movie, which had rewound back to the overdose scene so that the audience could be treated twice to the movie's most talked-about moment.

It was such a perfect way to introduce a Quentin Tarantino film, it was almost . . . *too* perfect. Later, few people believed the incident was on the level.

"I was sitting behind that guy, and you could practically see the SAG [Screen Actors Guild] card sticking out of his pocket," says one skeptic in the audience that night. "No way was that real. I saw him slumped over, being carried out by friends, and by the time he had reached the exit door he was standing and walking and talking, like his scene was over."

Who would pull such a stunt? All fingers point to Harvey Weinstein, the modern-day equivalent of such grand old movie showmen as William Castle, who in the fifties wired theater seats to give patrons an extra thrill during *The Tingler*.

"I did not do that," Harvey says, but he laughs, pleased that anyone would give him the credit. "In light of how some folks responded to the violence in *Reservoir Dogs*, that would have been the wrong cue on this movie, because as I was saying to Quentin, *Pulp Fiction* is fun, not violent."

And how did Harvey, a physically substantial person, get from the second-tier box to the main aisle of the orchestra in time to race to the twentieth row and be the first person on the scene?

Instinct, says Harvey. "In my other life, from the time I was nineteen to age twenty-four, I produced two thousand concerts. I had a pretty good track record at handling those situations. I know that in a situation like that there's always potential for a riot, or the person's health, if a decision isn't made quick enough. I've seen 168 kids faint from heat exhaustion at an outdoor concert with Genesis in Toronto. So for me, any time there's an incident in a theater, my adrenaline goes back to when I was twenty-four."

Whether or not Harvey staged The Big Faint, it proved one thing about Quentin's work. "Expect the unexpected," says Harvey. "That's why people love him."

CHAPTER 2
Little Q

I can take care of myself. I grew up in a tough neighborhood, and I've handled some pretty rough customers in my day.
—Wayne Gale *in* Natural
Born Killers *(Tarantino version)*

Teenage mom Connie Tarantino lugged her squalling infant Quentin Jerome across the hinterlands of America from the hillbilly hills of Tennessee to the inner city of South Central Los Angeles when she was only sixteen years old. "I hauled him in his cradle board," says Connie. "I wore out six pairs of moccasins doing it."

That's the Quentin Tarantino childhood myth, the one that has been widely reported and richly embellished with each retelling, and Connie—now Connie Zastoupil—is allowing herself a rare moment of fun with it. "Quentin would have you believe he was raised by wolves," she says sardonically. ("Discount everything she tells you by 20 percent," is Quentin's warning.)

Actually, Quentin is the product of a middle-class upbringing in a California beach suburb. It's true he spent time with his grandparents in Knoxville, Tennessee, when he was around ten or eleven, a period with a relative lack of supervision that made a distinct impression on the lad. And his grandparents minded him as a toddler while Connie was finishing college. But Connie is happy to dispell the romance of Quentin as some child of backwoods America. It's not the romanticizing that bothers her, it's that these stories depend on Connie taking the part of the trailer-trash mom, barefoot, pregnant and illiterate. "I take exception to the way I've been characterized," says Connie, who nevertheless agrees that there is a rags-to-riches story to be told—hers. "I have been called a wildly progressive mother, and that's probably true."

Part Irish, part Cherokee, Connie McHugh was born on September 3, 1946. She was a willful child—headstrong, bright, utterly determined, an often unwilling participant in a family full of rifts and shifting alliances. This fostered in her an early desire for independence and family stability. "My parents were not very attentive in the normal sense and that's why I lived with various members of the family whenever I wanted—usually at my own instigation," says Connie. "Although I doubt I instigated that at age two. But my mother was always running off doing different things and I preferred my grandmother and my aunt."

Connie was born in Tennessee—if anyone in the bloodline wanted to claim hillbilly roots she would be the one—but grew up in various parts of Ohio with family members, notably her grandmother. At age six she settled down in Cleveland with adoptive parents Betty and Ellis Shaffer. Connie Shaffer stayed in Cleveland through junior high school, but after spending a summer with an aunt who lived in California, she liked it there so much she moved in and attended a southern California high school, graduating at the tender age of fifteen. "Just very smart," she says in the clipped, secure cadences of a woman who knows herself and knows what she wants.

What she wanted was her freedom, and one of the routes to

that freedom was education. For her, knowledge was a drug and an escape hatch rolled into one. "I wanted out of that family and I saw education as a way of getting out of that environment," says Connie. "They never stopped me from accelerating in school, nor was there any recognition of it. I somehow imagined that I would become a full-fledged adult when I got that high school diploma and that I could go off to college and do what I wanted. Everyone else was going away to college and they said no, no, you still have to be home by ten. I know that sounds caring in its own way, but it wasn't, it was just an ignorant way of looking at things."

A drastic solution occurred to Connie when she was visiting a girlfriend whose father was a lawyer. She overheard her friend's parents discussing the subject of "emancipated minors," kids under eighteen who in California could legally live on their own under certain conditions. Connie understood it to mean that if she could just get married, she would no longer be subject to the control of her family. "So within a short period of time I got married and accidentally got pregnant, and that's why Quentin was born so early."

The young man who facilitated Connie's emancipation was Tony Tarantino, five years older, a law student who wanted to be an actor and appeared occasionally in productions at the Pasadena Playhouse. They met while horseback riding at a local stable. The marriage of convenience foundered almost immediately, and Connie departed for the University of Tennessee to get her bachelor's degree in microbiology and nursing. She toyed with changing her major to police science—the administration of justice—but stuck with medicine.

One of the strains on the marriage was the unexpected pregnancy; Connie had Quentin while she was still sixteen, nearly a child herself. "I was so angry over being pregnant because he had told me he couldn't have children. Of course, once I had Quentin I loved him dearly, but I wasn't planning on having a child while I was in college and having that kind of financial burden. And I was so angry with Tony that I didn't even tell him at first that he had a child. I didn't actually think he was settled enough to be a father anyway, so I didn't see any point in telling him."

Quentin was born in Knoxville, Tennessee, on March 27, 1963, and it was only after finishing college that Connie returned to Los Angeles and looked up Tony Tarantino to show him his baby boy. "He knew Quentin's name and he had a picture of him," says Connie; they even tried a brief reconciliation. "I went out with him on a couple of dates, and that was it. I wasn't any more interested than I was the first time. But I did have a beautiful son, and I thanked him for that."

The grown Quentin seems curiously apathetic about his biological father. "I've never had any desire to get in touch with him," he says. "I'm not mad at him or anything like that. It actually was my mom who left that relationship. I've just never had any desire to . . . it would just be more or less embarrassing to look at somebody who I'm supposed to feel something for, even though I don't know him at all."

Quentin was named after two characters—one from pop culture and the other from a more literary source. On the TV show *Gunsmoke*, Burt Reynolds had played a half-breed Indian blacksmith named Quint Asper. And there were two Quentins in Faulkner's *The Sound and the Fury*. "I decided when I was pregnant that whether he was a boy or a girl his name was going to be Quentin," says Connie, who often calls her son "Quent" or "Q," and is annoyed that other people are picking up on her pet names for him. One of her minor fears is that her son is so famous that a new generation of babies will come along carrying his moniker. Connie also gave a lot of thought to the middle name Jerome—"I actually thought QJZ just happened to be the best bachelor monogram I'd ever seen," she says, although the "Z" for Quentin's adoptive last name implies that this was an afterthought. In any case, Quentin's name underwent several fluctuations, including the stage name he designed for himself as an adolescent—Quint Jerome.

Connie loved little Q, but he did put a crimp in her career

plans. "I was a math/science major. I actually wanted to go to medical school. And I went through nurse's training as a means to be able to support myself while pursuing another endeavor of study. But when Quentin was born I couldn't afford to go on to med school. I didn't really stay in nursing for very long. I did it for a few years when Q was a young child, and then I immediately went into the business arena of the company that I was with."

Quentin was born while Connie was in college, and although at first she tried to manage with just a baby-sitter, toward the end of college she sent him to live with her mother twenty miles away, an unintended parallel to Connie's own early years, when she lived with her grandmother.

Quentin was a happy baby, "very active, very willful," says the active, willful Connie.

With degree in hand, Connie returned to L.A., and within six months sent for Quentin. She married a small-time musician named Curtis Zastoupil, of Bohemian-Czech origin, and when Quentin was still a toddler Connie asked Tony Tarantino to sign papers allowing Curt to adopt. Connie, always concerned about being in charge of her own destiny no matter the price, waived child support "so I could have exclusive control of Quentin. That is oftentimes the way to have your freedom, and to secure your children's freedom."

Connie, now divorced three times, is touchy about all of her ex-husbands. (Long after Curt was Jan Bohusch, an eight-year marriage that ended in such bitterness that each party has trouble saying the other's name; they substitute pronouns.) When asked whether Quentin takes after his biological father in any way, Connie snaps: "No. He's like *me*. He looks like *me*." When she says she won exclusive control of Quentin from Tony, she really means it.

Then she softens. "Actually, he was a very adorable little boy."

"He gets a lot of his drive from his mother," says Alexandre Rockwell, the director of *In the Soup,* who befriended Quentin at

the Sundance Film Festival in 1992. "He's always driving forward with a very positive kind of outlook. The articles that have
been written about him say he had some Li'l Abner upbringing
or something, but his mother isn't like that and Quentin isn't
like that. Of course, there's probably some darkness in there,
because he drives toward being positive to the point where you
feel there's something chasing him. I mean, you feel that there's
something that frightens him."

The time from babyhood until age nine or ten was golden
for Quentin, at least as far as having a father figure in his life
was concerned (although Quentin has referred disparagingly to
his adoptive father's musical career—"a musician, as in 'The
Ramada Inn presents Curt Zastoupil'"). Curt played guitar and
piano, in addition to writing poetry. During those years, Curt
and Quentin were tight. "Since Curt was a musician and I
worked in the daytime he actually spent most of his daytime
hours with his stepfather and they were very, very close," says
Connie. "Plus, we had a rather extended family. My younger
brother Roger lived with us—I took him out of my mother's
home because I didn't like the way he was being raised. He
lived with us from the time he was thirteen until he went into
the service. He was Quentin's constant baby-sitter and tormen-
tor. And Curt's brother, who was my age, lived with us too,
when we were about nineteen. So we were actually a bunch of
kids living together. Quentin had a great deal of male influence
at that period of time in his life—two uncles and his father and
they all spent their time together in the daytime while I was
working on my career. My brother said that it was like being
raised at Disneyland. We were totally focused on fun; that's
why Quentin went to so many movies."

Quentin also has an uncle Johnny who is five years
younger—as confusing as that may seem—with whom he
played when he spent that brief time in Tennessee.

Although Connie is Catholic, she encouraged Quentin to try
out different churches until he found something that appealed

to him. None of them really did, although for a while he test-drove a new one every Sunday. Curt was Protestant, and Connie describes Quentin as "some variety of Protestant."

Connie and Quentin were both studies in stubbornness, and Connie quickly found little Q a formidable opponent. While he was still a toddler, Q overheard the word *bullshit* while playing at a friend's house. Like most children, he immediately sensed the word's power and urgency, but he would not be intimidated out of repeating it. For the next several weeks, *bullshit* became his all-purpose response to any demand placed on him. "Q, pick up your toys," Connie would say. *"Bullshit!"* he would reply. "Q, turn out the lights and go to sleep." *"Bullshit! Bullshit!"*

It was not her favorite method of punishment, yet Connie felt there was something fitting about having Quentin wash his mouth out with soap. "It was very strategic, because I didn't want to beat him or anything," says Connie. "So I thought I had to do something, because it was getting out of control. So I took a bar of soap and I scraped it across his teeth. And he looked at me with bubbles coming out of his mouth, and he was about three years old, and defiance was flashing in his eyes, and he said, 'Well, *B!*' And I lost it and cracked up. What was I going to do? We both knew what he meant."

Early on, Q began to pick up other forbidden forms of expression. "Goddamn, son of a bitch!" Connie would hear Q saying from his room.

"What did you say?" she would demand, storming in.

"It wasn't me, Mommy," he'd protest. "It was G.I. Joe and Spiderman talking to Batman."

"His language was peppery, even as a child, but he wasn't allowed to say it out of the context of playing with the G.I. Joe dolls, where he'd be playing all the parts and providing all the voices. It wasn't just G.I. Joes; he had all the action figures. They were all the size of Barbie dolls."

Little Q was hard on his toys. "I think I spent most of his childhood on my hands and knees putting G.I. Joe dolls back together, putting their legs back on, trying to find their little combat boots," says Connie with a laugh. "It used to bother me, he used to mess up their wardrobe. I was always looking for their little bayonets."

Connie recalls that Quentin's games were elaborate and action-packed. "They all had *Pulp Fiction, Reservoir Dogs* overtones. There was always a fight. I can't say that I paid that much attention to the complexity of the story he was scripting, but it always resulted in an altercation of some sort. There was always action. I would say that his characters didn't have as many philosophical discussions as his present-day characters do."

Recently, Connie found an original, vintage G.I. Joe in a shop in Portland, Oregon, and bought it for her grown son, an avid collector of the detritus of childhood—dolls, board games, posters, artifacts. "It was hard to find one," said Connie. "Most of them didn't survive the carnage."

Another way in which Q would amuse himself as a youngster was to perform speeches and act out little plays. "He used to memorize things," says Connie. "There were long-play albums and he would memorize them, front and back. And recite them to me again and again. One of those albums was *José Jimenez in Space* or something. And he had adult-type comedy albums, and *The Jungle Book*, and all those things. He could recite all of them verbatim."

Quentin also showed an early proclivity for writing. At fourteen he wrote a screenplay called *Captain Peachfuzz and the Anchovy Bandit*, modeled after *Smokey and the Bandit*, about a man who robbed pizza parlors, involving car chases and complicated CB lingo. "He used to write all the time when he was a child," says Connie. "He used to write Mother's Day stories for me, little dramas. Every year I'd get a Mother's Day story. But he would always kill me off in the story. And then he'd tell me how badly he felt about me dying, and how much he loved me. I said, 'Well, Quentin, why can't I live, why can't you love me when I'm alive?'"

*   *   *

When Q was nine years old, he saw *Deliverance,* the movie in which inbred backwoods hillbillies make white-water rafter Ned Beatty squeal like a pig before raping him. *Deliverance* had a profound effect on the boy. The child in him vowed never to go camping again, and the future filmmaker in him would refer to it in what would become the "gimp" scene in *Pulp Fiction*.

He loved the visceral effect movies had on him, even when he didn't understand what was really going on. Connie and Curt would take Quint to the movies all the time, never censoring what he saw. "The stories that they tell about me taking him to see inappropriate movies are very true," says Connie with a touch of pride. "Of course, I didn't realize . . . you know, I wasn't screening the movies myself. I simply took him every place I went, so if I was seeing an inappropriate movie, he was seeing it too. I think he always had a real healthy appreciation for fantasy. He never had nightmares or showed any sign of distress. He just liked movies."

She took him to see *Carnal Knowledge* when he was eight. "You know the part where Art Garfunkel is trying to talk the girl into going all the way—'C'mon, let's do it!' 'I don't want to do it!' 'C'mon, let's do it!' Well, in the middle of the theater, Quentin piped up: 'What's he wanna do, Mom?' And the whole theater cracked up because it was obvious there was a child in there."

Connie wanted her son to have a chance at everything in life, so when she had access to season tickets for the Lakers, she tried to tempt him. To this day, Quentin is sour on sports, figuring that in the time it takes people to watch a match they could have watched a movie and had a better time. "He was never interested in any of that stuff," concurs Connie. "He just wanted to go to the movies. I could always take him out to dinner, he enjoyed that. Otherwise, every time I wanted to do something with him, he wanted to go to the movies."

Connie is triumphant that Quentin didn't like *Bambi*. "It was the only movie that upset him, and it's understandable— they killed Bambi's mother. And it was, Run, Bambi, run! I mean, hell, I cried too. I'm sure the last thing a dying mother thinks of is whether they're going to get her kid. So we were both upset over that movie."

Family outings often consisted of dinner and a martial-arts movie. Connie was a big Bruce Lee fan, and Quentin would see anything: "He was really quite eclectic in his tastes."

After Curt, Connie's third husband, Jan, happily enough, was "a movie freak." But there was so much tension between them, Connie had Jan go to the movies with Quentin without her. Says Jan, "We saw just tons, *Aliens*, *Die Hard*, any kind of action movies, the *Godfather* movies, *Scarface*, *Body Double*, *Apocalypse Now*, retrospectives at the Cinerama Dome," an L.A. theater. "On a typical Friday, we'd go to a three, a six, an eight, and a midnight movie. She"—meaning Connie—"never came along, they had a major personality and power problem, she thought Quentin was a worthless bum. We discussed the movies, what he thought, and I gave him advice on girlfriends, how to conduct himself, grooming habits."

Later, Jan contradicts himself and says Quentin "had no interest whatever in girls, he'd just sit in his room writing screenplays in longhand."

Education was the most important thing to Connie. It was education that had gotten her free of the control of her family, and it was education that was now responsible for those steady paychecks. Connie wanted most of all to instill in little Q a love of learning. She would read to him every night, and the two of them being strong-willed, they would fight over which book it would be. "I wanted *Gulliver's Travels* and he wanted Dr. Seuss, so I taught him to read when he was three years old. I was still so young, we had to play what I wanted to play, too. But he loved books and he loved to read, and that was one of his first passions."

Connie claims Quentin was reading at third-grade level by the time he entered kindergarten at age five in the San Gabriel Valley. "He had a marvelous kindergarten teacher he adored, and I think she had a great deal of fondness for him," says

Connie, laughing at the memory. "She recognized the stellar little man that he was."

Kindergarten would prove to be the high point of Quentin's school career. "He was very bright," says Connie. "One of the reasons that I didn't worry too much about him—well, I worried anyway—but I have an IQ of around 165 and I know Q was tested at least twice, once at 155 and once at 160, so I knew that there wasn't going to be a problem with him learning if he ever decided to settle down and learn. But he was very hyperactive. And I had been very hyperactive as a child too. The only difference is that when I was a child I was very shy so I didn't have anything to do but study. And he was very hyperactive and already a social whirlwind, and so he could find a lot of other things to do besides study."

As much as he adored his kindergarten teacher, he hated his first-grade teacher. "He got into trouble for telling her that his mother wasn't really a nurse, that I was Modesty Blaise" (the female James Bond of the literary world, played by Monica Vitti in a hit sixties film, and the heroine of the book John Travolta is reading in the loo when Bruce Willis blows him away in *Pulp Fiction*). "The teacher told me that he was a lying little . . ." Connie's voice trails off at the critical juncture. "At my first parent-teacher conference, I tried to explain to her the imagination of young children, but she was more concerned about him being truthful and living in the real world. She was a very uptight young lady."

"I actually found some of my old report cards two years ago," says Quentin, "and they kept talking about how I was really bright, but, all right, I had a problem focusing and stuff. It was funny because in kindergarten I did really good. But that first-grade teacher really hated me. She really really didn't like me at all. And she treated me like really mean, it was the meanest I'd ever been treated by a teacher. And she'd say things to me like, 'I don't see how your parents could love you.' It really turned me off from school."

Another bone of contention between Quentin and his first-grade teacher was an assignment that he finished before anyone else in the class and then refused to do over when the teacher didn't believe him. "She said he hadn't done it and he said yes I have and she said no you haven't," says Connie. "And so it was this thing about semantics. He actually refused to do it because she refused to acknowledge that he had already done it."

At the parent-teacher conference, according to Connie, the first-grade teacher found Connie as intractable as her son.

"Mrs. Zastoupil, your son is uncontrollable," fretted the teacher. "I cannot relate to him, I cannot handle him."

"I don't know what to say to an adult who can't handle a six-year-old," retorted Connie. "I can't help you. Maybe you shouldn't be a teacher."

"Well, maybe your son needs Ritalin."

Ritalin is a drug often given to hyperactive children to make them more manageable. What is considered in the adult Quentin to be an enviable amount of energy, personality and flair was considered in little Q to be disruptive and antisocial.

Connie, whose career was in medicine, refused to put her son on Ritalin. "I'm sorry I introduced this hellion into the school system," she told the teacher, "but you're going to have to deal with it because I'm not going to have him medicated."

Connie disagrees that Quentin was uncontrollable. "When he had an assignment he was interested in, he would be finished in those early days of school much faster than the rest of the class, and of course the teacher wanted him to be working at the same pace. He would become bored. He would rather have been doing what he wanted. He wanted to do those subjects that interested him most." (Quentin agrees that he was "probably hyperactive" throughout childhood.)

Second grade was a further torment for Q. That's the grade in which you learn to tell time. "Something misfired there," admits Connie, "and Q had trouble telling time. Someone recently asked me in an interview, How did you feel about that? And I said, He's a genius, who gives a shit if he can tell time or not? He can ask somebody the time. If he needs to know the time, he'll find out."

First grade, second grade . . . where Connie had conquered school in one burst of effort after another, Quentin was leaving a daunting trail of failures. Education was rapidly falling off the short list of things Quentin was interested in. And then another educational disaster struck in the third grade, when the family moved to El Segundo in the South Bay area and Quentin switched schools.

This would be Quentin's favorite childhood home, partly because it was near the Los Angeles International Airport, which sparked his imagination, and partly because the family was still doing the "Disneyland thing." But the private Hawthorne Christian School was certainly his least favorite school. It didn't conform to the hillbilly roots he liked to imagine for himself. Until sixth grade, Quentin wore a regulation school uniform, shirt and tie, to attend Hawthorne.

The neighborhoods of Los Angeles are a patchwork of different incomes and ethnicities; you can live in an upper-middle-class neighborhood and cross over a freeway to find yourself in a ghetto. Quentin lived in one of these middle-class patches but longed for the excitement of the lower classes. "We moved to several nearby places, including Manhattan Beach"—home of the future Video Archives store where Quentin would work—"and Torrance, which was a residential area that technically was an unincorporated piece of the county," says Connie. "I deliberately chose areas that were middle-class yet ethnically mixed, because I wanted Quentin to have that exposure. In fact, that was one of my side agendas for sending him to Tennessee, because it was so different. I wanted him to see that there was a different world and that it wasn't so nice as the one he was raised in."

Once he became famous, Quentin allowed interviewers to conclude that he had grown up in South Central Los Angeles, a famous ghetto that was geographically near where he actually lived. "I've never said anything that's not accurate about my childhood," he retorts. "The only problem is that sometimes the press doesn't know the difference between the South Bay and South Central. So I describe the South Bay and they write South Central."

But it may have been wishful thinking on his part to come from the ghetto, because the minute Quentin put on that hated private-school uniform, he wanted desperately to escape the world of neatly clipped hedges. "He hated that school," admits Connie. "He hated it with a passion. They were very strict. So he talked me into letting him go to a public junior high school. And of course the one he wanted to go to was in the ghetto, and I refused to do that."

Quentin's romanticizing of his childhood is a sore point with Connie. However, when asked about that house on El Segundo Boulevard, the one Quentin loved so much, she replies matter-of-factly that although she sold it in the early eighties, she believes it is no longer standing. "There was a big to-do, a drug dealer or somebody bought it, stashed drugs there, and the DEA [Drug Enforcement Agency] tore it up." A perfect fate for a Quentin landmark, or perhaps an easy answer to keep Quentin's early life shrouded in mystery.

The ways in which children rebel against their parents are calculated to hurt. Parents concerned with propriety raise children who dye their hair purple. Connie, who put more stock in the power of education than in any particular religion, wound up with a son who hated school.

At first, the arguments would be about which school Q should attend. He won the battle to go to public school, and for a brief shining moment he won the battle to attend an inner-city high school. "I thought I was furthering his ethnic orientation," says Connie with that sardonic tone she uses when describing the battles she lost to her son.

Nevertheless, Quentin still hated school, often hiding quietly in the downstairs bathroom until he heard his mother leave for work so he could play hooky. Quentin would later exaggerate and claim he'd been left back in the ninth grade about twelve times, but Connie figures he may have lost credits when he changed schools, making him slightly older than the other kids in his class. Quentin was enjoying acting tough, starting fights and walking through bad neighborhoods without fear. But his victory of choosing his own school was brief, because at age sixteen, the same age at which his mother had trudged on through college while pregnant, Quentin dropped out of school for good. He had only made it to the tenth grade, and the actual time he had logged in that grade was on a par with how much vermouth there is in a dry martini.

"He loved kindergarten," says Connie with a sigh. "Then it was all downhill."

When Quentin was nine or ten, Connie and Curt Zastoupil got a divorce. It's a time Quentin doesn't like to talk about much and which probably affected his already poor schooling for the worse. The split was inevitable once Curt had taken it into his head that he needed, in Connie's view, "time to contemplate his navel."

Connie tried to protect Quentin from the truth. "When he was too young to understand, I'd say, 'Your father can't see you because he works a long ways from where we live and he just can't come and see you.' But when he was older he realized what had happened." Quentin remained close to his Zastoupil relatives—Aunt Ginny and Uncle Conrad are mentioned near the end of *Pulp Fiction,* when Harvey Keitel offers to replace the Ginny-and-Conrad linens that get soaked with blood. But things were never the same again between Quentin and Curt. It was as if they had never been close, horsing around the house all day while Connie was out working, making every day like Disneyland. Curt became distant and emotionally unavailable.

"It's not awkward now at all," says Quentin, who runs into Curt at his aunt and uncle's house on holidays. "It's like we went through a weird period when I was sixteen or so, but now it's fine." Curt teaches guitar and lives without a phone "somewhere in the hills"; Quentin says he is not certain just where and, as with all his father figures, professes no curiosity.

"The divorce from Curt totally affected me at the time," says Quentin. "That was like going through a divorce like any kid that age is going through a divorce. But the other two [divorces] didn't necessarily bother me. Did it affect my work? If someone were to go through my movies and see that these characters are looking for father figures, that's all very interesting. Myself, I don't know. I mean, it might very well be, but none of it's conscious. And stuff like that I'd rather not give my opinion on. It's more like I'd like to hear what others have to say about it. All I know is, when I'm making a movie, I'm never thinking about that. After the fact, you can say, oh wow, look at this, look what I did, you know? That's always really interesting, but when I'm writing it's coming from more or less a subconscious level."

Both *Reservoir Dogs* and *Pulp Fiction* are rife with betrayals of and by father figures. In *Reservoir Dogs*, the undercover cop is comforted by the older Harvey Keitel when all along his very presence in the gang has spelled their doom. In *Pulp*, John Travolta is placed in an awkward Oedipal situation on a date with his boss's wife; boxer Bruce Willis double-crosses Marsellus but later gains his forgiveness by saving his life; the youths who steal Marsellus's briefcase are mortally punished.

"In a weird way, since I grew up basically without a father, you kind of go looking for your father in other places," admits Quentin. "One of the things that a father does, and why there's so many fucked-up kids in the world when a father doesn't do this, is that he comes to tell the boy, you know, what being a man is. What is expected of men and everything. It's really easy to write that off as something that's not important, but actually that is an important thing for a boy, because you know what, a boy is actually looking for that, whether they can articulate that or not. Looking for some guidance, you know, as far as being a man, and everything. Childhood's really weird for a boy. You get torn in all these different directions. When I was a kid I totally like didn't accept any of the prescribed things of right or wrong. I wanted to find a right or wrong inside my own heart.

And since I didn't have somebody who I admired showing me the way, I went looking for it, and in a way I guess I kind of found it with Howard Hawks's movies. I saw the ethic that he was proposing in his films, about men and their relationships with each other and with women. And I guess I recognized it in my own self and kind of adopted that. A girl I was talking to about this said I picked the right guy, he did a better job for me than half the fathers out there. I don't mean to drill this into my movies, I guess they end up coming to the surface."

Some of the things that formed Quentin's worldview undoubtedly happened during the time of Connie's divorce from Curt. Not only did he feel a sense of abandonment, but it was at this time that Connie was faced with a medical emergency and shipped Quentin off to his grandparents in a panic over what might become of him if anything happened to her.

Connie says it was for six months; Quentin says it was for a whole year, fifth grade plus the two summers that bracketed it. "It was very interesting there," admits Quentin. "It was just a whole other kind of way of life. It was kind of like a hillbilly life, actually. I don't know how to describe it other than that."

Quentin readily reveals that his grandmother, who was supposed to be taking care of him, was an alcoholic, "and she'd fall off the wagon and then go off on what they call in the South 'a drunk.' And she was drunk for days on end and just go out carousing and causing trouble. And my mom had not raised me like that at all. She didn't know that her mom was still doing this. So my mom was real mad when she found out that I was subjected to that, so she's actually never spoke to my grandmother since."

Quentin, too, is out of touch with his maternal grandparents out of loyalty to Connie; he still sees Curt's parents Dorothy and John during holidays.

Connie claims that Quentin has never shown any interest in meeting his biological father. "I don't even know that Tony is still alive," she says. And although Quentin has a "cordial" relationship with Curt, "I just don't believe that the father-son tie is there anymore. You notice he really only refers to his mother?"

It's true—Quentin never discusses his first two fathers, or Connie's subsequent husband, the trade-show promoter to whom Connie wound up paying alimony for four years. Connie met Jan on Thanksgiving 1981 in Florida, and they were married a month later, on December 31. Quentin was eighteen and lived in the house with them for two years before moving out on his own. Neither Connie nor Jan has anything good to say about each other or the marriage ("Do we have to talk about him?" says Connie; "She has no good qualities, none!" insists Jan).

"Jan is an example of someone who can snatch defeat from the jaws of victory," says Jerry Martinez, one of Quentin's friends from the video store where he worked in his early twenties. "This guy's like a cartoon. He had the capacity to be disgusting, but a really great character. He wanted in the worst way to be near the movies, and he got divorced just when Quentin was about to get famous. It must really kill him."

"He's a parasite without a host," snipes Connie.

In the years before Jan, with Curt gone from the picture, the struggles between Quentin and Connie over Q's autonomy intensified. Connie's focus shifted from worrying about Quentin's schooling to worrying about the proverbial "bad elements" he was hanging out with. "His reading skills were already superior so I knew he could always play catch-up on an education. I would have been far more concerned if he had had a reading disorder. And I was concerned that his math skills were not good. But when the time came that he started ditching school, and I knew that he was enamored of the bad crowd, I felt like you could force a child out of the house every day but then you don't know what they're doing with their daytime hours. I knew if I let him stay home that he'd be writing screenplays and stories, and glued to movies—I knew what he'd be doing with his free time if I allowed him to stay home. And I knew conversely that if I did push him out into the street that he may be out there getting into trouble. He had the ability to be a leader. And he was somewhat fearless."

Connie worried and Quentin fought, and finally he gave up the pretense of education and left school. "I was very disappointed," says Connie. "As a matter of fact, I was angry at him for years for not staying in school."

Trouble had been in the air for a while. When Quentin was thirteen, he showed signs of inheriting his mother's old distaste for curfews. "I didn't want to be a kid, I wanted to be an adult, to be treated like an adult and everything. I just, you know, hung out in really bad neighborhoods, stayed out late, drank and stuff like that."

Then, when he was fifteen, Quentin was arrested for shoplifting pulp fiction.

"It wasn't a legitimate shoplifting thing," quibbles Quentin. "I saw the book in the Kmart in the book section. And I wanted to read it, all right? And then I tried to con it out, I tried to say that I brought it in with me, or something like that. But I never actually stuck it in my jacket and tried to walk out with it, all right? Anyway, it wasn't working. And so I put it back and started to leave and then they grabbed me."

"Did you cross that line?" asked the store dick, pointing to an area on the floor near the checkout counter. "Then you officially shoplifted."

They hauled him off to the back of the store and called the police.

At least Quentin showed good taste as a would-be thief— the paperback he chose was called *The Switch*, and it was by a pulp-fiction writer Quentin had never tried before, Elmore Leonard. "I didn't know who he was, it just sounded like a good book," says Quentin.

The Switch was about the kidnapping of a tennis mom by two petty crooks, a black man and a white man, who try to shake down the woman's husband for the ransom. But the husband is down in the Bahamas with his illegal money and his illicit girlfriend, and has just filed for a divorce, so he doesn't care if they kill the wife as long as she's out of his life and he gets to keep his money. It was a quick read, too quick a read to have to pay for it.

He wound up paying for it in another way. Connie

answered the doorbell to see her Quent standing in the shadow of a uniformed policeman. In return for custody of her son, Connie promised the cop that she would "tear him apart limb from limb."

"Normally I worry about bringing a kid home to his mother because I found out on the way over here that his father doesn't live here," said the cop. "But I see you have it under control."

"We had an extensive library at home," says Connie. "Of all of the things I might have denied him, I never denied him books. I guess it was one of those things—he was there, the book was there, it was dangerous, he did it."

Connie was furious. Again she devised a punishment to suit the crime. She locked Q in his room, went out and bought dozens of books, unlocked his door and dumped them on his floor. "You want to read? Read!" she commanded. "That's all you're going to do this summer!"

Quentin spent the entire summer in the house reading the books. "He enjoyed it," muses Connie. "It wasn't much of a punishment."

"I actually went back to the Kmart the next week to buy the book," says Quentin. "I didn't want to have gone through all this for nothing." This time, he paid—although he admits that shoplifting it the second time around "would have been really ballsy, like, 'Fuck you, guys!'"

Connie began to feel guilty about the incident. "You administer the discipline and then at some point you think that maybe you've been a little rigid," says Connie. "I was at that stage for having grounded him for the whole summer when he came to me one day and asked if he could join the local community theater group. I thought, Well how much trouble could you get into in the local community theater?"

She gave him the twenty-five dollars it took to join the Torrance Community Theater. Eventually he came home and announced he had the lead in a play called *Two and Two Make Six*.

"Wonderful," said Connie. "Do you keep your clothes on?"

It was a play about partner-swapping between a middle-aged couple and a young couple. "But it was fairly innocent," says Connie. "As innocent as adultery can be."

Quentin became assistant stage manager and helped out on every play they staged; it was a more positive way of rebelling.

Still, Connie could see that the same way she could never really win the battle over little Q saying the word *bullshit,* she was never going to be able to keep him in school. "Fine, quit school," she told him. "You have my blessing. But one thing— you have to get a job."

Quentin did just that. He tried to work at a headhunting firm but was not cut out for placing people in jobs. So his first real job as a partly emancipated minor was to usher at the Pussycat Lounge, a porn theater in Torrance. He was sixteen years old, and as a further sign of his emancipation, he changed his last name back to Tarantino.

Today Connie is the executive vice president for sales and marketing and president of the California division of a health maintenance company headquartered in Maryland. She attended a party in her honor the night of her son's thirty-second birthday, the night he stood, all six-foot-four of him, at the podium at the sixty-seventh annual awards ceremony of the Academy of Motion Picture Arts and Sciences to accept his Oscar for Best Original Screenplay.

"I hope you'll be biologically grateful if you win an Oscar," Connie had told Quentin over dinner nine days before the event.

Quentin didn't thank Connie that night, but then, he didn't thank anyone specifically—possibly a first in Oscar history.

"I'm very proud of him as a man, even if he'd never taken Hollywood by storm," says Connie. "I think he's a very strong individual and a very good man. Yes, I was disappointed that he didn't get a formal education. But I knew how intelligent he was. I worried about him from a career point of view, but I never really lost confidence that he would pull off something."

CHAPTER 3

Video Archives

After working together these past coupla years, we're like well-oiled machinery. No, more like a Formula race car. No, scratch that one, too. What we're really like is a Swiss watch. Small, intricate, compact . . . it shouldn't work as well as it does, but it does. Because of the craftsmanship, the expertise, and the artist's loving hand.

> —Wayne Gale describing his camera
> crew buddies in Natural Born Killers
> (Tarantino version)

Quentin's five formative years behind the counter at a video store were vital to his shaping as a filmmaker and to the lives of those who worked with him. These were buddies who talked, watched and made films with Quentin, who picked him up from jail after he served time for parking fines, whose lives became fused with Quentin's. Today some are bitter, some loyal. One committed suicide in despair that he would never be as famous as Quentin. All of them do excellent Quentin imitations, the staccato laugh, the excited, rambling sentences.

"We eventually started picking up his mannerisms because we were all trying to compete, to be heard—the loud talking, the hand gyrations," says Jerry Martinez. "I knew that Quentin was going to make it. But I never thought that it would be like this, so fast. We all had a sense of history, we knew every filmmaker and what their story was and how they had made it. I thought that it would take Quentin at least a few more movies to get to this point. He's being perceived as the filmmaker of this particular generation, and that's pretty wild. When it's a friend, you try to be supportive, but it's hard to know in advance where the talk starts and the talent stops, or vice versa."

In late November 1994, the most famous video store in America went out of business. It hadn't survived an unpublicized move the previous June from Manhattan Beach to cheaper digs in Hermosa Beach, California. It hadn't survived indifferent management. Ultimately, it hadn't survived the loss of its most famous employee, Quentin Tarantino, who had gone off a few years before to become the rock star of movie directors.

For much of the mid-1980s, Video Archives was—at least in the eyes of its enthusiastic staff—the Manhattan Beach equivalent of the Left Bank. The guys who worked there were sharp and funny and spewed out wild monologues on their favorite subjects from the pop-culture catalogue. Just about every clerk in the store wanted to go into filmmaking or the arts. When they clicked, they really clicked, and when they fought, it was just like a Durwood Kirby burger from Jack Rabbit Slim's—bloody as hell. Quentin was known to have beaten up at least one colleague and one customer for various infractions. "The blood came out of the forehead area and sort of collected in the eye socket," said one pal about a Quentin fracas. The boys were constantly getting fired or banned from the store until things cooled off.

"The thing about Archives is we were all interested in some creative endeavor—movies and art primarily, but also writing," says Russell Vossler, who worked there from 1984 to 1991.

"The video store was a strange place, a family more than anything," says Jerry Martinez, another longtime employee. "In the ten years or so it was open, maybe twenty people who worked there could leave and come back and still be assured free rentals if they were in good standing. We were all friends. It wasn't like a regular place."

Video Archives—the coolest, hippest video rental counter in the county—was the offspring of Video Outtakes, not so cool, not so hip. Outtakes, in Redondo Beach, was owned by Dean McGill and managed by Lance Lawson. Working behind the counter was McGill's sensitive son Scott, who yearned to be a filmmaker, and the store attracted a slew of faithful cineast customers, all in their late teens or early twenties—like Quentin Tarantino, a local kid who had dropped out of high school and just liked being near all those videos.

Another guy who hung around was a carpenter named Eddie Karpinsky. "He was the sweetest, nicest guy in the world," says Jerry Martinez, a future Video Archives employee who met Eddie at a comics store. "Eddie would come in and fix the shelves and the drawers for no charge." Eddie was so nice that he was actually listed as "Nice Guy Eddie" in the computer, and Quentin later named the Chris Penn character after him in *Reservoir Dogs*. Eddie kept encouraging Martinez to stop by Video Outtakes and meet Lance, but every time they stopped by, Lance was strangely absent—an early sign of his troublesome managerial style. "Finally I learned he'd had a big falling-out with the owner, Dean McGill," says Jerry.

It must have been some falling-out; Lance took the staff and customers with him. He even took Dean's son, Scott.

Lance went in on the new video store with two brothers, Rick and Dennis Humbert. Rick worked at a record store named Licorice Pizza and Dennis managed card clubs. In October 1983, they opened Video Archives in two-thirds of what used to be a bicycle shop in a nondescript strip mall on North Sepulveda Boulevard in Manhattan Beach, an upper-middle-class suburb of Los Angeles. Later it expanded into a larger space in the same strip. Today a Tuxedo King outlet and a bakery occupy the spaces where Quentin Tarantino earned his Ph.D. in film.

Lance, Rick and Dennis hired some of their acquaintances from the neighborhood. One of the first hires was Stephen Polyi, a colorful, outspoken Sicilian from Licorice Pizza whom everyone called Stevo. Another hire was Scott McGill's friend from Video Outtakes, Roger Avary, an eighteen-year-old movie nut who wanted to write and direct, and who had known the much older Lance since he was a kid.

It wasn't a fancy store. In fact, it had wood where other stores had Plexiglas, and five customers could make it claustrophobic. Stevo liked to think of it as Henry Higgins regarded his bedchamber, as "an undiscovered tomb." At first, it didn't even have a cash register, only a countertop with a wooden drawer where the clerks kept the money. The videos, however, were catalogued by computer on inventory software designed by Roger and his friend Andy Blinn. Roger, Andy and Scott formed the nucleus of what would become the Video Archives gang, something like the gang from *Reservoir Dogs* but without the skinny ties. The store would be immortalized as the comics store where Clarence works for someone named Lance in *True Romance*.

Quentin, barely twenty, made the move from Outtakes to Archives as a faithful customer. He had quit high school at sixteen and spent his first year as an official adult ushering at the X-rated Pussycat Lounge in Torrance. "You sell popcorn, tear the tickets, you know, walk up and down the aisle and everything," says Quentin. "I lied about my age. And then when I was seventeen some kid I knew got mad at me and called up the theater and said, 'Your usher is underage!' They were grilling me and said I had to bring in my birth certificate if I wanted my job back."

He began acting lessons at the James Best Theater Company in 1981, and in 1983, when he was twenty, his mother's third husband, Jan, put him to work selling booth space to trade-show customers. "He's not at all self-centered," says Jan, "but he's an opinionated son of a bitch. He doesn't care if he steps on somebody, he'll do it if he wants to do it. He doesn't take advice very well, and quite frankly, if it weren't for the fact that he caught the rising star, he couldn't work for an authority figure."

But one authority figure decided to take a chance on him—Lance Lawson, the manager of Video Archives. Lance would hang out talking about movies so often with Quentin that he decided to put him to work, and in 1984, Quentin began an on-and-off relationship with the store that would last into 1990.

"Quentin was the kinda guy you'd look for in a job like that," says Roger Avary. "He was perfect video-store material, a walking film encyclopedia."

Not everyone was so thrilled. "Look how this guy fills out a credit card slip!" taunted a co-worker as he watched a flustered Quentin trying to tally numbers.

"What's forty times?" Quentin would ask, trying to multiply. "Forty times *what*?" came the answer as the other guys shook their heads in disbelief.

"He had no concept of numbers or mathematics or even east or west—you can't give him directions, you have to take him by the hand and show him," recalls Stevo Polyi.

During what Stevo calls "the heyday" of Video Archives, Jerry Martinez was hired, then Russell Vossler, then Rowland Wafford. But this heyday had a rocky start. Although each employee had his own area of expertise, Quentin had the most forceful personality and voice, and was always fully caffeinated. His integration into the Archives bunch was not without friction, because Roger also prided himself on his knowledge of film, and the two were highly competitive. He and Quentin were assigned to the same shift, and they would argue and one-up each other constantly. A truce came only after they realized that they both loved the same movies, even titles other people would be too ashamed to cop to.

"We were the video-store generation, right after the film-school generation, the first generation of people who wanted to be filmmakers who had grown up alongside computers, videos, the information highway," says Roger. "It's only natural to gravitate toward what you love. And I gravitated toward the video store. And so did other like-minded people, one of them being Quentin." They would become writing partners, with Roger's contributions making their way into nearly every script Quentin would touch, up to and including their pièce de résistance, the Oscar-winning screenplay for *Pulp Fiction*.

As a child, Roger had been interested in cartooning and animation. In school, he experimented with cel animation, pixillation, and simple stop-motion animation using clay figures. He monkeyed around with Super-8 and video cameras. Briefly, he attended the Art Center College of Design in Pasadena, where the students made advertising reels; he dropped out "because I realized the best way to learn about making movies was by watching movies. And why would you give somebody tuition money to teach you how to make films when the best way to do it is just by using that tuition money to try to make one yourself?"

Roger would work at the video store, then take off for school or another job, then return as part of the constant ebb and flow of the Video Archives staff. During one of his times away, Roger worked for the producer Charles Band at Empire, "the closest thing to Roger Corman there was."

Six months after Quentin was hired, Gerald Martinez came aboard. At twenty, the swarthy, goateed Jerry was a frequent customer who, like Quentin and Roger before him, wanted to be on the other side of the counter. "I had heard about Quentin," says Jerry. "I kept hearing that I had to meet this guy."

Their initial meeting was not auspicious. Jerry had been to a sneak preview of the Joe Dante film *Gremlins* and hated it. Quentin, who loved Dante's frequent allusions to comics, Warner Brothers cartoons and *Famous Monsters* magazine, loved it. "Part of the Video Archives scene was you got together and talked about movies," says Jerry. "So I finally meet this guy everyone says I should meet and he argues with me. Maybe I was being a little bit of a snob, a little judgmental about films at that time.

That's one thing I really learned from Quentin is that all of these films have a value, there isn't one that should be more important than another one if it's true to itself. You could make some little mindless comedy, but if it comes from a pure place then it's every bit as valid as *Gandhi*. I learned not to pass judgment on films before seeing them. He really opened up my mind a lot."

Quentin would come over to Jerry's for family functions and for the annual Christmas tamale party. "For a while, he didn't have any other place to go for Christmas," says Jerry. "When I first met him, he was kind of estranged from his mother, Connie. For about three years, they weren't getting along. Connie would tell me how sick she was of Quentin's story about Dogpatch. She's a self-made woman and kind of pulled herself up by her bootstraps and really made something of her life. She's a very successful woman, an executive. To do that and be unmarried, how horribly disappointed she must have been in Quentin. Financially she can send her son to any school, and he can be whatever, and he decides to be an actor, and later a filmmaker. It must have been very disheartening, even though she was trying to be supportive. Like any parent, you see the impracticality of your child's situation. For her, Quentin was a disappointment at that time."

Jerry had a brother named Steve who was considered part of the group, although he never actually worked at the store. "I pride myself on that fact, that I was the outsider," says Steve. "I was a real friend, I didn't need video-ness to work my way in."

Steve, a painter, would tease the gang about their movie enthusiasm. "I liked Quentin because he's a positive guy, easily moved to laughter, and that attracted me," says Steve. "It wasn't a movie thing."

One night, Quentin called Steve at 10 P.M., dying to find someone who would accompany him to the Chevy Chase movie *Fletch*. "I felt bad, he wanted go to the movies so bad. He was begging, begging." Steve went on movie outings with the guys, but they would impose a ban—"You can come but if you're a jerk, if you're a jackass this time, you're never coming again." Jerkdom applied to anyone who chatted during the opening credits. "They get so reverent about their movies. We'd be sitting watching a video, and I'd make a remark, and they'd all go, 'Shut up! You're taking us out of the movie!'"

Steve almost lost his video privileges with Quentin when, during the action flick *American Ninja,* he made wisecracks. "I wrecked the movie for him," admits Steve. "After that, I was on probation."

Another time, the two fought bitterly over *Cobra,* a lesser Stallone movie. "This is something I take very seriously!" Quentin yelled before storming out.

Jerry Martinez was taking an art class at the time he joined the Archives staff, and he threw some temp work over to his classmate Russell Vossler. Russ would fill in when needed, and eventually asked Lance for a full-time gig.

Russ was introduced to Quentin at the store, but his first vivid memory was when Quentin drove him home one night in his messy Honda Civic, which he occasionally slept in. "I was a Hitchcock geek, and he was a big fan of Brian De Palma. That was fertile ground for an argument. I didn't even really know him and we were already having a big argument, Hitchcock versus De Palma," says Russ, who sounds like a true Quentin convert, with a contrite "I was lost and now I'm found" quality to his tale. "Quentin was very adamant. When he has an opinion about a film, it's like gospel truth. At the time I had a very narrow view of things, and I was thinking how De Palma had been accused of stealing from Hitchcock, bastardizing Hitchcock throughout his career. I think I was talking about *Body Double,* and how the character spies on someone pulling diamonds out of a safe, and how diamonds were supposed to mean something, and Quentin kinda scoffed at the idea. It was getting really obscure and minute. I guess I was petty and anal about details."

Since De Palma's *Blow Out* is one of Quentin's favorite movies, it was obvious where he stood on the Hitchcock–De Palma debate. Quentin has dismissed Hitchcock lovers as "Fanboy Film Guy 101." Russ thinks there's more to Quentin's love of De Palma than that. "He saw those movies at a very impressionable age and they stayed with him," says Russ. "And Quentin admired his career. When he was younger, De Palma was doing very small indie-type films like *Greetings* and *Hi, Mom!* and he discovered De Niro, and then he made big, super-stylish, really emotional films. That impressed Quentin."

Quentin loved to follow the careers of his favorite directors so much that at one point he conducted a series of interviews with a few of them. "I wasn't lying to them, I was actually going to write a book. I earnestly went out there to do that," says Quentin. "But I realized that I didn't have the disposition to write a film book."

He interviewed Joe Dante, John Milius and others, not really asking them reporter-style questions but simply talking with them about their career paths and storing that information away for later. It became a way to justify having movie conversations with people who were actually in the field.

Lance Lawson was everything you'd want in a boss, except good at business. He drew a salary from the cash drawer, but was never around. An early edict that the boys could get free lunch while they were working was eventually reinterpreted to mean a free meal every time they happened to be in the store, and since some of them were practically living there, the cash drawer came into play for pizza, burgers and snacks at all hours. "It's not like we stole or bought clothing or anything," says Jerry. "We just used it for food."

If Quentin had grown up in a Disneyland home environment, he recaptured that sense of fun at Video Archives, where the guys all had keys to the place; sometimes they even slept in the back of the store. They put their favorite videos up on the monitor and worked out scenarios for possible future screenplays, rarely getting beyond page 60.

Lance was in his early thirties when he opened Video Archives, and to the twentysomething clerks he seemed like an aging hippie. "He was the overriding force behind the store, the soul of the store," says Jerry. "We kind of revered him, because the store was everything to us at the time."

Lance was a film enthusiast who ignored the dictates of the marketplace by stocking the shelves with foreign films, classics and documentaries, the more obscure the better. "A minority of the customers really knew how great a place we were," says Jerry. "We were probably one of the best stores in California, only because there were very few places that even came close to us in the selection we carried."

As the store gained a cult following, "we took it over," says Jerry. "It was a horrible position to be in, because we ran the store but we couldn't write a check or order tapes. Important films came out—we didn't have *Bringing Up Baby*—and it would piss us off because Lance was neglecting things."

To lend the store more personality, they dreamed up the white-glove-named May We Suggest section to highlight the tastes of the staff. Rowland Wafford would push early Robert Zemeckis, like *Used Cars* and *I Want to Hold Your Hand*. Quentin would stack the rack with kung fu flicks, blaxploitation classics like *Coffy*, and anything else starring Pam Grier. At one time or another, Quentin would promote his personal favorites: *Blow Out*, *One-Eyed Jacks*, *Rio Bravo*, *For a Few Dollars More*, *Bande à Part*, *Rolling Thunder*, *Breathless* (1983), *Le Doulos*, *His Girl Friday*, *They Live by Night*, *The Long Goodbye*.

Eventually, in order to keep pace with more traditional video outlets, they had to change the May We Suggest section to New Releases, because that's where most customers head first. But they still maintained a Farewell section for dearly departed filmmakers, until Quentin mistakenly stocked it with a Kurosawa retrospective, not realizing the Japanese master was still alive and kicking.

Rowland Wafford doesn't remember the first time he met Quentin—"knowing Quentin is kinda like a blur"—but he does remember Quentin's most salient quality, "you couldn't get a short story out of him." Rowland was the rare Video Archives clerk who wasn't interested in becoming a director. He wanted to edit, work the cameras, write or produce.

Stevo Polyi, one of the first hires at Video Archives (and one of the last to leave), thinks of 1986 to 1987 as the "meaty years" of the Archives experience. During that time, Stevo and Quentin roomed together for two years in a ramshackle house right behind the store, at 1130 Twenty-second Street. When Michael Rapaport in *True Romance* refers forlornly to his pothead room-mate Brad Pitt, it was in memory of Quentin's time in that house. "It was like a roommate dude house, one bathroom, three bed-rooms, an overgrown backyard," says Stevo, who is five years older than Quentin. "The toilet backed up every six months. Thank god Archives was just down the way." Before that, Quentin had been living off Imperial Highway "in a depressed apartment in a bad area. He was living with Eugene, a black guy. The apartment was known as Quentin's Cave."

Stevo describes Quentin as "an okay roommate. He cleaned up his messes in the kitchen, but his own room and his personal hygiene were rather sloppy. He would come out of the bedroom in the morning and the smell just rolled out after him."

The rent was $1100, split three ways. Good humor prevailed in the frat environment, except for the time Quentin got unchar-acteristically angry at the roommate they called Dave the British Guy. "He had no job and he was doing nasty things around the house. Finally we had a confrontation. Quentin got so mad he slammed the door."

The "heyday" that Stevo recalls seems to coincide with the time he had Quentin mostly to himself. "We used to stay after work and watch movies together, call out for pizza. Roger was off at school. It was basically just Quentin and I."

For Stevo's birthday one September, the perpetually broke (and, say friends, cheap) Quentin gave him a "favor card." The hand-drawn card was an IOU, promising the bearer he could trade it in for "any favor at any time no matter how big, no mat-ter how small, no notice be given."

"It's in his horrible handwriting," says Stevo. "It has no expiration date."

Stevo says he never met Quentin's mother, Connie, during all that time because things between mother and son were chilly in the aftermath of Quentin quitting school. Stevo also claims that Quentin only took back his biological father's name of Tarantino because he couldn't stand being called Zastoupil—"in school, they had called him Disaster-Pill"—and that he once visited a plastic surgeon about his "Dudley Do-Right jaw, to see if it could be shortened" so he could get more acting roles. (The doctor told him he had a "characteristic look" and he should keep it.)

After two years in the rooming house, Quentin wanted to move closer to Hollywood, where the action was. He was the manager of the store at that time, but often he would simply fail to show up. Dennis Humbert fired Quentin, but as with all the Archivists who were fired or banned, it was temporary. Quentin was back on weekends in late 1989 to help underwrite his screenwriting habit. For a few years, he lived rent-free in Connie's house while she was away on business.

"Quentin can be a real sweet guy, a nice guy when he wants to be, but only when it's in his interests. He looks out for himself more than other people do," says Stevo. "He's kind of a trickster, too, always getting people to do his bidding. When he had free passes to the movies, he wouldn't share them. He once talked me into going to see *DreamChild*, and while I was sitting there he went into another theater in the Beverly Center to check out another movie. He never came back. Maybe he's like that because he had to fend for himself so much. I had real cool parents, they've always helped me out or taken care of me. Maybe Quentin decided he should take what he can while he's there."

Video Archives proved a great place not only to screen and talk movies, but to pick up girls. Quentin, who by all accounts has an innocent, romantic notion of dating, developed a routine whereby he would note the membership number of a customer who caught his fancy, then go into the computer and change her name to something like Dreamgirl. Then he would call her to the counter and act concerned, telling her there seemed to be a problem with the account, and show her that she was registered as Dreamgirl. "It worked," says Jerry. "He must have seen it in the movies. Or a girl would come in, rent a movie, and Quentin would write down her account number and then call her at home and be as charming and sincere as he could. He'd tell them he just thought they were very sweet, and wanted to go to a movie with them."

Jerry and his older brother, Steve, were living with their mother, Lydia, who was pressed into service on one of Quentin's dates. "He didn't have time to go out because he was working," says Lydia. "He wanted to take a girl on a picnic in the parking lot of the video store. He needed a picnic basket and tablecloth, like an old-fashioned picnic."

"Too bad you don't have any ants, that would really do it," Quentin told Lydia, who was impressed by Quentin's imagination, even if a parking lot isn't the most romantic spot. "It was unique, something no one else would have thought about. It goes to show how his mind works. He's a unique person, he just goes ahead and does what he feels he wants to do, and doesn't care who thinks what, or if it's stupid or dumb."

Several small romances unfolded in this manner. "I don't get the impression he was having torrid affairs or anything," says Jerry. "Quentin gets caught up in the romance of dating. He's a romantic guy. It's not just to get into their pants."

Quentin had a lot of dates through the video store, but none of them ever clicked—until Grace Lovelace came along.

Grace was a customer who was studying to be an English teacher. Quentin was attracted and used his recent managerial status to get her hired. They didn't start dating until four or five months later. Although all of the guys took a liking to her, at first they were annoyed that Quentin had gotten her on the limited payroll. "Yes, she's cute," says Jerry, "but we always tried to hire people who would strengthen the store, who had something to offer, like a specialty. Russell was the Cartoon Guy, he knew all about Warner Brothers animation. I was the Foreign Guy, I knew a lot about German and Japanese movies. Grace is quiet and intelligent and loves movies, but not on the scale that the rest of us did. I was pissed off when Quentin hired her."

Jerry's brother Steve was part of the cabal that would meet Sunday nights to watch *Shadow Warriors*, a popular TV series from Japan (there called *Kage No Gundo*) starring Sonny Chiba that unfolded as feudal morality plays. In each episode, samurai and ninjas would battle for the hearts, minds and bodies of some Japanese village. At the end, Sonny Chiba would make a grand speech about righteousness and the tyranny of evil men. "The last person to hear that speech would soon be a dead man," is how Quentin describes his fascination with the show; he incorporated that into the character of Jules in *Pulp Fiction*.

Those Sonny Chiba evenings in the summer of 1989 would go sometimes until 5 A.M. Grace Lovelace would attend, but she was never much of a *Shadow Warriors* fan, and often she fell asleep on the couch. One night, Steve Martinez thought that the sleeping Grace would make a nice subject for a painting, so he sketched her lying there. The result was a portrait named *Grace Watching Shadow Warriors*, and of course the joke is that her eyes are closed. People outside the group didn't get it, and accused Steve of giving it an arty name. When he changed the title briefly, Quentin called him "a big jackass." Although a doctor offered money for the painting, his wife hated it; Grace's mother also offered to buy it. But Quentin wound up with the painting for free in his living room, where it hung even after Grace left him in 1991 to further her education, and where it hangs today now that Grace is back in his life.

At least Quentin gravitated toward strong women. "He was very influenced by his mother," says Jerry, "and he certainly doesn't go out with weak sisters. I don't think he puts up with dumb or shallow people. He's not a creep or anything, he's respectful of women. I don't believe what people say, that his movies are a male-oriented power fantasy. I've never seen him use his celebrity now to take advantage of women."

*   *   *

Scott McGill, the son of the owner of Archives predecessor Video Outtakes, was Roger Avary's best friend. But as a budding filmmaker himself, he gravitated toward Quentin, and before long the two were working together on a modest little movie called *Lovebirds in Bondage*. Scott, who was several years younger than everybody else, had once shot a short film for Roger that had won a prize at a festival, so he knew some of the basics about putting a film together. Scott worked the camera on *Lovebirds* while Quentin directed and starred. They never finished it.

"We co-wrote and co-directed it," says Quentin. "It was about a guy who was in love with a girl who got in an auto accident. Then she's a total vegetable, well, maybe not total, just brain-damaged, crazy. So he's all messed up about it, and decides he wants to be with her, so he gets himself committed. I played the guy. We never got as far as casting the girl, we only shot the guy stuff. It came out really good, and the next thing I knew he said his mom destroyed the footage. But later, I thought he had probably destroyed it himself."

"I don't think Quentin knew it at the time, but Scott wasn't really happy with him as a director," says one of the people who saw the finished footage. "Quentin didn't know what he was doing back then. And Scott was really the one who seemed like he had all the talent. He was the most sensitive potential filmmaker of the bunch."

"Scott was one of us, a writer, director, producer, whatever," says another member of the gang. "He was extremely talented. I think out of all of us I'd probably give him the most credit for having a defined style at an early age."

Later Scott would help Quentin on another film he would try to make, *My Best Friend's Birthday*. But Scott was more sensitive than the other guys. He couldn't take the vicious banter that passed for friendship, so in the end he only helped out occasionally on *My Best Friend's Birthday*.

Eventually, Scott got work as an assistant editor with Don Coscarelli, who had made *Phantasm*, one of Scott's favorite films. This, to everyone at the video store, was considered The Big Time, and it looked like Scott would be the first of them to make it in Hollywood.

On July 4, 1987, having waited until his best friend Roger was safely out of the way on a trip to Europe, Scott McGill went into the bathroom of his apartment and slashed timidly at his wrist and throat. The cuts weren't deep enough. He took a moment to sop up the blood from the floor so that the mess wouldn't be a bother to anyone else, then walked up the stairs to the roof of his building and leaped to his death.

He left behind an elaborate journal and audiotape for Roger, who was emotionally unable to examine them until much time had passed. In these memoirs Scott explained that he was afraid he would never be as successful a filmmaker as either Roger or Quentin. He felt he couldn't compete.

"The way our group was, we just gave each other such shit all the time. It was a running joke that was part of the joy of being together, it was just hilarious to everybody," says Rand Vossler, Russell's brother who never worked at Archives but who had roomed with Scott for a while. "Somehow I had the impression that it just was not that funny to Scott. And in a lot of ways I think he eventually got overwhelmed with every- thing. I know that he was envious of the attention that Quentin got and I think that in some way he felt that he was better. Nobody really paid that much attention to him and he was very humble about his work, extremely humble. He didn't show me any of his stuff until a year after I met him."

Obviously Scott's troubles ran deeper and for a longer time than anyone realized. Nevertheless, the group felt varying degrees of guilt. "We weren't there for him enough," mourns one.

"Scott and I were really close," says Quentin. "He had left a nine-page letter and tape for Roger, but we found the letter not quite two years after his death, it was just floating around and I came across it from someone who had it. The letter explained it all, adding up to the fact that he wanted to be a filmmaker and didn't think he'd ever be able to do it, he didn't have the stamina. Everything he had tried, he'd start out with piss and vinegar and then lose his steam. He figured that eventually he'd always be disappointed, living with his mother, and he didn't want to live life like that."

A memorial service for friends was held sometime after the funeral. Quentin didn't show. Neither did most of the gang. Of all the activities the Archivists engaged in, introspection was not one.

Video Archives was more than a place to work, it was a home away from home, a place where like-minded people congregated, a treasure trove of movie lore. But because it didn't cater to the Blockbuster crowd, the store never really prospered, and the move in 1994 to Hermosa Beach finally killed it. "It was a microcommunity of artists," says Jerry. "The move was never advertised, there was no promotion done so the customers would know where to find it. Everyone could see the writing on the wall."

By then, almost everyone had left. The "Two Reds," redheads Laura Rush and Julie McLean, who had joined the store in the late eighties and wound up running the place, had already quit. Robert Silvey, who joined after Quentin was starting to be famous and was such a fan that he practically fainted when Quentin consented to play a board game with him, stayed on to the bitter end. Jerry helped out when he could right before he got his new job at Disneyland.

"It was a block from the beach and no parking," says Stevo. "I hadn't gotten paid in four weeks. Hermosa Beach killed it. It wasn't the same old Archives. It was like beating a dead horse."

"That store was ours," says Jerry Martinez. "We made it ours, and it was the most important thing to us. It was more than just a store, it was our family, and Lance was kind of the absentee father or something. He just wouldn't show up, he'd never be there. There was always someplace else he wanted to be, or preferred to be, or had to go to. For us, this was a great place, we'd go there even when we weren't working."

*   *   *

The old gang went on to other things, together and separately.

Russ Vossler and Jerry Martinez returned to their basic love—not movies, but art. Russ does illustration work at the Varner Studios, a sculpting studio where he helps design toys for fast-food promotional gigs. For *Pulp Fiction*, he drew the original Jack Rabbit Slim character—later redesigned by Jerry— and the Big Jerry's cab logo, which is a caricature of his pal Jerry. "The back of my head can be seen in *Four Rooms*, that's the extent of my acting ability," says Russ.

Although Russ stays in touch with Quentin, there can be six-month stretches between sightings. He thinks the old friends who take Quentin's absences to heart "hate themselves" and take it out on Quentin by bad-mouthing him. "When Quentin hears about that, he's kind of saddened by it, not in a pitying way, but he's just a little bit hurt by it. What's really neat is that within his circle of people, he gets a lot of support and goodwill."

Jerry Martinez has shaved off his goatee because his new employers at Disneyland don't go for that sort of thing. In the Watch Shop on Main Street, Jerry sits at an animation desk and draws preapproved drawings of Disney characters, which get reduced onto watch faces to be sold as souvenirs along with the original artwork. Jerry still sees Quentin and is very protective of him.

Quentin had befriended the Two Reds, who joined Video Archives after "the heyday." The women appear briefly in Quentin's segment of the omnibus movie *Four Rooms*.

Rowland Wafford has stayed best friends with Stevo Polyi, and together they traveled to France in January 1995 to act in *Mr. Stitch*, a movie Roger Avary wrote and directed. Roger created those roles specifically for Rowland and Stevo out of friendship. Rowland and Stevo had never been out of the country before, so they are as gushing on the subject of Roger Avary as the other guys are on the subject of Quentin; sometimes it seems the Archivists have chosen sides.

Rowland appears briefly in *Reservoir Dogs*, in the coffee

shop flashback where Tim Roth walks in. "You see my back, my hair is so big it covers up my wife who's sitting with me. Tim Roth walks right by me, and I threw in a little bit of action, I picked up a coffee cup." (Jerry Martinez can also be glimpsed briefly in another booth in that scene.)

Like most of the old gang, things Rowland said to Quentin have wound up in Quentin's screenplays. "When Steve Buscemi and Harvey Keitel are arguing in *Reservoir Dogs* and Michael Madsen comes in and says that someone's going to end up crying, that's my grandma talking to me and my cousins," says Rowland.

In May 1994, Rowland borrowed from Quentin a letterboxed laser disc edition of the 1966 Japanese monster movie *War of the Gargantuas*. Quentin hates to lend anything from his beloved laser disc collection, so he made Rowland promise to return it right away. "I kept leaving messages on his machine," says Rowland. "He wanted it right back, and he doesn't return my calls."

He wouldn't returns calls, yet out of the blue, Quentin invited Rowland to a special screening of James Cameron's *True Lies*. He invited a handful of former Archivists, about as many of them as there are members of the *Reservoir Dogs* gang. "Quentin does these things," says Rowland, now the Public Access Guy for the MultiVision cable company in Hermosa Beach. "The thing is, you can't really describe him, he's just Quentin."

Stevo Polyi claims he was the source of many of Quentin's famous movie monologues. When Dennis Hopper taunts Christopher Walken about the mixed heritage of Sicilians in *True Romance*, that, says Stevo, came from him. "I'm the guy who's Sicilian, I made that up. You've gotta be careful what you say around Quentin, because he picks it up and uses it," a sentiment that is echoed by other members of the old gang.

Quentin demurs. "Stevo couldn't put those words together if he tried," he says. "I started doing the Christopher Walken speech to him, to get him mad, and then I realized it really works. Where it actually came from is Don Watts, the brother of my mother's longtime friend Jackie Watts. Don used to say those things, and he thinks it's true."

In *Reservoir Dogs,* undercover cop Tim Roth tells an anecdote about trying to watch *The Lost Boys* during a drug buy. Again, says Stevo, that was his own story, a slice of his life. Others corroborate this. "At first I was flattered, then it pissed me off royally," says Stevo. "Tim Roth goes around saying how that scene is pure fucking Quentin, and I'm like, that's *me*! Quentin feels that whoever makes it first gets it, like a free-for-all. Nothing we said was ever copyrighted. Quentin's room was next to mine, he would listen to me on the phone and then come out and question me about things I'd just said. It took me a long time to get around to *Reservoir Dogs,* and I'm afraid to see *Pulp Fiction,* I don't want to see anything else of mine. Quentin believes it's first come, first served. He's told me and Roger to our face, 'We'll just see who gets it done first, buddy-boy.' Nothing really bothers him much, it's like water off a duck's back."

Quentin agrees that trying to watch *The Lost Boys* while the telephone is ringing is "totally Stevo. And it's understandable that Stevo might think he was affected by the 1986 marijuana drought. Maybe it affected him the most. But does he have a copyright on the 1986 marijuana drought? It's not like he ever walked into a bathroom with a bunch of cops."

Stevo provided the prototype for the Brad Pitt character in *True Romance* and the Eric Stoltz character in *Pulp Fiction,* "because Stevo always wore bathrobes around the house."

Stevo appears briefly in *Reservoir Dogs* as "Sheriff No. 4" in the Tim Roth bathroom scene. He was asked to audition for the Dean Martin waiter role in *Pulp Fiction,* but he blew off the audition, miffed that Quentin hadn't called him personally.

Although he seems bitter about how Quentin "borrowed" his material, there is the sense that what makes Stevo most upset is having lost access to his friend. "He changed his phone number on me," he gripes. But he still carries around Quentin's "favor card" in his wallet, like a snapshot of a loved one.

He tried to call in the favor when he was out of work for a few months in 1994. "You're a big man now, if you can help me out, great," Stevo told him. "It took a lot for me to ask him, too.

But he just gave me the silent treatment. He didn't want to do me that favor. He's very much into himself right now, he's busy reinventing himself, much like Madonna used to every year. I think I represent something from a time Quentin wants to forget, a Quentin who was sloppy and not dressed nice, who spent time in the county jail for outstanding traffic violations. We tried to bail him out, but they kept upping the bail, until finally he spent ten days in jail for everything."

Quentin had been so bad about the upkeep of his cars and the status of his traffic tickets that one time, when his car broke down, he had called a friend to pick him up; when the friend arrived, they pushed the old wreck into the driveway of a Thom McAn shoe store and just abandoned it there. Those subsequent ten days in jail were worth it to Quentin—it absolved him of a $7,000 backlog of fines, and he absorbed some legitimate jailhouse dialogue.

Today, Stevo gets out of bed around 1 P.M. and works on his screenplay, "sort of Disney meets David Lynch." Quentin agrees that he should have called Stevo back about that favor card, but says it had been a time when people were after him "like piranhas" for favors.

Steve Martinez, who painted Grace asleep on the sofa, is a struggling artist with a studio in his mother's garage. During the week, he works three shifts as a security guard in downtown Los Angeles. His painting of Uma Thurman lounging on a sofa appears in one scene of *Pulp Fiction* behind the heroin-hazed John Travolta.

Grace Lovelace broke up with Quentin right after the filming of *Reservoir Dogs*, but Quentin persisted in thinking of her as the love of his life, the one that got away. He named a character after her in the original screenplay of *Natural Born Killers*—the character gets knifed in the head—and named Bruce Willis's *Pulp Fiction* chopper after her.

Grace now teaches English at the University of California at Irvine, and she and Quentin resumed their relationship after *Pulp Fiction*. Everyone from the old gang likes Grace and calls her "sweet" and "smart," but all of them have to be prompted to remember whether she was present at any of the activities they describe. It's almost as if in their minds, Grace is forever asleep on the couch during *Shadow Warriors*, with them but not of them.

Lance Lawson continues to make himself appear to be missing in action. After the Oscar nominations were announced, he changed his outgoing phone message to a recording of a radio ad promoting *Pulp Fiction*. The man whom Jerry Martinez described as "the absentee father figure" talks frequently on the phone to Quentin, someone who has known a few absentee fathers in his time.

In March 1995, Quentin arranged to buy up all of Video Archives' video stock (Roger Avary bought up the laser discs). He realized it would be nice if he could buy the rights to the name of the store and start it up again himself, "but with the name goes a lot of other things, like lawsuits."

Of the other two original owners, Rick Humbert cashed in his Video Archives chips years ago and moved to Amsterdam like Vincent Vega; today he lives with his mother in Japan. Dennis Humbert returned to the real estate business he was in years ago.

Roger Avary fared the best and the worst of the whole lot. He collaborated with Quentin so often that their material mingled to a point where only the two of them knew who contributed what. Roger claims an early screenplay he wrote called *The Open Road* turned into Quentin's script for *True Romance*. Little bits that Roger wrote for other scripts found their way into all of Quentin's work. Although Roger was originally to share screenwriting credit with Quentin on *Pulp Fiction*, the credit went to Quentin alone, with Roger sharing a "stories by" credit; in the round of critical awards that followed, some included Roger, some didn't. His major acknowledgment came when he and Quentin won an Oscar for Best Original Screenplay.

None of the guys denies Roger's heavy influence on Quentin's work; even the most hardcore Quentin loyalists admit Roger was screwed along the way. Roger went on to write and direct *Killing Zoe*, about major betrayals between boy-

hood pals during a bank heist; some describe it as a thinly
veiled re-creation of Roger and Quentin's relationship.

"If Quentin didn't make it in the film business," Roger is
fond of saying, "it's very likely he'd have ended up a serial
killer."

CHAPTER 4

My Best Friend's Birthday

*Nothing much happens in Torrance. But occasionally you can
have a bad night there.*

> —*Legend on first page of script for*
> My Best Friend's Birthday, *Quentin*
> *Tarantino and Craig Hamann, c. 1985*

Like Quentin, Craig Hamann had an aversion to authority figures. It's not that Quentin or Craig didn't want to learn, it's just
that they were suspicious of inflexible rules, especially as those
rules applied to them.

With this outlaw outlook, it's little wonder that Craig
Hamann was eventually kicked out of the James Best Theater
Company after just seven months. Quentin stayed on longer, but
the two remained friends from January 1981, when they met in

acting class, until just before Quentin made *Reservoir Dogs* in 1991.

"One of the reasons why we hit it off right away was because we had both seen lots of movies and liked the same type of movies," says Craig. "He was the most talented actor in the class, and probably the least appreciated, which really used to anger me. I mean, here's a guy with a wealth of knowledge about movies, who clearly knew more than any of the instructors. But in acting schools, in my view, the instructors become gurus, and the students do things a certain way to please the gurus, but Quentin wouldn't do that. Within a matter of months he outgrew the school. The other students didn't know shit about anything. They only cared how photos and résumés look. Quentin was a consummate authority on film, he honestly saw the art of it. He was full of energy and life, and it was hard for him to contain himself onstage. He wanted to get to the heart of any scene he did and was just so passionate about the roles he was playing."

Quentin and Craig became best friends and wrote little scenes for themselves to act in, instead of memorizing the traditional monologues found in drama bookstores. Quentin would take Craig to the movies to introduce him to Hong Kong action pictures and Italian horror films.

In late 1984, Craig came up with the idea for *My Best Friend's Birthday*. He wrote a forty-one-page script, "fairly autobiographical," about how a gregarious best friend tries to do something special for Craig on his birthday, only everything he tries goes wrong and it turns into the worst day of his life. "Quentin and I started adding scenes, then we had about eighty pages of script. Quentin and I co-wrote, co-produced, co-starred. I was the best friend, he was playing this loud rockabilly boy. Quentin directed it." The purpose of the film would be to showcase the acting talents of Craig and Quentin and get them some work in Hollywood.

Quentin's character was named Clarence Pool, and Craig played Mickey Burnett, named after Mickey Rourke. Later Quentin would give the name Clarence to his alter ego in *True*

Romance, and the name Mickey to the protagonist in *Natural Born Killers*.

Mickey is fired from his job the night before his birthday, and Clarence decides to show Mickey a great time by hiring him a prostitute, just the way Lance would do for Clarence in *True Romance*. Clarence gives the hooker, Misty Knight, a key to Mickey's house and she lets herself in when Mickey doesn't expect her. Her pimp shows up too, shades of Clarence's confrontation with the pimp in *True Romance*.

Meanwhile, Mickey's girlfriend has dumped him, and he meets another girl who ends up being the girl Clarence is dating on the side, who simultaneously is dating a sadistic cop. Quentin added a scene for Craig where the ex-girlfriend reappears, pretending she's interested in getting back together, when all she wants is to reclaim her Rod Stewart tapes. "Everything that can go wrong that night gets worse," says Craig. "Thanks to Clarence, Mickey gets in a fight with the pimp and the cop and gets rejected by two different girls, while Clarence falls in love with the prostitute. Clarence and Mickey have a big fight and Mickey falls into the birthday cake."

At the end of the night, Mickey and Clarence are outside a bar. Mickey forgives Clarence and sits on the hood of a car. Clarence gives him a joint. "Just smoke this, relax, and when you feel calm, you come back in the bar and I'll buy you a beer," says Clarence, who goes inside.

Mickey lights up the joint, then the car turns on its lights to reveal that Mickey is sitting on the hood of a cop car. *My Best Friend's Birthday* ends with Mickey being busted for drugs.

"The humor is sometimes very dry, or absurd," says Craig. "None of the characters is very smart. Their cumulative IQ would make a good golf score."

Longtime actor Allen Garfield had been teaching his craft at the Lee Strasberg Theater Institute, but when Strasberg died, Allen opened his own Actors' Shelter in 1985. His very first student was Quentin Tarantino.

"Quentin sought me out because he had seen the first two films that I had done in New York with De Niro and De Palma called *Greetings* and *Hi, Mom!* And so Quentin, being enamored of those films, sought me out to study acting, writing and directing. He told me he wanted to work with the actor who had worked with Brian De Palma."

Classes were held on weekends in a theater in Beverly Hills. "From the inception what I had in front of my eyes was a very, very beautiful, pure, raw, unharnessed talent," says Allen. "And also a fellow who has all of the hunger to act, write and direct, and all of the insecurity about how to go about doing it. And not knowing if he would be acceptable in the marketplace at any time because of his feeling that he marched to such a different drummer."

Allen remembers that Quentin would come to class with "all of these rambling, uncharted monologues."

One of the things Allen tried to talk Quentin out of was his fascination with De Palma. "I told him the De Palma that I worked with is no longer the De Palma that I worked with—meaning that the films he spontaneously and courageously made in the sixties and seventies weren't the films he was making in the eighties. You're talking about somebody now who has ventured into bloodletting and copying other masters. And Quentin would argue, yes, but he has such a sense of moving the camera. And we would have these amusing, intense arguments with me telling him that if he wants to emulate somebody, emulate Cassavetes, don't come and study with me and then go and copy De Palma. If I seemed to be coming down too hard on his adoration of De Palma, it was only because it would be a pity to see him squandering his original, rawboned talent by trying to be derivative of somebody else who already abandoned his original bold streaks."

Classes cost $200 a month for two marathon classes a week; Quentin didn't always have the money, but Allen often let him slide over the five or so years Quentin studied with him. Quentin had incentive to stay beyond even the free ride: Allen would often tell him he had "the germ of being in your own generation another Orson Welles."

"His countenance, it was very unusual visually for an actor," says Allen. "His face had a very wonderful, uncommon sculptured look, and his talent had the possibility of a triple threat, not unlike Welles. But with even more of a possibility of having an uninterrupted genius career, as opposed to a genius like Mr. Welles who floundered and just surfaced every once in a while after the first hurrah."

Quentin and some of the Archivists would hang out at Allen's apartment in West Hollywood, editing together a sample reel of Allen's work from videos they borrowed from the store. It was then that Quentin asked his teacher if he would donate one night a week to acting in a little film he was planning to make. Allen would play "an entertainment magnate." "That was our first taste of acting with each other," says Allen.

Ten years later, they would act together again in *Destiny Turns On the Radio*, a film from Savoy Pictures with Quentin in a pivotal role as a magical figure named Johnny Destiny.

My Best Friend's Birthday would be a labor of love for everyone involved—it had to be, because there was no money in it. The $5000 the movie cost came out of everyone's pockets, and filming would be halted until another payday came around at Video Archives, the store where Quentin worked and that supplied much of the cast and crew.

One of the actors was a former James Best classmate of Craig's and Quentin's—Rich Turner, a fellow South Bay resident who would later play the sheriff in *Reservoir Dogs*, the one who recites a story in the bathroom while Tim Roth is washing his hands. Rich would also have a small part as a bank hostage in Roger Avary's *Killing Zoe*. In *My Best Friend's Birthday*, Rich played the new boyfriend of the girl who dumps Craig. It wasn't so far-fetched a premise, since in real life, Linda Kaye, who plays the ex-girlfriend, dated both Russ Vossler from the video store and Quentin. She would later appear briefly in both *Reservoir*

Dogs (she is pulled out of her car) and *Pulp Fiction* (she is shot while trying to help Bruce Willis).

Russ Vossler's brother Rand had taken some film classes at Los Angeles Community College. Rand was desperate to get hold of equipment and work on as many projects as he could in whatever capacity was available—producing, shooting, editing, directing. Russ told Rand about Quentin's plans to shoot a movie on Super-8, so Rand hooked up with the Archivists and served as producer and cinematographer.

But first, he had to audition.

Even though there was no pay involved, and the movie would be nothing but a glorified student film, Quentin wanted to make sure everyone was right for the job. Rand met with Quentin in late 1984 or January 1985 and was sent on a trial run to shoot a short movie, *Jukebox at the End of Time*, with Scott McGill and their friend Al Harrell. It starred Craig Hamann.

"We jokingly referred to it as *My Dinner with Mad Max*, a film with the pace of *My Dinner with André*, but the way we shot it and assumed it would cut together I don't think we had a take that lasted more than three seconds," says Rand. "It would have to be cut like an action film to make it work."

Rand and Scott both handled the photography for the two days it took to make *Jukebox*. Then they plunged into *My Best Friend's Birthday*. It was mapped out over the kitchen table at the Harbor City home of Quentin's mother, who was away on business.

"Quentin was very hot on screwball comedy at the time," says Rand. "He was a huge Howard Hawks fan and was going through this screwball comedy phase. He immersed himself in Peter Bogdanovich as a kind of second-generation screwball director."

It was a lucky thing Connie was out of town. For one thing, her despised third husband, Jan, was currying Quentin's favor by secretly slipping him money to help him make his film. For another thing, much of the movie was shot in Connie's house "and if she had been around at any time we were there she would have freaked out and closed it down," according to Rand. In fact, they all schemed to send Connie off to a hotel for two weeks so that she wouldn't see how they were messing up her house. "We just ransacked the place."

Jan says Connie never went to a hotel, that she went to stay at a friend's house closer to Glendale, where she was working at the time and where she and Jan would move after Quentin moved out on his own. Jan relays this as if Connie had committed a crime: "She was a *workaholic*," he spits.

"Jan wasn't a bad guy," says Jerry Martinez from the video store, "but he was as close to a used-car salesman as you can get."

Although the idea had always been to make a low-budget film, Rand convinced Quentin—"not that he needed too much prodding"—to expand the script with some additional material and make a feature-length film. "It was right around the time of *She's Gotta Have It* and *Stranger Than Paradise,* and we were both fired up. This was gonna be our ticket, boy! This was gonna be our first feature film, and as Orson Welles was always fond of saying—'Have the confidence of ignorance.' We certainly had that. We had no idea the extent of the commitment it was going to be. We became passionate partners instantly."

Rand Vossler's presence caused a minor rift on the set. Scott McGill, the sensitive Video Archivist who in 1987 would commit suicide, was to be the director of photography, but he quit after the first four days.

"It was one of those screwy things," says Rand. "Scott and I actually became good friends after a while. But he had never shot 16-mm film and he was intimidated by that. The first two days I was working as his assistant and it was obvious that he was overwhelmed, so he asked me to step in for him, so I would shoot the film and he would help me. That became a matter of contention with Craig, because Craig really wanted Scott to shoot the film. We eventually got Scott to come back and work on the film, but it was one of the big melodramas on the set."

Rand was managing a Musicland record store. Quentin had his seven dollars an hour from Video Archives. Craig borrowed up to his limit on his Visa card. "Basically, between Craig, Quentin and myself, we pooled all the money we had and took two weeks off and shot as much as we could. We finished about a third of the script in that time and we were all bone-dry broke and couldn't afford to do anything more with it. We couldn't even afford to develop the film. We set all the film aside and went back to work until we could afford to shoot again, and I think it was maybe three weeks later that we pooled our money again and shot for a long three-day weekend. We basically did this every weekend or every other weekend for months."

The opening scene of the movie turned out to be the funniest. It takes place in a deejay's booth of K-Billy's radio station and was filmed in the breakfast nook of Rand's mother's house. The kitchen had a pass-through window where they hung a sheet of Plexiglas to simulate a control booth. They disguised the fact that it was a kitchen by hanging movie posters on the walls and an American flag over a window that looked out onto a patio.

Rowland Wafford, another Archivist, plays a character named Lenny Otis, head of the southern California chapter of the Eddie Cochran Fan Club. Mickey, played by Quentin, is a deejay who is interviewing Lenny on the air. Stevo Polyi, also from the video store, plays another deejay who tells a story "about how wacky it was to get stoned in a magic shop," says Rowland. Stevo's character has brought back itching powder from the magic store, and during a station break he enters the booth where Quentin is interviewing Rowland. "He pulls out this white industrial itching powder, it's in a baggie. Quentin automatically assumes it's cocaine, and before he can be told that it's itching powder, Stevo gets a call from an old girlfriend that he's been arguing with, and leaves the room. So right before we go back on the air, Quentin says, 'Let's do some of this up.' So he snorts this itching powder, flicks on the radio, they're on the air, he freaks out and everything just really goes wacky before the opening credits."

As preposterous as it seems, Rowland is dumbfounded when reminded that the scene bears similarities to the one in

Pulp Fiction where Uma Thurman snorts heroin from a bag of white powder she mistakes for cocaine. "I never made that connection," he says, awed.

Rand Vossler says that's not the only scene that underwent a sea change into a future Quentin screenplay. Several speeches and scenarios from the amateur effort went into *True Romance*, including the opening Elvis speech that Clarence gives as he's looking for someone to go to the movies with. The K-Billy radio station finds its way into the background of *Reservoir Dogs*, where it provides the musical accompaniment to the ear-slicing scene. And Quentin's voice is heard as the deejay Panhandle Slim on a similar radio station in the short film *The Coriolus Effect*.

Somehow, the boys got an introduction to Fred Olen Ray, maker of super-low-budget grade-Z films; at the time, he had yet to make his seminal *Hollywood Chainsaw Hookers*.

"We talked him into lending us a 16-mm camera that he had lying around," says Rand. "It was like, 'Oh my god! We have a free camera!' We couldn't believe we were going to be able to shoot forever. And that's one of the reasons we had the luxury of shooting every weekend; we didn't have to rent all this material."

"We all threw some money in there, we got money any way we could," says Craig Hamann. "We got that equipment by hook or by crook. That camera we borrowed held like two and a half minutes of film in each roll, and we kept lying to Fred about when we would return it."

They used a crystal synch tape recorder for the dialogue along with the borrowed camera.

"I think we didn't see one frame of footage until about five or six months later, after we had shot the majority of the film and we could finally afford to process some of the material," says Rand.

There are two ways to shoot film—you can shoot with negative film, which when processed provides a work print that looks like a photograph negative; it still needs to be reversed in another process. Or you can shoot in reversal so that you save a step and get a positive image after processing. "We shot in reversal 16-mm

film because we wanted to get a cleaner image and we didn't
think we could afford shooting with negative film," says Rand.

When they finally processed their first batch of film, "the
screening was incredibly encouraging. Even though we weren't
seeing it yet with sound, we were just jumping up and down
and hugging each other. We thought it was the greatest thing. It
just looked so great. The projectionist was watching the film
with us and he came out and told us we should keep going
because it was some of the best black-and-white footage he'd
seen. Quentin and I couldn't contain ourselves."

Unfortunately, once they matched the synch sound to the
footage, they realized that the battered old camera had not been
running at the same rate as the tape recorder. The sound was
totally out of synch. Now they knew why Fred had been so
quick to loan them that camera.

"Oh, it was a major drag," says Rand. But Craig Hamann
knew someone who had worked with the businessman Armand
Hammer on some documentaries about Hammer's art excur-
sions to Russia. The guy had flatbed editing equipment in the
Hammer offices and he would let Rand and Quentin in to hand-
tool *My Best Friend's Birthday,* linking the sound to the picture
frame by frame, counting on visual cues like door slams or
actors saying the letter "p" to try to synchronize the dialogue.

"Usually you synch a film up with the slap of the slate, but
our film didn't have that," says Rand. "It was all over the place,
and sometimes it went out of synch every five seconds. Any
time someone said a line of dialogue I would have to cut out
frames or add frames to fill in the blanks, which I did for the
whole film. It took at least three weeks."

By now it was spring of 1986 and Scott McGill was working
for Don Coscarelli, the wunderkind who had put together
1979's *Phantasm* like a one-man band. He was working on
Phantasm II and *Survival Quest,* and Scott got Rand a job alongside him. Quentin was left with the raw footage of *My Best
Friend's Birthday,* and Rand fell out of touch with him.

"Quentin was always kinda funny about friends of his that

had any kind of success, because he always felt that he should be the one who should be having the success," says Rand. "He and I had really saturated each other with our presence and I had gone on to bigger and better things. He was bitter that I would be doing this feature film and he was still trying to cut *My Best Friend's Birthday* together."

Connie's husband, Jan, rented some flatbed editing equipment so that Quentin could splice the footage together in his apartment. Jan, who is practically rabid on the subject of how many of Quentin's bills he paid—"I've got receipts! I have them right here!"—says he took out display ads in *Variety* and *The Hollywood Reporter*, and that Gene Kirkwood, producer of *The Pope of Greenwich Village*, showed up to take a look at the unfinished movie. "Quentin answered the door in a dirty T-shirt, pair of shorts and no shoes and no socks," says Jan. "He was very unkempt, a doing-his-own-thing guy. I said to him, How dare you wear a filthy T-shirt when it's a guy from Twentieth Century Fox? And he said, 'They're coming here to look at my work and not me.'"

Kirkwood said to call him when the movie was finished. But as Quentin worked on it, he realized there were holes in the story. Six months later, in December 1986, he called back the entire cast and crew and asked them to shoot some additional scenes he had written. This time, they rented a camera that would keep the sound in synch. Jan slipped Quentin the keys to his office, Turner Bradshaw, located in Westwood around the corner from where Jim McBride filmed a scene from his 1983 remake of *Breathless*, one of Quentin's favorite movies. At night, the boys would slip in and shoot a few scenes, hightailing it out of there before the sun came up.

The guys who worked on the movie say it cost a total of $5000 that they all chipped in over time; Jan says it was closer to $8000, and that he footed most of the bills. "I put a whole lot of equipment rental on my credit cards," he says. "I took out a $2000 loan and gave him the money and he never repaid it. I've got receipts for $2000 worth of stuff that I purchased."

"We'd go over to Los Angeles Community College and say we're working on a student film and we needed lighting equipment," says Craig Hamann of one of the many scams the boys pulled to get raw material. "We had situations where we only had a location for one night, and if the actors didn't show, Quentin would call up his friends who weren't actors and he'd coach them on the spot, giving them a crash course on how to act. Quentin had that capacity even then."

"We would start Friday afternoon and shoot for over seventy-two hours until we had to return the equipment on Monday morning," says Rand. "We shot all over town. Sometimes we'd drive over to Jan's office in the middle of the night and shoot until the sun was coming up. To give you an idea of just how slapdash it was, all of our batteries went dead one night and we had to pull out one of the car batteries and run the camera off the car battery."

Rand remembers that it was a friend, soundman Dov Schwarz, who provided the car battery. Stevo Polyi claims it was his car and his battery, and that he was roused from sleep at 2 A.M. to provide them.

"A lot of people worked with us along the way but nobody stuck with it," says Rand. "We lost people like crazy. It basically became a project where Craig, Quentin, Dov and I would be the only guys working. Any time we needed another actor we'd get one for four hours and we had to be really ready for him. From that time I have nothing but fond memories of the experience. It's an example of why Quentin and I got involved in film, just the camaraderie of putting together a project, the passion involved. It is just a tremendous experience."

Another location they "stole" was a bar in Westchester near the airport. It has since been torn down and rebuilt. "It was like this hole in the wall, one pool table and a crappy little jukebox," says Rand. "That was just heaven for us 'cause we would get there at like four in the morning. I don't even know if the owners knew we were there, we were just kinda let in by a waitress, and we knew that we had to leave by a certain point before anyone showed in the morning."

The waitress eventually tired of staying up so late to let the boys in, so she gave them a set of keys. "It was great because they had all this ginger ale and little sandwiches so we never had to worry about lunch. We just kinda made it our home for a while; it seemed like weeks."

During this time, both Quentin and Rand had full-time jobs, and they were working on maybe three hours of sleep a night. "It eventually broke us down a couple of times," says Rand. "There were a couple of days where Quentin just didn't show and so we would shut down. There was one day when I woke up completely disoriented, I had no idea who I was. We were both headed toward nervous breakdowns."

Then it was back to the lab to process this second batch of footage, and once again it was a disaster. Three critical scenes were destroyed in the lab during a power outage while the film was being transferred. Two and a half of those scenes had been shot at the bar, and the crew had already lost their bar privileges. The whole thing was so discouraging that Quentin finally gave up.

"After we lost two rolls of film in the lab accident, we never could complete the movie," says Craig. "Quentin has said, and I agree, that this was our film school. We learned more doing that than if we had gone to film school."

"He wrote off the film as an experience," says Rand, who likes to take credit for teaching Quentin some of the ropes. "He had never shot a single frame of film before and was relying on me basically to get him through. He hadn't developed his directorial style at all. He had gone into the project as an actor as opposed to a director, so I think he was very charged up and happy about directing the film, even though he had none of the basic training. He didn't know how to shoot a conversation back and forth, just the physical elements of filmmaking. He had no concept of the 180-degree rule, in which the camera has to stay on one side of the action so the audience keeps the same perspective throughout a scene. Things like that."

"Rand pretty much taught Quentin the basics of making a film, not necessarily the creative stuff, but the technical stuff," agrees Russ Vossler, Rand's brother who worked at Video Archives.

By the end of the film, Quentin had absorbed those technical aspects, and he mined the footage to create a video full of outtakes that could serve as a calling card for future acting jobs. "It's crude and primitive," he says today of the unfinished movie, "but you can tell that I made it."

"It's a real diamond in the rough," says Craig. "You can see Quentin's style starting to form, the beginnings are there. We used all rockabilly music, although we didn't exactly clear the rights to it. We didn't really know what we were doing at the time. The fun thing about it is we threw caution to the wind and just decided to make a movie. Quentin's genius was obvious even back then; he was extraordinary. He took what should have been a bad student film and ended up with a French farce, or a very funny film noir. The idea that it's about two guys in Torrance who think they're cool, that alone is a contradiction in terms."

Craig considered Quentin his best friend for many years, but after *My Best Friend's Birthday*, the relationship withered. "We drifted apart," says Craig. "I didn't want to, but it just kinda happened. He started hanging out with other people."

Craig is mentioned in the closing credits of *Reservoir Dogs*; he helped around the set and provided some of the background voices. After that, he didn't hear from Quentin again until *Pulp Fiction*. Quentin called in Craig to teach Uma Thurman and John Travolta what it was like to OD on heroin. "I described to him what Uma should be going through. When you OD on heroin, if you snort, it's like bad nose drops, you bleed from your nose. I met him and Uma at a Thai restaurant, and later I worked with Travolta a couple of times in his trailer."

Today Craig is an actor and a screenwriter, and is philosophical about his former best friend. "I'm aware there are people around me who think that Quentin has forsaken me, or left me behind in the dust, or turned his back on me. All I can say is, face-to-face when we've talked, to this day he treats me with respect, and as a friend. And I'm not going to ask him for anything more. I don't want success in my career to be dependent on anyone else except me."

CHAPTER 5

True Romance

*Look, goddammit, I never asked you for a goddamn thing! I've
tried to make your parental obligation as easy as possible.
After Mom divorced you did I ever ask you for anything? When
I wouldn't see ya for six months to a year at a time, did I ever
get in your shit about it? No! . . . You see, I know that you're
just a bad parent. You're not really very good at it. But I know
you love me.*

—Clarence in True Romance,
screenplay by Quentin Tarantino

After all the hard work, *My Best Friend's Birthday* was a washout.
Quentin was discouraged, but the fires were still burning. He
began cannibalizing the screenplay for a new project, *True
Romance,* about a couple of lovebirds on the run with a suitcase
full of coke. Clarence, the hero, spends the movie trying to
unload the coke, for which he can't get full value because he's not
in a bargaining position—a metaphor for what would happen

with Quentin's precious screenplay. He couldn't unload it for love or money, certainly not with himself attached as director.

True Romance was completed in 1987 and was sent to just about everyone in Hollywood over the next four years, sometimes C.O.D. The rejection letters were unusually cruel. "How dare you send me this fucking piece of shit, are you out of your fucking mind?" reads one letter, addressed to Quentin's manager at the time, Cathryn Jaymes.

Apparently few producers could get beyond the opening scene, in which a bunch of pimps and drug dealers sit around discussing the manliness of performing cunnilingus, until one of them blows the others away with a shotgun. Then the action moves back and forth in time through flashbacks and a fractured narrative to tell the story of Clarence and Alabama, two newlyweds who love pie, Sonny Chiba triple-bills, Elvis, and Mickey Rourke. Quentin was inspired by one of his favorite movies, *They Live by Night*, Nicholas Ray's directorial debut about lovers on the lam from the law; despite their bad deeds, they are innocents. "I've always wanted to hold hands with a girl in a movie," is Farley Granger's most fervent wish.

At the end of *True Romance*, Clarence dies with blood clouding his eyes the way Mr. Brown would later die in *Reservoir Dogs*.

The show-stopping scene was the one in which Clarence's estranged dad, who has never done anything for him since the divorce, refuses to give up his son's whereabouts to a mobster. The father sees his situation is hopeless, so in order to buy himself a quick death, he taunts the mobster by telling him that long ago, the Moors tainted the bloodline of the Sicilians. "Your ancestors were niggers," he says in Quentin's original script. "Your great, great, great, great, great grandmother was fucked by a nigger, and had a half-nigger kid. That is a fact. Now tell me, am I lyin'?"

The mobster shoots him in the face. "I haven't killed anybody since 1974," he complains.

Finally there was a nibble. British producer Stanley Margolis, whose credits included the far different *Roller Boogie* in 1979 with Linda Blair on roller skates, thought the script was brilliant. Cathryn Jaymes had sent the script over to Stanley for him to form a limited partnership so that Quentin could shoot the movie himself on 16-mm for $60,000. Naturally, Quentin had no money, so the idea was for Stanley to prepare the prospectus and then get a percentage of profits down the road. "I read the first seven pages of the script, and as I was reading I was thinking, 'What the hell, what on earth am I reading? What is this all about?'" says Stanley. "And I felt the audience is going to react to watching this the same way as I reacted reading it. For the first six minutes, half the audience is going to be embarrassed by the language, the other half is going to be laughing, and what happens at the end of that six minutes is going to blow them all away, it's going to be like a roller coaster ride. I didn't really care what the rest of the script was. The first six minutes were such a great hook, this was a moviemaker here, different than any I'd ever read in the past."

Stanley met with Quentin and Roger Avary, who was Quentin's writing partner. "This is too good to shoot on 16-mm for $60,000," said Stanley. "Let me option it and see if I can raise the money."

That first option was a joint agreement with Quentin; later, when no one was interested in having Quentin direct, Stanley took a second option, mortgaging his house in the process and planning a $2.7 million budget.

The rejection letters Stanley got were no better than those Cathryn had received. "Why would you ever want to make a film about two such despicable characters?" reads a typical rejection. "We got turned down by everyone in town, including the people who wound up making it," says Stanley. "I was getting so frustrated."

He eventually signed a deal with Davis Films, whose head, Samuel Hadida, initially agreed with Quentin's early choice of Bill Lustig as director. Bill had started his career directing porn films like *Violation of Claudia* and *Hot Honey*. His more recent claims to fame were *Relentless*, with Judd Nelson, and *Maniac Cop*.

"Bill was totally wrong for it," says Stanley.

Cathryn agrees. "Bill had no understanding of Quentin's work and Quentin's unique ability to tell a story in nonlinear fashion. He didn't understand the out-of-synch storytelling aspect."

Even Quentin agrees, although there was a time when he thought *True Romance* was just the material a talented, underappreciated exploitation filmmaker like Bill needed. "I always got a kick out of Bill's stuff," says Quentin. "I met Bill through my friend Scott Spiegel and we'd talk about doing *Relentless* 2 together. I showed him *True Romance* and he said he really liked it. But he didn't really like it. He realized it was good writing, all right. But he was like, yeah, it's a little too weird, a little too this, a little too that. Basically, he didn't understand it. It's not his kind of movie. He wanted something more straightforward."

Bill invited Quentin over to his house in Topanga Canyon in the summer of 1990 and ran a videotape of John Woo's *The Killer*. They enthused about their mutual interest in Hong Kong cinema and talked about how they would be the next Scorsese and Schrader, the partnership that had yielded *Taxi Driver* and *Raging Bull*.

"I thought this would be a real breakout movie for him," says Quentin. "But it just became obvious that it was not a case where this guy is like a groovy B-movie director who has just been saddled with a bunch of junk, and now he's got a good script and boy, he's gonna take it to the moon. No, he was going to turn it into more B-movie junk. He described it as being 'Pretty Woman with a gun.'"

At first, Quentin was cooperative about making changes in the script; then he began to balk. "My impression was that he was an incredible dialogue writer," says Bill Lustig. "I was impressed with his commitment to his project. When I had made suggestions for changes, normally a writer will just buckle: 'Okay, I'll do it, and I'll do anything else you want, do you want me to wash the windows of your car?' Quentin stood firm despite the fact it could have meant some money for him."

Bill and Stanley hooked up in October 1990 independently of Quentin, with manager Cathryn Jaymes's blessing. "I told Cathryn that Quentin was against the changes but she said not to worry," says Bill.

Stanley agreed with Bill about straightening out the narrative, although he wasn't happy about tacking on a happy ending. "In the script Quentin wrote, Clarence dies at the end, he gets killed. Which was the right ending, no question about it," says Stanley. "But no one liked it, they wanted an upbeat ending. Quentin wouldn't do it. He flatly refused. He simply would not change a word. And I called in Roger Avary to rewrite the ending."

Roger added a voice-over narration by the Alabama character, and at the end, Clarence lives. The two run off to an island paradise and name their baby Elvis. (In the movie, the baby is played by Patricia Arquette's real son, Enzo.)

"The way the script was written was very much in the style of *Reservoir Dogs* where it had flashbacks," says Bill. "One part was even a flashback of a flashback. It was quite inventive but it seemed to get in the way of the story. What I basically did was make the script linear."

The subject of authorship is a thorn in Quentin's side. "Bill is very good at what he does," he says, "but you know, my stuff may look like exploitation movies, and they obviously don't consider themselves better than exploitation movies, but there is more there. And Bill wasn't seeing the more that was there."

Bill went ahead with location scouting in Detroit and went to Cannes in 1991 to drum up foreign support. "We couldn't get interest from foreign buyers. They were put off by the script and didn't know what to make of it. It was really bizarre, the first time on a project that I had to sit with the distributors and explain the movie. I can see where they were put off. Here you have a group of black guys in the first scene talking about how white men have fucked up their women by eating their pussies."

After Cannes, Bill set up a production office and had Roger Avary make more revisions, which wasn't helping his already strained friendship with Quentin. "Roger was reluctant to change the ending—we both hated it, that corny thing about naming the kid Elvis," says Bill. "But it came down to that we were not going to be able to sell this picture with the ending that was there. So by this time Quentin was mad that we were changing the ending and rightfully so. By this time I think he was pissed at me because he felt that I betrayed him. Whatever, that's life."

What goes around comes around. Bill was eventually fired from the project by Sammy Hadida, and the way he found out was by reading it in *Variety* in December 1991. "There was an interview with Quentin in which he announced that Tony Scott was going to direct the film. I wrote a letter to my producer [Sammy Hadida] in Paris and he never responded. In February 1992 I got a phone call that said, 'Well, you know you are being replaced by Tony Scott, and that's that.' There was a whole web of betrayal around me, of the producers and of Quentin himself. The bottom line was, I was the last guy to know I was fired."

Actually, it was Quentin who pushed Tony Scott to convince Sammy Hadida to fire Bill Lustig. Quentin had sent the script to Tony through a mutual friend, Catalaine Knell, an associate producer at CineTel who hired Quentin in 1990 to do a script rewrite.

"I thought Quentin was a really interesting, crazy personality, and I'm always drawn to people like that," says Tony. "I was just finishing shooting *The Last Boy Scout* and I took a week off and was recovering in a hotel in Italy. I find it very difficult to read scripts in one sitting. And I read this in one night and said, Fuck, this is phenomenal." Quentin was excited by the prospect of having Tony Scott at the helm, so he egged him on. "Well, these guys own it, and they're going to do it with Bill Lustig," Quentin says he told Tony. "So why don't you see what you can do? I would rather you do it.'"

Bill Lustig takes solace in his belief that the Tony Scott version "is exactly the way I laid it out, with the exception of a few pages. But the approach is entirely different than what I had in mind. Tony's film seemed to be more in the world of Hollywood slick; what I had in mind was like Don Siegel, a much grittier picture. I felt that the whole idea of Clarence was a guy very much like Quentin, who is not a particularly handsome person but through his gift of gab becomes attractive. The kind of actor I had in mind was someone like Kevin Dillon, a more ordinary-looking guy with an ability to talk and be charming."

Bill didn't do too badly. He had a pay-or-play contract, so he received his full fee, plus he says he had four "points"—meaning he would make a percentage back once the movie turned a profit. The movie never did turn a profit, "but the frustration of it is that there's no recognition for my contribution on the picture, and I feel kinda hurt. I must admit that the experience was kinda demoralizing. I had so much passion for this business and making movies and all that, and the experience of *True Romance* just sort of took the passion out of me. Now I kinda think about making movies and making a living. I still have hopes and dreams of doing something that would be special, but when this happens to you and you're burned, you're so reluctant to go through that experience again. You take a project, you breathe life into it, only to see everyone else run off and you're left behind. But I bear Quentin no grudge. His films have a heartbeat in a Hollywood that makes soulless pictures. He has had the incredible good fortune to be able to break through and make films with a vision and a point of view, and I think that's what people respond to. A lot of it was being at the right place at the right time."

Unfortunately, it was Stanley Margolis who seemed to be in the wrong place at the wrong time. Stanley got stuck with a lawsuit by CineTel when it appeared that both CineTel and Hadida's Davis Films had dibs on *True Romance* at the same time. CineTel won the suit, but by that time, Tony Scott was off and running with *True Romance*, backed by Morgan Creek and Warner Brothers. What had started as a $60,000 project was now a slick, $12.5 million Hollywood production starring Christian Slater as Quentin's alter ego, Patricia Arquette as Alabama,

Dennis Hopper as the estranged father and Christopher Walken as the Sicilian whose blood boils over.

"It would have been a better movie if it had been made at $3 million," says Stanley Margolis today. "Because that was a movie that really required a low-budget feel to it. It didn't require a Tony Scott image to it. You know, Tony Scott's a very good director, but not for a subject like *True Romance*."

There was a brief period during which Miramax almost made the movie in partnership with Davis Films. "I was looking at James Foley to direct for about $6 or $7 million," says Miramax's Harvey Weinstein. "But Sammy [Hadida] wanted to make a $20 million movie with Tony. So basically we were in for a fee plus a piece of the action." Harvey and Bob Weinstein received executive producer credit for doing just about nothing.

Catalaine Knell of CineTel says it was Bill Lustig's fault that Stanley Margolis got sued. Bill claims CineTel never really optioned the script, "they were stringing us along and never really closed. They claimed they had a deal in principle. But when CineTel seemed like a dead end I brought the script to Sammy Hadida and Sammy optioned the project without reading the script. CineTel never gave us any money, never gave us a contract."

Later, when the alliances on *True Romance* were as tangled as the final shootout in that movie, Catalaine still took some satisfaction in knowing that her former boss, Tony Scott, wound up as the director. "If there was ever a writer Tony should be in business with, it's Quentin," says Cat. "By the time we won the litigation, they were already shooting the movie. Bill Lustig made out like a bandit with something like $200,000. Quentin got something like $40,000. Stanley Margolis"—the producer who had put up his house as collateral on the movie—"took the biggest hit; he wound up paying for Bill's bad behavior. But at least Bill didn't direct that movie. Tony Scott went to the guy Bill sold it to and said he was interested. And they said, Bill Lustig or Tony Scott? Bill Lustig or Tony Scott?" Catalaine laughs triumphantly. "Who do you think they went with?"

"If people say I lost my house because I mortgaged it to exercise the option on *True Romance*, that's totally untrue," says Stanley Margolis of the messy aftermath. "Anyway, what happened with CineTel had nothing to do with Quentin. The guy is a great filmmaker. He's one of the great filmmakers in America today. Just don't expect people to say he's a nice guy as well."

To Quentin, who had planned *True Romance* as a $60,000 backyard enterprise, the new budget was stratospheric. But Tony Scott, director of the hits *Beverly Hills Cop 2* and *Top Gun*, was now working with about half his usual budget by taking on *True Romance*, which he pegs at $14.5 million. "It's a lot of money for a movie, but not compared with the sort of budgets I've been working with," says Tony. "It was the right amount for this movie, because you have to appeal to the general public. Unfortunately, it didn't."

The movie, made by Morgan Creek and released through Warner Brothers, grossed a disappointing $12 million at the U.S. box office.

"I think it's my favorite movie of those I directed," says Tony ruefully. "But it didn't make the money it should have." In 1995, Tony would work once again with Quentin on an uncredited rewrite of his submarine drama *Crimson Tide*.

Tony started casting *True Romance* with Christian Slater in the lead, and from there followed his gut instinct. "You start with one person and, you know, one color leads to another. I felt Christian and Patricia Arquette were a perfect balance. I mean, the movie is very much seen from Patricia's point of view. It's about two kids who are in pursuit of a dream."

During rehearsals, Christian Slater met with Quentin for about four hours, "just to see what type of person he really was." Quentin turned out to be exactly the way Christian had imagined him from reading the script; after all, Quentin had meant the protagonist to serve as his alter ego. "But then in thinking more about it and working with Tony in order to create the character, I saw that the challenge was to create someone who is sympathetic in all of this utter chaos and madness, someone sympathetic in this type of a nightmare experience," says Christian. "That kind of guy can't be too much of a character, you know, he has to be much more human, much more down-to-earth."

Tony allowed Christian to change their plan of patterning Clarence on Quentin. "It's very difficult to emulate Quentin Tarantino," says Tony. "The character was still crazy in terms of his concepts, but a lot mellower in the flesh."

Tony brought back Roger Avary to pare down the shooting script from 130 pages to 115. "Roger and Quentin were thick as thieves," says Tony. "The only thing that Quentin and I had a difference of opinion about was the happy ending. I did it not for commercial reasons, but because I fell in love with these characters and I wanted to see them survive. I'm sort of a romantic at heart. I wanted to smile with them. I always defer to Quentin because he's so smart, so I shot both endings and cut them together, and I still in my heart reached out for the happy ending."

In one scene Patricia Arquette's character, Alabama, is severely beaten, and only manages to escape after stabbing her assailant in the foot with a corkscrew and bashing him over the head with a toilet-tank cover. "I looked at it from a feminist viewpoint, like, does this say it's okay to beat women?" says Patricia. "Sure, this just perpetuates it. But that's going on in the world anyway, and besides, there certainly will be some sick people who'll look at this and even find me more attractive because of it, like, ooh, that's sexy, I'd like to slap you around. To me that is not sexy, and it puts me in a little bit of a dangerous position by even taking the role. But the thing I thought about it is, it's sexist to even look at this as a woman instead of as a man. No one would judge it if it were a man in the scene. What Quentin does is he writes these characters and makes you get to know something about them before he kills them. We're so desensitized by violence on TV, that's the real violence."

Patricia was also interested in what killing her assailant

would do to her character emotionally. "How does that affect you? Can you live with yourself knowing you killed someone? Is it an easy decision for you, or is it emotionally painful? There will always be repercussions from something like this."

The violence in that scene has a strongly sexual element, with the assailant (James Gandolfini) appraising Alabama's body before slugging her; after the slug he indulges in a moment of private euphoria. "In a way, she is more familiar with the truly dark side of human nature than Clarence is," says Patricia. "He was familiar with it from a voyeuristic viewpoint of watching Sonny Chiba movies. But she had already come from a history we don't know much about, a prostitute with a scary pimp. When she walks into the hotel room for that scene it's almost as if they're playmates in this black playground, they know the game, they know each other, it's a whole seduction from the start. It's a world she wants to walk away from, but first she has to stay and play the game in order to survive."

It was Patricia's stunt double, Joanie Avery, who went smashing through the candy-glass shower door. "We have the same jawbone so you don't realize it's her," says Patricia, who is annoyed by the charges of excessive violence leveled at the movie. "This is an art medium, like painting, like singing. I think it's just a matter of laziness on everyone's part if they don't take the responsibility of deciding who they are. If you're looking for a hero, don't come to see this movie. This is not a movie to tell you who to be. This is a movie where every good guy has horrible things he has to do, and where every bad guy has beautiful, interesting things that they do too. As far as my experience of trying to learn how to be a woman, I never learned it from watching any movie. There's probably been a handful of movies that have ever affected me in a humanistic way. And there's been a million movies that have taught me many many things. But deciding who I had to be as a woman, and how I felt about everything, my sexuality, my spirituality, I had to figure those things from within."

Dennis Hopper also rejects the charges that the screenplay

is violent or racist. It is Dennis who delivers the speech about black blood coursing through the veins of Sicilians; the main appeal of that to an actor is that screenplays so rarely give them speeches to work with. "A producer looks at a script and says, my god, this is a speech, we can't have this in the movie, cut it down to three lines!" says Dennis. "But Quentin sets up these incredible imaginary circumstances where it allows you to be able to give speeches. The scene with Chris Walken, I know I'm going to die in that scene, there's no way I can give up my son and tell him where my son is. He's going to kill me either way. So I'm not getting out of that scene alive. The only thing I can do is infuriate him to a point that he kills me without torturing me and getting the information."

Dennis, who only met Quentin after the movie when they happened on each other at the urinals of a newly opened night-club, figured the speech "would probably rub a few people the wrong way," but he describes it as "a very human speech. It may be pathetic that the outcome is what it is, but the human-ness of it is what's interesting to me. That isn't offensive. What's involved is offensive, what's implied and the outcome is offen-sive, but these are phenomena of our times, and the scene is a very real scene."

He sees what Quentin does as "putting our culture in a Waring blender and redistributing it as an artistic, entertaining phenomenon. I think of Tarantino as the Mark Twain of the nineties, that he's dealing with the same things as a couple of guys running away on a riverboat going down the river on the Mississippi. I know that's a strange juxtaposition, but we're in the nineties now and we live in a violent society. Now how can you write about this and create something in this time and not make some reflection on your culture?"

The Sicilian speech has gone on to its own kind of cult fame. Miramax honcho Harvey Weinstein was out to dinner one night at the Tribeca Grill with Al Pacino and Fisher Stevens, and the two actors suddenly launched into it, word for word, Fisher taking the Dennis Hopper role and Al doing Chris

Walken. "They did it perfectly from memory," says Harvey. "I was falling on the floor laughing."

Bronson Pinchot, who plays the comic-relief role of Eliot Blitzer, the middleman in the coke deal between Clarence and a Hollywood producer, says that the role "garnered more work for me than anything since the original *Beverly Hills Cop* ten years ago. I feel a debt to *True Romance* and to Quentin."

Bronson wanted the role because it was "juicy," and because his character shows up in several scenes to link the action. He has one particularly funny bit where he fears that Clarence has figured out he's been wired by the police, and he breaks down, begging for mercy.

"At first I couldn't make any linear sort of sense of the character," says Bronson. "I knew then it was going to be a fascinating part to play. I read it and I thought this has to do with pain, this character is in pain and I know there is a lot going on with him. But after seven years of doing television scripts, where you know what it's going to be before you even turn the page, I didn't exactly know what the role was going to amount to. There was a hell of a lot of room for interpretation. As a matter of fact, you were supposed to cheer when the character died. By the time it came to my death, Tony Scott said to me that devilishly, mischievously, surreptitiously and quietly I had constructed a character who is sympathetic. 'I can't end you the way I wanted to end you, I wanted to blow your head off and see your head fly across the room, but I don't think the audience will accept that anymore.' That leeway was obvious in the script because it was very ambiguous, it wasn't an easy A-B-C-D-E-F-G kind of story."

Although Bronson didn't meet the author until they were both doing publicity for the movie in 1993, he describes Quentin as "a little bit like somebody you'd meet underneath the table at a family Thanksgiving when you've finished your turkey and crawled underneath to giggle." As for the violence of the material, he points out that "the earliest piece of fiction that the Western world has is something ten times more violent than Quentin Tarantino, which is Homer's *Iliad*, and there are far more gory deaths in that, and that's the most revered piece of literature."

True Romance didn't come out quite the way Quentin had envisioned it, but he didn't distance himself from it the way he later would from Oliver Stone's *Natural Born Killers*. Except for the happy ending and the reconstructed sequence of events, it had everything he put into the original script. Roger Avary got a mere "special thanks" in the end credits for the rewrites that drove a wedge into his friendship with Quentin. Stanley Margolis got an "executive producer" credit. All the veiled references to the Video Archives crew are intact. Said Quentin, "It was like watching a big-budget feature of your home movies."

CHAPTER 6

Natural Born Killers

Am I God or what?

> —*TV filmmaker Wayne Gale in*
> Natural Born Killers

Natural Born Killers took a chunk out of everyone, laying waste to friendships, hopes and dreams. Quentin, who was disgusted with the fruitless years he had spent trying to make a go of *True Romance*, dashed off the *NBK* script in a few weeks, tailoring it specifically to be a vehicle for his directing debut. He eventually came to hope it would never be made. "I may catch it someday if I'm in a hotel and it's on pay-per-view," he said derisively about the version Oliver Stone made in 1994.

Quentin wasn't the only one scorched by the experience of *NBK*. His old-time pal Rand Vossler, who quit his production-company job to devote himself to trying to produce *NBK,* not only lost his own opportunity to direct it after Quentin went off to make *Reservoir Dogs,* he lost his best friend as well. Quentin stopped returning phone calls the deeper Rand became ensnared in litigation and ill will. Aggressive young producers Don Murphy and Jane Hamsher, who saw *NBK* as their ticket to fame, wound up in an ongoing war with Quentin made public in *Premiere* magazine in January 1995. And Oliver Stone, who rewrote the script to make more of a comment on the nature of violence and the media's complicity, wound up being nearly undone by the media himself, thanks to a ratings controversy over whether the movie promoted violence, and criticisms that his rewrite was a disservice to the newly famous Quentin Tarantino. "No one emerges with a rosy sheen on their cheeks," admits Don Murphy today.

When *NBK* opened overseas in the fall of 1994—it was banned from theaters in Great Britain until February 1995—Stone traveled with the movie to meet the press and bang the drum. "In Europe and everywhere we went, we'd arrive in a country and [Quentin] had just been there [with *Pulp Fiction*], so at any interview we were getting these questions—Well, why does Mr. Tarantino say this? Why did you trash his movie? What's your problem with him? What did you do to his sacred script?" says Stone. "We were in an uncomfortable position because you can't knock somebody who's a first-time filmmaker when you're the big shot, and you can't really defend yourself against that. So it hurt the business because it put a stain on the movie, as if the writer had walked out on it and that therefore it was a disaster. And he'd not even seen the movie. It was hardly fair. His hubris was enormous."

The first draft of *Natural Born Killers* was time-stamped by the Writers Guild of America on September 13, 1989. It featured two married serial killers, Mickey and Mallory Knox. Quentin liked to use names that honored people and places that caught his imagination. One of the characters in the Elmore Leonard novel he had swiped as a teenager had been named Mickey, and it stuck in his mind, but Mickey Knox was more of a nod to Mickey Rourke, a grunge actor Quentin loved. The last name, Knox, was a sawed-off version of Knoxville, Tennessee, home of his grandparents and seat of his romanticized childhood notions of a trailer-trash upbringing.

Mickey and Mallory are murderers of the school of "kill 'em to watch their expression change," yet Quentin saw it—as he perversely liked to see most of his ideas—as a love story. "Amidst the violence and murder and carnage, you've got the structure of a Wagnerian love story," comments one character, and a few pages later, the Knoxes' "operatic devotion to each other" is cited.

He also saw it as a black comedy, in which a tabloid-TV camera crew—"commando journalists"—trails along hoping for an exclusive interview with Mickey for their *American Maniacs* show. The crew—Scott, the cameraman; Roger, the soundman; and Unruly Julie, the assistant—were all named after friends from Video Archives, where he still worked from time to time when he needed money. Scott was named after the doomed Scott McGill, the quiet one who had served as cameraman on *My Best Friend's Birthday*. Roger was Roger Avary, Quentin's writing partner who had tried for years to help him get a green light for *True Romance*. And Julie was Julie McLean, a late hire after the glory years of Video Archives.

The leader of this crew is a character named Wayne Gale, a TV reporter patterned, according to the script, on Geraldo Rivera. Wayne Gale provides the movie's point of view—"Am I God or what?" he crows when he lands an exclusive interview with the serial killer. In his pursuit of the story while constantly worrying about how to photograph, stage and promote it, Wayne is Quentin's alter ego, the guy who is as concerned with the filming of the action as with the action itself. (In fact, Quentin originally wanted to play the role.) Wayne's crew eats donuts and banters at a "rapid-fire *His Girl Friday* pace," according to the script notes, not unlike a typical day at the video store.

There are other mentions in the script of the Video Archives gang. A character named Russell Vossler shows up as a Harvard law student being interviewed about the appeal of the killers. A character named Grace Mulberry is knifed in the head while testifying on the witness stand, and if there's any doubt that this was a nod to Quentin's Video Archives girlfriend Grace Lovelace, the name *Lovelace* is accidentally substituted for *Mulberry* several times in the original script.

The characters go off into Tarantinia—about whether Raquel Welch is an underrated actress, about Spielberg selling out his "cool" audience when he made *Indiana Jones and the Last Crusade*—and they make frequent references to pop-culture touchstones like the *Batman* TV series.

There are also passages that are the kind you might expect from the child of a bitter divorce. Mickey and Mallory are separated by a sadistic judge who explains: "The husband and wife would have no contact or correspondence with each other for the rest of their lives. And they would never receive any word or information about the other . . . They'll never even know when the other dies," reminiscent of how Quentin's mom Connie talks about his biological father ("I wouldn't even know if he's still alive").

What Quentin hoped for *NBK* is what he had hoped for *True Romance*, and he has Wayne Gale sum that up as he explains to his crew what an interview with Mickey Knox could do for their careers: "This is Elton John confessing his bisexuality to *Rolling Stone*! This is the tearful reporting of the Hindenburg disaster! This is Truffaut setting the record straight on Hitchcock . . . This is the Maysles brothers at Altamont . . . "

"This is Raymond Burr witnessing the destruction of Tokyo by Godzilla!" adds Roger.

"Fuck video," says Wayne on the next page of the script. "This is just too damned important. This is for posterity. No, we're using high-contrast 16-mm black and white, and I mean *black and white*, where the black's black and the white's white. *Film . . . film . . . film!*"

Of all the analogies in the script, the Hindenburg was most apt.

The friendship between Quentin and Roger Avary was feeling the strain after years of disappointment on *True Romance*. So Quentin sent his script of *NBK* to his old buddy Rand Vossler. They hadn't been in touch for years, not since they'd burnt out on making *My Best Friend's Birthday*. There were competitive feelings between them. But at this point, Rand had something in his favor—a job.

Not just any job. Rand was the feature-development guy for Lewis B. Chesler over at MGM. Chesler had been executive producer of the *Hitchhiker* series, and he and Rand had developed three pilot episodes for HBO called *The Edge*, a collection of twenty-minute noir shorts that were stylistically right up Quentin's alley.

"One thing about Quentin, he had never really considered himself a writer, but would write scenes that he would just play out in his mind," says Rand. "I think a lot of the material for *NBK* was already written and stored in files, and out of frustration he went into the files and took out a bunch of cool scenes with a loosely structured plot."

Quentin and Rand set up shop over burgers at Denny's Gower Gulch, on the corner of Sunset and Gower, in November 1989. "I remember zipping out there. I had just read the script and was kinda pumped up about it and kinda intrigued with the material," says Rand. "It was a great piece of writing."

As time would tell, no one disagreed with Rand's assessment of the script. On the other hand, no one wanted to make the movie. The subject matter was too grisly, the tone too outrageous. The fractured narrative structure was too confusing, the humor too black.

Rand had two initial concerns. He wondered how Roger Avary would feel being displaced from Quentin's side as producer. Quentin assured him that Roger didn't like *NBK* all that much, and anyway, they both had cabin fever from being cooped up together too long. Another thing bothering Rand was the fate of his own project, a road-picture screenplay he was working on. But Quentin struck a deal: If Rand would produce for Quentin on *NBK*, Quentin would turn around and produce a film for Rand that they would write together, and with which Rand could make his own directing debut. You scratch my back, I'll scratch yours. Quentin even kept an eye out for material that might suit Rand. One, the pulp-noir novel the *Ticket to Hell* by Harry Whittington, was about a bagman who has to deliver a million smackers to the goons who kidnapped a senator's son. The book so impressed Quentin that he drew up an 8½-by-11 presentation of how the movie poster might look: *Ticket to Hell! Directed by Rand Vossler! Produced by Quentin Tarantino! Starring Sean Young and Quentin Tarantino!*

Quentin's drafting abilities left something to be desired, even though he had taken a few lessons, but his choice of Sean Young wasn't so far-fetched; Rand had been Sean's personal assistant on *The Boost*. The movie was as good as cast!

With visions of his own future directorial debut dancing in his head, Rand brought *NBK* to his boss, Lewis Chesler, who was looking to make low-budget noir pictures in the $2 million range. "We did a whole big pitch with him, and he handed it off to one of his other development people who didn't 'get' it, and subsequently Lewis didn't do the project," is how Rand describes the beginning of the tortuous route *NBK* would take.

Working together, Rand and Quentin developed a routine for business meetings. Rand would go in first and pump up Quentin, "create a mythological guy." It worked in reverse too— Quentin would go in and pitch Rand as a giant of filmmaking, then Rand would saunter in and soak up the reflected rays. The working relationship was good; all they lacked was the deal.

And the dough. The boys were broke. Rand quit his job to devote himself full-time to *NBK*, maintaining a small office at Chessler's with Xerox, fax, phone and coffeemaker privileges in return for occasional consulting work. They called themselves Natural Born Filmmakers. Whenever the well went dry,

Quentin would pick up a few shifts at Video Archives. Around this time, Quentin also got turned on to a script rewrite over at CineTel, and then another script rewrite for producing team Ron Hamady and George Braunstein, "some pirate thing about a guy whose wife and son are killed aboard his sixty-foot yacht, basically a revenge film," says Rand. "They offered Quentin $40,000 to do this. He and I hit the roof! We'd use that money to shoot a sequence for *NBK*. Quentin was working out of his mother's house in Glendale. He didn't have a car, although there was Jan's Porsche, but Jan and Connie were having trouble and Connie didn't want Quentin driving it." In the interim, Rand loaned Quentin his 1975 Camaro while Rand tooled about on his motorcycle.

Hamady and Braunstein loaned Quentin a fax machine so he could relay script pages hot off the typewriter. Quentin let his creativity run amok, turning a lackluster melodrama into "a gut-splitting Hong Kong kung fu movie, which was really kinda cool," according to Rand. But not so cool with the producers, who after only a couple of weeks made Quentin walk the plank, a token payment in his pocket.

"It didn't work out so bad," says Quentin. "I only wrote about fifty pages and they gave me $10,000, a quick influx of cash, and my commitment was over with! I didn't have to do any more! It wasn't that fucking strung-out process that happens all the time."

Now Quentin and Rand were both out of work, spending twelve- and fourteen-hour days working on the script or pursuing finance leads. They slept either at Connie's house or at Rand's mother's house. When things got really desperate, it was time to call in the Hun Brothers.

The Hun Brothers were giant Nordic bodybuilders who wanted an acting career. Their manager promised $275,000 if Quentin and Rand could match the money and add a scene that featured the brothers; such a scene duly materialized on page 44 of the script. Actually, it was Roger Avary who wrote it, because Quentin was too disgusted. "It seemed like just too much of a commercial consideration, like I was too much of a prostitute," says Quentin.

In the Hun Brothers scene, Mickey and Mallory are taking a chainsaw to the Hun legs when they recognize them for the Huns that they are. "Hey, these are the Brothers Hun!" says Mallory. It turns out that she and Mickey have been strongly influenced by the Hun film *Conquering Huns of Neptune*. So they spare the Huns, who live to give an interview to Wayne Gale's *American Maniacs* TV show.

(The Hun scene was actually shot, and although it was cut from Oliver Stone's theatrical version, it was to be reinstated in the special laser disc version. However, the Huns were played by the Barbarian Brothers, Peter and David Paul, who had fifteen minutes of fame in 1987 with *The Barbarians,* a *Conan* send-up.)

Around this time, Quentin considered making a twenty-minute short modeled after *The Edge* episodes that Rand and his boss had made for HBO. Because the episodes were only twenty minutes long, you'd come into the story in the middle of the climax, with very little backstory. "You're left to figure everything out during a real-time climax instead of a little twist ending which had been prevalent in anthology films of the time," explains Rand. "I said don't worry about creating the whole beginning, middle and end, just shoot the climax!"

They brainstormed, and after half an hour, Quentin revealed a plan for a heist film he had been keeping on the back burner. It would involve only one location, a warehouse, where all the guys would gather after a robbery you don't see. One of the guys would be an undercover cop, who is already wounded as the film opens. "We figured we'd take whatever money he'd get from *True Romance* and use it to shoot this short film, then use that to continue to sell him as a director in order to get financing for *NBK*," says Rand. The twenty-minute short would be a "calling card," something less than a film and more than a show reel that film-school students often make to get their foot in a producer's door.

Quentin's new pal, filmmaker Scott Spiegel, was on line for a midnight double feature when he introduced Quentin and Rand to Lawrence Bender. Lawrence had produced Scotty's own directorial debut, *Intruder*. Months later, Quentin and Rand would again run into Lawrence, only this time Rand says he tried to get the fledgling producer interested in coming aboard *NBK*. "He embraced it at first, but he had problems with the script."

Quentin continued to polish his script for the twenty-minute short, the one that would get *NBK* financed. It was October 1990. Only problem was, Quentin's ideas could not be contained by a twenty-minute time frame. "Rand, I have good news and bad news," Quentin said after Rand returned from a friend's wedding in Hawaii. He had been away only ten days, and the bottom of his world was about to drop out. "The good news is that I've finished writing *Reservoir Dogs*."

"Super cool!" said Rand as they drove along the highway.

"The bad news is that it's no longer a twenty-minute short, it's a feature-length movie, and I'm going to direct it and Lawrence Bender is going to produce it."

Quentin was abandoning *Natural Born Killers*, the project Rand had given up his job for. Rand insists to this day that the Hun money was just about to pour in.

Quentin Tarantino had a theory about first films. A director's first movie has got to make a big splash. Everything in your life up to that point has to go into that film. You pull no punches, you take no prisoners. "That's the mentality Quentin had when he wrote *NBK*," says Rand. "In its wildness and eclectic qualities—our version, not the Stone piece of crap thing it ended up being."

The facts of what happened next are simple, but the truth of it depends on your point of view. One fact is that Quentin gave the distraught Rand his blessing to go ahead and direct *NBK* himself, advising him to shoot it guerrilla-style in 16-mm, just the way they had made *My Best Friend's Birthday* in the mid-eighties. Another fact is that Rand believed he had an airtight contract to direct *NBK*, no matter what. A third fact is that Rand

Vossler never directed a frame of it; Oliver Stone brought it in as a big-budget movie for Warner Brothers.

Those are the facts. The truth is more elusive. "It's like any rock," says one source who briefly toyed with the idea of producing *NBK* himself. "When you turn it over, it's crawling with slugs."

According to one person close to the action, Quentin encouraged Rand only because he thought it would never come to much, that it wouldn't be "a real movie." Another source says that producers Don Murphy and Jane Hamsher, who were helping Rand get his money, sold him out—something the two vigorously deny. Don wrote a now-famous letter to *Premiere* magazine accusing Quentin of a history of selling out friends and stealing material. "In reality no one can 'steal' a script from anyone, since the author is required to sign numerous chain-of-title documents attributing originality of authorship," reads the letter in part. "When the time came to look for directors, Quentin not only okayed the search, but met some of them with us." Oliver Stone says that by the time he started working on the project, Don and Jane had clear ownership of the property, that the problem with Rand had been ironed out, and that the worst thing about Quentin's behavior at the time was that he lacked enthusiasm for Stone's project.

The upshot, despite quibbles over the semantics of such words as *blame* and *hate*, is that Quentin blames Rand for losing possession of the script, Rand blames Quentin for not standing by him, Rand and Quentin each hate Don and Don hates them in return, and despite numerous claims that they've "made up," Quentin and Oliver are anathema to each other.

Don Murphy and Jane Hamsher were relatively new in town, recent graduates of the University of Southern California. Jane had been in the Peter Stark producer's program there, endowed and begun in the late seventies by legendary producer Ray Stark after his son Peter died. Producer Bruce Binkow was an early graduate of the program and agreed to meet the recent

grads out of a sense of school ties. Don and Jane had put down a
fraction of the option money on *NBK* and were looking to raise
about half a million dollars for Rand Vossler to direct now that
the writer, Quentin Tarantino, was busy with his new project.

Binkow read the script and gave the kids his honest assessment: "Guys, you're missing the big picture. This is good
enough that we can get you a deal."

By "deal," he meant more than just chump change. Binkow
had been working at Robert Greenwald Productions and was
about to form Thunderbird Pictures with Peter McAlevey, a former entertainment reporter for *Newsweek* who was running
Michael Douglas's Stonebridge Entertainment. Bruce and Pete
thought this might be the project to launch their new partnership, so they set up a few meetings.

One of these meetings was with Brad Krevoy at Motion
Picture Corporation of America. Pete and Brad went way back to
their early days in Hollywood, when Peter was still at *Newsweek*
and Brad was learning the ropes with Roger Corman. Pete and
Brad had double-dated a set of Persian twins. Brad must have
been fascinated with twins, because he was making *Double
Trouble* with twin weight lifters Peter and David Paul, the so-
called Barbarian Brothers, who would later figure in *NBK*.

Brad wanted to get to a higher level of filmmaking. In his
office that day, Brad told Don, Jane, Bruce and Pete that he
would make their movie for $3 million, provided only that
Albert Magnoli, the director of *Purple Rain*, be at the helm, and
that shooting would commence in less than two months, on
January 2, 1991, the minute everyone got back from holiday.

"Well, guys, you got yourselves a deal," beamed Pete
McAlevey, using his still-in-effect Stonebridge expense account
to buy everyone a round of capuccinos from the frozen-yogurt
stand on the corner. "But you gotta tell me now if there's anything you're concerned about, anything that bothers you."

"Well, it all sounds very nice," said Don, sipping his capuc-
cino. "You should just know there's one caveat. Jane and I must
have complete creative control."

Pete almost did a spit-take. "You two are kids just out of school! Michael fucking *Douglas* doesn't even get creative control!"

Don says today that he never asked for complete creative control, he was just protecting his and Jane's interests against the more seasoned producers.

Pete walked off the deal. What he didn't know then was that in time, Michael Douglas would become one of the few players in Hollywood who indeed had creative control, and that *Natural Born Killers* would be a major, multimillion-dollar motion picture from Warner Brothers with Oliver Stone directing.

Brad Krevoy didn't cry long over spilt milk. He graduated from the twin Persians and the twin bodybuilders to a different set of twins—in 1995, he produced the Jim Carrey–Jeff Daniels box-office smash *Dumb and Dumber* and made out like a bandit.

The version of *NBK* that made the rounds of Hollywood under the aegis of Don and Jane was date-stamped March 12, 1991. It was 127 pages long, and the title page was marked "Directed by Rand Vossler." Rand will not confirm or deny the chain of events that erased his name from that title page—his legal settlement contains a clause that forbids him to discuss it. But sources close to the project who are not thus constrained, including some of the guys from Video Archives, say that Rand temporarily signed his rights over to Don and Jane so that he could shoot the *American Maniacs* segment of *NBK* in a combination of several formats, including Super-8, HDTV, 16-mm, and Beta SP. Like the twenty-minute short that *Reservoir Dogs* was originally meant to be, this segment would be Rand's calling card to Hollywood, to prove he could direct and to provide a taste of *NBK* to potential investors. Don and Jane wanted to hold the rights as insurance that Rand wouldn't just shoot and run. "We were spending the money to shoot it," explains Don. According to his friends, Rand complied only as a formality, feeling protected by another legal document which promised he would be the director come hell or high water. He auditioned hundreds of actors for his short, including Drew Barrymore, Patricia Arquette and Billy Wirth. Everyone from the cinematographer to the editor agreed to work for free, such was the power of a Quentin Tarantino script even before anyone had really heard of Quentin Tarantino.

Two sources say that within a few days of Rand signing over his rights, Don and Jane fired him in order to go after bigger fish. Again, Don and Jane vigorously deny this. "When it came time to put those rights down to paper, Quentin's attorneys made clear they did not support Rand's position that he had those rights," says Don. "Those were hollow promises Quentin made to Rand."

Rand, hurt and confused, filed a lawsuit against Don and Jane.

The night before Rand was no longer officially to be the director of *NBK*, Quentin showed up at his house to watch *Stuntmasters* on TV. The show was doing a feature about a Steve Buscemi stunt from the just-filmed *Reservoir Dogs*. Quentin later explained that he had come over that night to "reestablish our friendship and to know that he still considered me a friend," says Rand. But he soon found his pipeline to Quentin drying up; as the lawsuit intensified and Quentin became more famous, there was no contact between the two except through the mediation of Lawrence Bender.

"Where I'm at now I have nothing but love and respect for the man, even if he is Joe Hollywood or Mister Academy Awards," says Rand today. "The things he did to hurt me were out of carelessness. In his heart, regardless of his motivations, once the film became a real film he didn't want it made. In a selfish way, he was enthusiastic about the lawsuit, because it would make the film impossible to make. Litigation would keep people from putting money toward the film, and he'd get the film back. He forgot that a lawsuit takes money, and I had no money. My lawyer worked on a contingency basis on a reduced hourly rate. But I was still going broke; I was busting a nut to afford that lawsuit."

Oliver Stone wasn't involved at this juncture. And even when he was, his first thought was to executive produce the movie with Sean Penn directing, something Quentin admits he was enthusiastic about. Rand's lawsuit was eventually settled, presumably to everyone's satisfaction—at least in the legal and financial sense. Money was paid, rights were cleared. The movie was made.

Rand saw his former best friend at the annual Christmas tamale party thrown by the Martinez brothers in December 1992. Things between Quentin and Rand were cordial but cool; the wounds had been plastered over but were not yet dry to the touch. "Quentin's a weird guy," says Rand. "I still send him congratulatory notes. But he's so big now I couldn't get near him if I wanted to. I can't bear the thought of going through an agent to get close to my friend. We had been like brothers, we were inseparable. We had a natural camaraderie born out of our mutual passion for film, a flame-burns-twice-as-bright syndrome."

At the tamale party, Quentin seemed reserved around Rand, although they still kidded and there are photographs of them playing tackle in the hallway. "He told somebody that he hated talking to me because he felt he was bragging; he twisted that around so that he somehow thinks I couldn't bear to be around him because I feel I should be doing what he's doing." Rand pauses, and says firmly: "In reality, I do believe I should be doing what he's doing. I should be making movies."

At one point in the party, Quentin pulled Rand aside. "I gotta talk to you about stuff Oliver Stone is saying," he said. But it wasn't the time.

The time never came. Rand called and left a message. He called a few times, but didn't want to overdo it. He sent Quentin an invitation to his wedding to longtime girlfriend Janice in July 1993 and received no response. "I finally got Quentin on the phone and he gave me one of those things, the Hollywood 'babe' treatment, where he's heading out the door right now and can't talk. That's when I gave up trying to contact him," says Rand, although he believes it comes with the territory. "I've always known this about him. Quentin and I have always talked about the theories of creating success—always be the weakest link in the chain, don't hang out with your pals from Torrance when you can hang out with John Travolta and Uma Thurman. We once had a talk about it when Quentin was sleeping on my mother's floor in the old days. Some of the guys at Video Archives were complaining that they never heard from him anymore. He had heard an interview with some filmmaker who had learned that what you have to do is immerse yourself in what you're doing even at the cost of alienating your past. That's what Quentin did. He cut as many ties as he could to isolate himself. He finally got an apartment out in Hollywood, some rattrap studio apartment with mounds of dirty clothes, a VCR, a bed. That's where he chose to be. He was in Hollywood, and that was important to him, cutting ties with his go-nowhere friends to get out of a stagnant pond. There was something exciting about being in the boundary of Hollywood for him. I never thought he would turn his back on us all; in fact, I do believe things will come around some day."

Regrets run high in the *NBK* saga. One theory, an inevitable one, is that Quentin Tarantino got too famous too fast and, to use a Tarantino phrase, started disappearing up his own ass. "I want you to understand just how Hollywood this person became the moment he had a modest amount of success," says Don Murphy. "It didn't happen fast, this fame. But when he hit, he hit big. When he hit, he hit huge. When he hit, his head swelled nineteen times."

Friends who forgive his bouts of egomania put it kindly: the naturally gregarious Quentin just spread himself thin making promises and commitments he couldn't keep. Disgruntled former friends feel differently. "At the eleventh hour he fucked them over," is how one puts it. "And he does it time and again. He really, really believes that he is like the coming of Christ, because in England, you know, he is. The reality is if you're well-grounded you get famous and maybe you get a little bit of an ego, right? If you're not well-grounded you just go insane."

("I've handled the pressure better than anyone I know," responds Quentin quietly.)

Those in the anti-Quentin camp are not without a sense of humor, albeit a nasty one, aimed at what they term Quentin's "Cro-Magnon forehead." Don Murphy and his friends have taken to calling Quentin "Unfrozen Caveman Director," after a recurring routine called "Unfrozen Caveman Lawyer" on *Saturday Night Live*. In the television skit, a caveman is thawed, dressed up, and deposited in a courtroom, where he lumberingly tries cases using Ice Age logic; it's a sort of "you can dress him up but you can't take him out" routine. Don and company sit around watching Quentin do the talk-show circuit while catcalling at the screen in stentorian tones: *"Your ways of walking are strange to me! Your celluloid scares me! But I do know this—you are Unfrozen Caveman Director!"*

It should be noted, however, that even the most bitter former friend of Quentin's is never as disrespectful as the "Unfrozen Caveman Director" contingent. Former friends are more apt to be saddened than nasty, and even now make excuses for him; above all, they miss him.

The bad feelings between Don Murphy and the Quentin camp have, if anything, intensified over time. "When anybody becomes as successful as Quentin has become out of nowhere, there's going to be a backlash and there are going to be crazy people who want to take potshots," says Stacey Sher, currently president of Jersey Films, which set up the original deal for *Pulp Fiction*.

Stacey is one of several sources who claim that Don Murphy sent out damaging faxes—one to the *L.A. Weekly* in Lawrence Bender's name, "saying that Quentin wanted to cast Steve Guttenberg in *Reservoir Dogs* but that it was Lawrence's idea to get Harvey Keitel." The *L.A. Weekly* smelled a rat and didn't run the letter. The William Morris Agency used supersleuth Gavin De Becker to investigate, but meanwhile someone noticed a unique streak running across the middle of the page, similar to previous faxes that had been sent from Don

Murphy's office. "Don confessed and said that he sent it as a joke to try to get closer to Quentin," says Stacey. Don's apology letter is dated November 2, 1992, and was sent to Lawrence, with copies to nine other people, seven of whom confirm receiving it. "We sent a letter to Don's lawyer saying that what he has done is a federal offense. It's fraud, and he's lucky we are not pressing charges against him," Stacey says.

"Stacey's comments are interesting, if obviously skewed by the fury of a woman who used to go out with Quentin and was dropped like a hot potato as soon as he got famous," says Don. Stacey and Quentin dated during 1991 and 1992; his detractors say he dated her just long enough for her to set up his *Pulp Fiction* deal. "As for any letters that may have been sent to the *L.A. Weekly* or elsewhere, my only comment is, some people see fraud in everything in our litigious society, and they are usually the people who severely need a sense-of-humor transfusion."

Now that the dust has settled on the *NBK* debacle, Rand Vossler is working on some new screenplays of his own and intends to produce *Cheapskates* with screenwriting partner Josh Olson. In the months following his loss of *NBK*, Rand was despondent and didn't know what to do with himself, so he called Quentin and asked if he could take a crack at finishing up their long-ago project, *My Best Friend's Birthday*. Half the footage is sitting in Rand's house in Torrance, half is in Quentin's duplex in West Hollywood, like a couple who split custody of the kids. "Actually, I'm looking forward to messing with that on my own free time," Quentin told Rand. "I'll be finishing that film myself."

On February 22, 1995, Rand invited his brother Russ and some of their old Video Archives buddies over for a little laser disc party. He had a copy of *Andrei Rublev*, the 1966 Andrei Tarkovsky film about a fifteenth-century artist's moral dilemma between art and conscience. Everybody was psyched to come over and watch. "And then, bam! bam! bam! everyone called up to say they couldn't make it. Quentin had invited them over to watch him on *All-American Girl*"—a TV sitcom in which Quentin made an appearance lampooning *Pulp Fiction.*

Rand, though weathered, is still able at times to do what the other Video Archives guys do, which is to adopt a kind of Zen attitude—"Quentin is just Quentin" they have all said at one time or another to explain the ineffable.

"I wasn't out of there twenty minutes before Rand signed it over to Don and Jane," says Quentin. "I never would have let them get their hands on it. If Rand had just done it the way I told him, shoot it guerrilla-style, you know, just keep shooting till he finishes it on 16-mm, if he'd have done that I would have given it to him for nothing. We had a little contract together that just said basically, you make it that way and we'll split the money when the film's over. Then they say they're gonna make it for $5 million, so I said, well if you're going to make it for that, then I want to be paid, I'm not going to give you a free option. So they came up with $10,000, something like that. But me and my lawyer went out *big-time* to create a situation where the contract read that I was selling the rights to Rand, not to Don and Jane. And as soon as I'm out of the room, he signs it over to *them*. Four days later they say, Rand, you're not directing the movie anymore. I knew they were thinking about it. But it was a weird situation, because, see, Rand was actually flipping out. He got bit by a case of egomania like I've never seen before. And it was really crazy. I do believe that in the beginning, Don and Jane were honorable about it, they actually wanted to work with him. Then they just totally realized he wasn't the guy to make the movie, and they were stuck. So now you can understand why they did what they did, but that doesn't make it *right*. There's no way on god's green earth I would ever give Don and Jane the rights to that script."

The funny thing is that not only does Quentin still think of Rand as his friend, but that when he gave Rand his blessing to run with *NBK* and direct it himself, Quentin felt it was the grandest, most selfless gift he had ever given anyone. Rand's brother, Russ Vossler, remembers Quentin being awed by his own generosity. "He felt," says Russ, "that giving *Natural Born Killers* to Rand was his ticket into heaven."

"It's like I had a baby and I killed it for him," says Quentin, laughing. "I did. I stabbed my baby in the heart for him. And yeah, at the end of the day I can feel good in my own heart that, you know, when it came down to the test I was there for him. I now know that I would do that for a friend. But the friendship can't be the same anymore. You can't help but have a little bit of resentment, having killed your baby."

Natural Born Killers, directed by Oliver Stone, opened wide in 1500 theaters on August 26, 1994. Within a week, it had tacked on another 400 screens.

Rand Vossler received a co-producer credit, which was his contractual right. The screenwriting credit went to Oliver Stone, David Veloz and Richard Rutoski, while Quentin declined to be listed in that category and settled instead for a "story by" credit, claiming he still owned the rights to the characters he had created.

Natural Born Killers, with Woody Harrelson as Mickey and Juliette Lewis as Mallory, met with the usual reaction to an Oliver Stone picture—half the critics loathed it and thought it self-indulgent and over-the-top (Dave Kehr dismissed it as ultimately being about "the ritual elimination of authority figures"), and half the critics thought it was one of the most important, trenchant social commentaries ever made. Stone had wedded form to function, using different kinds of film stock and techniques to create a visual extravaganza. He tightened the narrative, made it more linear, reduced the role of the *American Maniacs* camera crew and increased the role of the prison warden and of the police detective who can tell Mallory's been at the scene of a murder by the imprint of her ass on the hood of a car. The detective picks up a lone pubic hair and inspects it. "Mallory!" he breathes.

One person who hated *NBK* and had made this known for months in advance—but who had never seen it—was Quentin Tarantino. So far, the only things that have been known to slow down the motormouthed Quentin are moments when he is bliss-fully in love and whenever the subject of Oliver Stone arises.

"I wish Oliver Stone had just ripped it off rather than rewrite it," said Quentin testily over lunch at Cannes, a full three months before the picture opened. Nearly a year later, he still hadn't seen it, and didn't intend to. "You can't just change my work and expect me to say it's okay. Forget the fact that I'm coming from an ugly place when it comes to this project any-way"—meaning the trouble between Quentin and Rand, Quentin and Don Murphy. "I'll never feel good about this movie, all right, it's just insult to injury. I have to *pretend* that it's okay? Well, it's *not* okay."

Quentin even withheld a couple of pages from the script, a sort of death scene for Mallory, so that he could recycle it in a future movie. "My feeling was, you buy *The Big Sleep*, you don't get all the Raymond Chandler books too."

Oliver Stone has been stewing about Quentin's attitude for a long time. On the day before he flew to London for the long-delayed opening of *NBK* after a protracted fight over whether his movie—or any movie—fosters copycat crime, he let his thoughts be known.

Oliver only met Quentin once or twice, and their memories of those meetings diverge completely. If Oliver's angry about it, he has it under control. For a guy who makes movies that hit you over the head, Oliver in person can be quiet, dignified, gen-tlemanly, even self-effacing. He is, dare one say it, sweet. He doesn't dodge questions; he doesn't hide behind "off the record" comments. "The things Quentin said about me, they hurt. He hurt me," says Oliver quietly and with genuine sad-ness. If he is not truly this sincere, then he is a damn fine actor and should get a SAG card.

"I was hurt by his comments, to be honest," says Oliver. "Filmmakers knocking one another—we get so much shit from critics, I know I get a lot, why do we have to get it from another filmmaker? It's like, you know, I have to have Spike Lee put me down also? And it almost affirms what they want to believe. It's just against my code for a filmmaker to knock another film-maker."

Quentin, whose strength and weakness is that he says what's on his mind, remembers telling Oliver that he was a "Stanley Kramer with style," among other quasi-insults.

"He's said terrible things about [James] Ivory too," says Oliver. "And I've heard him knock a few films. What is it? Hubris, I guess, that first surge when you think you know everything about movies because you've seen a lot of them. That arrogance of youth when you believe that you can do any-thing. And when people call you a god or a giant it's easy to believe. If you go to film school, film school teaches you a cer-tain amount of humility, because you see where you come from and you see the long tradition that you're in. So when you real-ize the number of good filmmakers that there has been, it makes you a little bit more humble about the things you've said."

As one can guess, Stone went to film school—NYU film school by way of Yale. His Ivy League background is tempered by his tour of duty in Vietnam; he's literally lived life in the trenches. Tarantino, by contrast, is a high school dropout intimidated by the game show *Jeopardy*, yet he remembers every film he's ever seen. He has an innate sense of the medium and has devoted himself to capturing the parlance of the underclass. "If you just love movies enough, you can make a good one," Quentin told a crowd at London's National Film Theatre. "You don't have to go to school, you don't have to know a lens from a bag of sand."

Oliver is well-schooled, Quentin is self-taught; there's a case to be made for each.

"I actually thought I was giving Oliver a bit of credit by saying I haven't seen the movie," says Quentin. "I am not talk-ing about anything that I have seen. So it's not like I'm saying he made a shitty movie. I don't know if he made a shitty movie or not. I know he didn't make the movie that I wrote, and I don't like him doing that."

"I think you could look at *Pulp Fiction* in two years and you could look at *Natural Born Killers* and say it's apples and oranges," says Oliver. "They're not that close—a whole different style, a whole different attitude towards life. It's a different feeling. One is a film made by a man in his forties, and the other is by a man in his early thirties. Coming from different places. I mean, I'm coming from violence that I've lived, and between Vietnam and the Merchant Marines, I've been haunted by violence. It's obviously in my films; you've seen them. You can see that I'm wrestling with some problem with violence. And that's what characterizes NBK, that's why it disgusts a lot of people, it's not an easy film to like, it doesn't access easily into the culture. I'm amazed that it did, what, $52 million. It's really avant-garde, and the techniques are fast, it's hard, six things are coming at you at the same time."

Oliver carefully considers before he speaks, giving the computer of his mind time to reboot. Even then, he speaks carefully and deliberately, unlike Quentin, who sprays conversation as if from a machine gun. "What hurt me," says Oliver, "was his assessment of me as, in a sense, a filmmaker who could only say one thing. And I think that's unfair because if you see the movie, NBK to me is very complex, it's not just about the media, it's about the forces of violence. And there's an ambiguity in the movie that's not easily understandable on one viewing or six viewings. There's a lot of textures."

One of the things Quentin says he discussed with Oliver was the difference between "films" and "movies," one of those points of distinction only made by people "in the business." Quentin loves even the lowliest "movie" and has accused Oliver of trying to make high-falutin' "films."

"I don't remember that conversation," says Stone. "Because I don't think in those terms. I make movies, too. I love movies. Maybe he's just angry at me for tampering with his bible. To me, yeah, film should be about life experience. When I was in film school, a lot of the kids were doing technically brilliant films, but they based them on other movies. So it's important for movies to break through that barrier and try to be about your own felt experience."

Personally, Oliver prefers *Reservoir Dogs* to *Pulp Fiction*. "The question is, can he expand his worldview beyond that genre, the combination of violence and humor? Pop-culture icons, references to Madonna and Michael Jackson—it's fun. But that's not what you can live on. You can't dine out on it for the rest of your life, in my opinion. You can make fun movies, or pulpy movies, but I don't know, is there really something being said?"

In its raw version, the *NBK* screenplay held a lot of appeal for Stone. But that's what it was to him—raw material that he bought for the express purpose of shaping it to his own ends. "When you have the luxury in this business of finally getting development funds, then you have the money to buy material and to work with writers to develop it. It's the nature of the business," says Oliver. "Most writer-directors tend to stop writing, because it's easier to develop stuff, there are so many good minds. Why do you have to do it yourself? I still write, but I'm trying to be smart in terms of using that development money to try to get the best of all the minds there are that can work on a project. And that includes Quentin. So I don't look at it as if it's his screenplay or my screenplay, you know. That seems to be a dispute that the Writer's Guild makes up, people who want to separate us into two different entities, which is what happened on this film, unfortunately for me. I didn't see that coming, and I never thought about it. I just said, well, this is a great piece of material, let's move it forward into another area."

Oliver agrees with what Quentin himself has said, that *NBK* was meant to be a first film. Oliver says that it read like one. "It was written like *Slacker* or like *S.F.W.*—you know, it was that kind of a loose, Roger Corman–esque trashing of a sort of B-film but intersecting it with a nineties look at the media," says Oliver. "In other words, taking an old Roger Corman movie, two people on the run, but they meet the media in the nineties and then the media takes over. And it's mostly about Wayne Gale. There was the film crew, they all had an identity, and there were extended jokes about donuts and about being inside of a prison and getting knocked off one by one. And Mickey and

Mallory were essentially, to me, stick figures. They were two wild and crazy people, they'd been busted, and they used the media very cleverly to get out of the prison and they were free, and they were kissing again, and they were stock lovers who were kissing all the time. I thought it was brilliant because of the dialogue and because it was funny. And I really had wanted to direct a gangster film, so when I read this, I said this is perfect for me, because it combines the road movie with the prison movie, and it's a great combination, and at the same time it's about gangsters, but it's gangsters in a nineties fashion. But I really was not as interested in Wayne Gale, who is good only in small doses, and I just wasn't interested in making a movie about Geraldo Rivera."

In fact, the Wayne Gale character in Stone's version is patterned after the Australian éminence grise Steve Dunleavy, a former *New York Post* metropolitan editor who became the star reporter of Rupert Murdoch's *A Current Affair* tabloid-TV show. Robert Downey Jr. trailed after Dunleavy on the job for a while, returning from his research with a dead-on impression of a reporter who makes himself the star of his own reports. Dunleavy lambasted the movie, but those who know him say the characterization was remarkably accurate.

During the rewrite process, Stone envisioned Mickey and Mallory as a modern Bonnie and Clyde. He wanted to give them more backstory—the original script showed them only in brief flashback killing off their respective parents—so he devised an *I Love Mallory* sitcom, in which Mallory's dad's threats to molest her are met with canned laughter from a studio audience. Of the segments Stone added (including a mystical desert scene in which Mickey undergoes a transformation when he kills a Native American shaman), the *I Love Mallory* sequence is most in line with Quentin's own style.

"Their twisted love affair would be the motive, but there would be a sense that Mickey when he gives his interview like Manson is no longer the shallow young guy in the beginning of the movie. After a year in prison, he's in a different place. He's articulate now, he's philosophical, he talks about his father, the root causes of violence. He talks about the nature of every man having violence in him. So these were themes that I wanted to develop through the visual style of the movie, to show violence throughout the movie, where everybody was haunted by the concept of the demon within, the beast. On the other hand, I thought we used the best parts of Quentin's script."

There were scenes shot in which the camera crew maintained their personalities, but to keep the pace and also keep it near the two-hour mark, those scenes hit the trim bin. "There was more humor that we had to cut, but I think the movie is dead-on in capturing a coldness and a madness of this decade. It's not just about the media, it's about building more prisons, it's about more oppression, it's about the police forces becoming more corrupt. Parents who are not raising their children correctly, a society with its emphasis on violence. Everything you see on TV is wrestling matches, movies, violence begets violence. And this is a biblical theme, so it's not just about Wayne Gale to me. It's more like a *Wall Street*, a commentary on the nineties. It's sociopolitical, we threw in Hitler and Stalin, the concept is genocide begets genocide. And what is violence? Killing fifty-two people is wrong, yes. But what is it relative to the environmental damage that's shown in the movie, porpoises and whales and waters being ruined? I guess the movie's about capitalism, raging capitalism. And Mickey sees through it and understands it. At the end of the day I hoped that the movie would be sort of a deconstructivist experience, where you're aware that you're watching a movie, it's not like watching *Speed* where you just go along with the action. You're aware of the violence. And a lot of people told me they watched the violence like they were wearing virtual reality goggles or something. Mickey and Mallory find it fun to kill, and the audience is disgusted because they're enjoying watching it. You cannot walk out of that movie without being in some way disturbed by it, which is sort of the point."

Quentin met with Oliver when Oliver first came aboard,

and asked him not to make the film. He was still smarting over Don and Jane getting the rights to his screenplay; "I feel real bad that I ever let those guys ever get their hands on the script, and that Oliver was ever in the position to do what he did, and that I let the material go, when I could have either made it later or raped and pillaged it and used it for other things." Oliver says he came on board after "a paper trail" of legal documents that proved Don and Jane did indeed have the rights. The Rand Vossler problem was solved through lawyers. But again, there's fact and there's truth—the fact is that everything was legal by the time Oliver Stone settled into the director's chair, but the truth is that there was a puddle of bad blood left behind, and when Quentin refers to the "skulduggerous theft" of his script, he is not speaking literally or legally, but about how the chain of events plays back to him in his heart.

That Quentin didn't want his movie made was understandable, at least from the point of view of a screenwriter who wanted his material filmed with his own dialogue and sensibilities intact. Oliver Stone was unswayed, yet he of all people could sympathize. Oliver's screenplay for *Midnight Express* was directed by Alan Parker. *Scarface* was directed by Brian De Palma. *Year of the Dragon* was directed by Michael Cimino. As he reels off the names of the men who have reshaped Oliver Stone's clay, his face tightens almost imperceptibly. "But I didn't squawk, I didn't go public with it—I mean, I did a little bit later, but years after the picture came out. It really does damage the film, especially in this case because he"—Oliver rarely refers to Quentin by name—"became a god overnight, a myth, a legend. His is probably the most acclaimed single debut that I know of. I've never seen anything like it."

Oliver says Quentin was paid in the neighborhood of $400,000 for his *NBK* script; Quentin confirms that. "It was a big payday for him, and he has a tremendous bonus system. So he makes more money if the film does well. He has some kind of leveraged profit system, and he's collecting money now, still."

Quentin had a special provision whereby if the budget of

the movie went over $3 million, he got a percentage of the budget; the budget blossomed to $40 million. "Yes, I cashed the check," says Quentin, "but I didn't get that money just because they were cool guys. If that clause hadn't been put in by my lawyer, I'd have gotten paid like $45,000."

The unpleasantness still sticks in the craws of both filmmakers. "Per contract, he's not supposed to badmouth the film," says Oliver. "That's a given. We could probably sue the shit out of him and win. Because to be honest, it's just not done, a writer who becomes famous and then trashes his own movie. I feel like it's a code, it's a samurai code that you live with. The director makes the final choice."

CHAPTER 7

From Dusk Till Dawn

The path of the righteous man and defender is beset on all sides by the iniquities of the selfish and the tyranny of evil men. Blessed is he who in the name of charity and good will shepherds the weak through the valley of darkness. For he is truly his brother's keeper, and the father of lost children. And I will execute great vengeance upon them with furious anger, who poison and destroy my brothers. And they shall know I am the lord when I raise my vengeance upon them. (Ezekiel 25:17)

—From Dusk Till Dawn, *pages 65 and 66 of original draft by Quentin Tarantino, from a story by Robert Kurtzman and John Esposito, 1991*

—*. . . and then again in* Pulp Fiction, *1994*

Robert Kurtzman is the "K" in KNB EFX Group, a special-effects company formed by a trio of pals who met in 1987 while mixing and applying facial goo for Sam Raimi's *Evil Dead 2: Dead by Dawn*. The "N" is Greg Nicotero; the "B" is Howard Berger.

Raimi's sets are relatively relaxed affairs, thanks to the easy-going disposition of the floppy-haired horror director. His crew members are usually as young and enthusiastic as he is, fans of the same sort of goofy Three-Stooges-Meet-the-Beast-with-Five-Fingers style of filmmaking. On *Evil Dead 2*, Kurtzman, Nicotero and Berger also met Scott Spiegel, Raimi's boyhood chum, who co-wrote the screenplay with Sam. When Scott finally realized his dream of becoming a director with the slasher movie *Intruder* the following year, Kurtzman, Nicotero and Berger banded together more formally under the KNB banner.

Over the years, KNB would create "animatronics, creatures, puppets," including the calf Norman in *City Slickers*, the buffalo for *Dances with Wolves*, the Harryhausen-like army of skeletal warriors for Raimi's *Army of Darkness*, and, mostly as a favor, the severed ear for Quentin Tarantino's *Reservoir Dogs*.

Bob Kurtzman had been an Ohio kid obsessed with monster flicks. He studied art but gravitated to southern California where the movies were, and narrowed his artistic focus to cinematic makeup—which is how he wound up in Raimi's gore camp.

But like everyone else in Hollywood—at least everyone who didn't plan on becoming a screenwriter—what Bob really wanted was to direct.

With his writing partner John Esposito, who was working on the screenplay for Stephen King's *Graveyard Shift* at the time, Bob Kurtzman worked up a twenty-page treatment for a movie he wanted to direct, *From Dusk Till Dawn*. It was a "gangster-vampire" movie set in a Texas border-town topless joint, full of ample opportunity for KNB to whip up gore, slime and anima-tronic bats. The best opportunity of all was that it would be Bob's glorious debut as a director.

What Kurtzman needed in late 1990 was a writer to flesh out his movie treatment, and he began auditioning talent. One

day two unproduced scripts arrived on his doorstep C.O.D.—
True Romance and *Natural Born Killers*. Cool, thought Bob. This
Quentin Tarantino sure can write.

At this point in his still-nonexistent movie career, Quentin
was attending pitch meetings with the guarded hopefulness
with which he also went out on casting calls. He took the bus
over to the KNB studio, where Kurtzman and his partner
pitched him the vampire flick. Using the same enthusiasm and
alacrity that had once led his first-grade teacher to prescribe the
sedative Ritalin, Quentin went right to work and turned the
treatment into a screenplay in no time at all. "I think me and
John were the first people to hire Quentin to actually write
something," says Kurtzman, and Quentin confirms this.

Under Quentin's poor penmanship but brilliant ear for dialogue, Kurtzman's twenty-page treatment mutated into an
eighty-eight-page screenplay. "He added a few things, but for
the most part he was pretty true to the story," says Kurtzman.

"The characters were clichés," says Quentin. "The whole
thing was set up to be more or less a showcase for KNB
makeup effects. They gave me a pretty detailed outline—this
happens and this happens and this happens. Since that's what
they wanted, there was less for me to write."

In Tarantino's original version, *From Dusk Till Dawn* opens
much the way *Natural Born Killers* does, with a couple—in this
case brothers Richard and Seth Gecko—in the middle of a
killing spree. They take out the occupants of a dusty roadside
diner, then continue on the lam with a suitcase of loot from a
bank robbery. They take refuge from dusk till dawn in an eerie
strip joint called the Titty Twister.

"Is it safe to assume since the law enforcement authorities
in the great state of Texas are homosexuals of a sick and deviate
nature, that they will be too busy fucking each other up the ass
to actually catch the Gecko brothers?" says one brother, in imitation of a TV newscaster. "I would say that's a very safe
assumption," answers the other brother in "an FBI voice."

The brothers take hostage a family—an ex-preacher dad, his

nubile daughter and his adopted Vietnamese son—and there is a sprinkling of remarks about incestuous possibilities. "What's the story with you two?" asks Richard of the father and adopted son. "You a couple of fags? Is this some sorta homo honeymoon?"

Richard then asks the adopted son whether he ever has an urge for his sister—"I bet she keeps your dick harder than Chinese arithmetic."

Quentin, possibly remembering his adoptive dad Curt Zastoupil's abrupt departure from the family, wrote a scene in which the Vietnamese boy's adoptive dad turns on him: "A totally evil Jacob, with only half a face, matches stares with the boy he once called his son."

Tarantino's favorite subjects find their way into this early screenplay. The character Richard eats Cap'n Crunch cereal with Crunch Berries, dry from the box. A bar bouncer is compared to Godzilla, a bartender to Rodan. Much of the dialogue is snappy and outrageous: "Those acts of god really stick it in and break it off, don't they?"

With the hostage family in tow, the Gecko brothers arrive at the Titty Twister, "the rudest, sleaziest, most crab-infested top-less strip joint, honky-tonk whorehouse in all of Mexico." The neon sign advertising the place consists of a buxom neon woman whose breast is being twisted by a neon hand.

The barker outside the bar entices customers with this rap:

"All pussy must go! At the Titty Twister we're slashin' pussy in half! This is a pussy blowout! Make us an offer on our vast selection of pussy! We got hot pussy, cold pussy, wet pussy, tight pussy, fat pussy, hairy pussy, smelly pussy, snappin' pussy! If we don't have it, you don't want it! . . . Take advantage of our penny pussy sale. Buy any piece of pussy at our regular price, you get another piece of pussy of equal or lesser value, for a penny. Now try and beat pussy for a penny! If you can find cheaper pussy anywhere, fuck it!"

It turns out the staff of the Titty Twister are vampires, and they wind up attacking the customers and turning the unlucky ones into fellow creatures of the night. The scenario gets *Night of the Living Dead*–ish, with the hostage family and the Gecko brothers trying to ward off the vampire bats who are boring in from outside and the occasional indigenous vampire from within. The creative killings are also very early Sam Raimi.

Although Kurtzman had paid Quentin only $1500 to write the script, he knew it was worth more, and he was filled with gratitude. It seemed that Quentin truly understood the importance of a directing debut—in fact, Quentin was soon to make his own with *Reservoir Dogs,* which was to begin filming just as soon as he could scrape up the money. Thrilled with his script, Bob agreed to have his KNB crew work on *Reservoir Dogs* for pennies. If truth be told, Bob wound up paying out of his own pocket, but he didn't mind; "Quentin wrote that screenplay for me and it was kind of a favor thing."

On *Reservoir Dogs,* the KNB gang made up some dummies, did some blood gags, and made a prosthetic ear of foam latex that Michael Madsen would slice right off a cop's face. "We actually glued the actor's ear down and then attached a prosthetic with a hairpiece that simulated his missing hair," says Kurtzman, a handsome, laid-back guy just a year younger than Quentin. Later, KNB would also work on *Pulp Fiction,* making Bruce Willis's samurai slash look realistic, and also creating Marvin's exploding head, which didn't make it into the movie, "probably for ratings; it was pretty bloody."

Tarantino also brought back the KNB boys in 1995 for a gag in *Four Rooms,* for which they devised a urethane finger.

After *Reservoir Dogs,* Kurtzman spent a few years vainly trying to get *From Dusk Till Dawn* off the ground with himself attached as director and his effects company on board for the gore. He faced what Quentin had faced when trying to get *True Romance* and *Natural Born Killers* made—nobody wanted an untested director. *From Dusk Till Dawn* was turned down more often than a bed in a hot-sheet motel. Even *Fangoria,* the magazine for horror fans, which had set up a movie-production arm, rejected the script. "Fango Films weren't the swiftest, and they were very cliquish," admits Tony Timpone, editor of the respected *Fangoria* magazine and a big Tarantino fan—he remembers Quentin hanging out at the annual Fango conventions before he was famous, trying to get FX wizard Tom Savini to make a personal appearance at Video Archives. After *Reservoir Dogs*, Quentin still hung out with the Fango crowd and cheerfully filled in when a guest presenter didn't show at the second annual Fango Chainsaw Awards in 1993. "Gosh, I haven't even seen all of those, I'll have to rent them!" Quentin expostulated after watching clips of the nominees in the straight-to-video category.

Still, a rejection of *From Dusk Till Dawn* by Fango Films was a blow. "Eventually, you know, it got to the point where we decided to set it up with another director cause it was an easier thing to do," says Kurtzman with resignation.

That new director would be Robert Rodriguez, who set his sights on the script as early as September 1992.

Every year at the Sundance festival, there is a new kid on the block whose movie breaks a record for being the cheapest one ever made. San Antonio–born Robert Rodriguez won that distinction—along with the audience prize—in 1992, the year Quentin Tarantino's *Reservoir Dogs* was also in competition. Robert had made *El Mariachi* for the laughable sum of $7000. He had borrowed $4000 from a friend and raised the other $3000 by volunteering for a month as a guinea pig in a research experiment of a new cholesterol drug.

El Mariachi, shot for the Mexican home-video market but destined for finer things, won Robert a two-year writing-directing deal with Columbia Pictures, and also won him a fancy agent at ICM. One of the first things this agent, Robert Newman, would do would be to figure out his new client's tastes in order to steer him in appropriate directions. "You gotta see *Reservoir Dogs*," he told Rodriguez. "It's about a bunch of guys doing cool stuff."

Although Robert and Quentin's movies were up against each other at Sundance in January 1992, they didn't actually meet until September of that year at the Toronto International

Film Festival (then still grandly titled the "Festival of Festivals"). Robert had caught *Reservoir Dogs* at the Telluride festival two weeks beforehand; Quentin had yet to see *El Mariachi*, but he knew all about it. The two were going to be on a filmmakers panel together in Toronto, and on the way into the conference room while everything was being set up, they did the filmmaking equivalent of the secret handshake—"We talked about Chinese cinema and all the different influences that were in his films, and that I thought he would see in mine," says Robert. This established them as members of the same clique.

Robert was intrigued by the notation in Quentin's panelist bio that he'd written an unproduced script called *From Dusk Till Dawn*, a border-town vampire movie. Quentin told him it was like two movies for the price of one; "at first you see an action movie, and then it becomes a vampire film all of a sudden."

Robert now describes it as being "about a couple of serial killers getting chased through Texas, killing a coupla Texas Rangers, shooting their way to a Mexican border town, then waiting in a whorehouse that turns out to be a den of vampire monster banshees who eat all the truckers. Then it turns into T*he Evil Dead*."

Quentin had left the land of $1500 scripts the minute *Reservoir Dogs* unspooled at Sundance. Never again would he have to stand by while other people made his movies. Anyway, no producers had wanted to pay Bob Kurtzman to direct the movie. Robert Rodriguez figured it would be easy enough for Quentin to buy back the rights "from the makeup guys."

The makeup guys found at this point that with Quentin getting famous, there was indeed interest in the property. But by then, the script needed a rewrite, "and they couldn't find a writer willing to rewrite Quentin Tarantino," says a source close to the project. "No one wanted to be accused of rewriting him."

"The Italian producers bought an option on the rights for like $35,000, something like that," says Quentin. "The deal was that when they'd get the film made, Bob Kurtzman would get like $200,000 or something."

Robert says Quentin was offered his own film back, but he didn't want it; however, he leaned on the producers to go with Rodriguez. "I wasn't really interested in doing it, it was like the old Quentin script, and I'd have to compete with all his other movies. Any good idea I'd come up with people would attribute to him, and any bad stuff would be attributed to me. Why would I put myself in that position? But when he told me that he was interested in doing a rewrite if I directed it, that would be cool."

In fact, the two had gotten along so well in Toronto that in 1995, Robert would direct a quarter of Quentin's *Four Rooms* project at the same time that he was completing his *El Mariachi* sequel. By this time, *From Dusk Till Dawn* had metamorphosed from a modest genre picture to a $17 million feature scheduled for a high-profile Christmas 1995 release from the new Dimension division of Miramax, to be marketed with the sly slogan: "Vampires. No Interviews."

In a deal memo procured by Mike Fleming for his Buzz column in *Variety*, $2.35 million was set aside up front for Rodriguez to executive produce and direct and for Tarantino to executive produce and put a spit-shine on the ol' script. "The prices go up if either acts in the film. Also included is first-dollar gross back-end participation that starts at 15 percent, escalates to 35 percent of gross after $70 million, and 40 percent of gross after $80 million. That money is split between Rodriguez, Tarantino and producers Meir Teper and Gianni Nunnari, who'll also get $1.2 million up front for producing, with Lawrence Bender pocketing $500,000 up front. The filmmakers keep the soundtrack rights and Rodriguez also gets final cut," wrote Fleming. Of that budget, $1.5 million was set aside to pay the actors; filming was to begin June 1995. The Fleming column was subtitled "Goodbye, Bargains."

If that seems like too much money for Quentin, Miramax chief Harvey Weinstein explains that his boy wasn't just making a couple of corrections on the script. "Quentin doesn't rewrite like, okay, I'll change a line," says Harvey. "He's *rewriting*."

"I started making the characters really three-dimensional," says Quentin, who was planning to play the younger Gecko brother, Richie. "Now that I wasn't just trying to showcase the makeup effects anymore, I was trying to actually tell the story. Now the big thing is at the end, as opposed to big giant masks walking around."

Today, Robert Kurtzman continues to make animatronics, creatures, puppets. In his spare time, "I'm just working on some screenplays and, you know, trying to get some things going." He still hopes to make his directing debut one day.

But it won't be on the gangster-vampire movie he dreamed up in 1990. On *From Dusk Till Dawn*, Kurtzman and his writing partner will get story and co-producer credit. And he and the KNB boys will do for his baby what they've been doing all along. "I'm handling the creature effects," he says without a trace of irony or bitterness.

CHAPTER 8

Past Midnight

For a serial killer, he's a damn fine-lookin' guy.
          —Past Midnight, *uncredited screenplay*
          by Quentin Tarantino

There were days when Scott Spiegel had to push aside the nagging thought that his friends were right, that nice guys finish last. Cheerful, earnest, loyal, generous—maybe these were bad qualities for a future Hollywood director to have after all. No natural-born killer he. Maybe that was why everyone in his circumference seemed to be getting directing gigs while Scotty was still plugging away at screenplays, just like he did at the beginning of his career when he and junior high school pal Sam Raimi out of Detroit co-wrote *Evil Dead 2: Dead by Dawn* in 1987.

"What in the crap is going on, this is so cool!" is Scotty's ebullient response to old pal Quentin Tarantino's meteoric rise, spoken with Scotty's trademark mixture of glee and childlike awe. "That guy was so broke! He was the brokest!"

"I have Scott to thank for getting me in the film industry," says Quentin.

When you're pals with Scotty, you're pals for life. He has had a cameo in every subsequent Sam Raimi picture since their co-writing days; he turned stomachs aplenty as the Gold Teeth Man in *The Quick and the Dead*, a character whose life expectancy is as short as his teeth are rotten. These sets are good places to meet future pals for life, because the crews tend to bond under highly pressured conditions, forging friendships like forging steel. For instance, on Raimi's *Darkman* in 1990, Scotty did a bit part as a dockworker alongside Bill Lustig, a man he had met five years before, a former pornographer who turned legit when he directed the low-rent slasher movie *Maniac* in 1980. Some people loved Bill, some hated him—one who worked with him at CineTel still refers to him as "that slimeball," only partly because of Lustig's habitually rumpled and shaggy appearance. But one thing you could say for Bill, he had carved his niche (or dug his grave, depending how you look at it) with the *Maniac Cop* franchise beginning in 1988, which is why Quentin initially backed him as the right director for *True Romance*.

"Ironically, before I knew Bill, I was afraid of him," says Scotty. "But he got me my first writing gig on *Hit List*, and he turned into a fairly decent filmmaker himself." And on the subject of Lawrence Bender, a former dancer and struggling actor who produced the only film Scotty had yet directed, he was just as happy to intercede against a smear campaign in later years when Bender needed good word-of-mouth to help Quentin Tarantino get *Reservoir Dogs* made over at LIVE Entertainment.

Three of the nicest things nice-guy Scotty would do would be to introduce Quentin to Bob Kurtzman, who had an idea for a screenplay called *From Dusk till Dawn;* to Bill Lustig, who almost directed *True Romance;* and to Lawrence Bender, who became the producer who finally made things happen for Quentin. "I could have kicked myself—here, Quentin! Here's Lawrence Bender!" jokes Scotty about setting up the winning team at a time when Scotty himself desperately needed help with his *Nutty Nut* comedy. Certainly Scotty could have leaned on Bender to work with him again as he had on *Intruder,* except "I knew slapstick comedy isn't Lawrence's cup of meat at all. But the bottom line is, Sam Raimi has Robert Tapert, and Quentin Tarantino has Lawrence Bender. Every director needs a strong producer who can really produce results. But when you throw guys up together and hope something sticks to the wall, it doesn't always work. I'm glad Quentin and Lawrence were able to get their vision out there, basically unencumbered by studio pressure. They've retained a tremendous amount of autonomy."

As Scotty counted down the days to Quentin's big night at the Oscars in 1995, it seemed very remote from the times when Quentin would drop by with a handful of rented videos to crash on Scotty's couch for the weekend. "My roommate does an impression of Quentin," offers Scotty, going into the breathy-intense Quentin voice. *"Hey, Scott, can I have a bowl of cereal?"*

"I knew he was something," says Scotty. "But I didn't realize he would become this instant Martin Scorsese. When we were all just starting out, it was like Moe Howard said in *Movie Maniacs,* 'Well, there's 50,000 people in Hollywood that don't know anything about making movies. Three more won't make a difference!'"

Quentin Tarantino did not meet Scott Spiegel by chance. Although fate was responsible for throwing possibilities in his path, Quentin had some of his mother's "self-made" philosophy. He knew the difference between good and bum luck was the person who could pull possibilites out of the air and wrestle them to the ground, leaving very little to chance. The plan behind leaving Video Archives for a low-paying, dead-end salesman job at Imperial Entertainment was to make contacts, to get closer to the pulse.

Imperial was a small Cannon wanna-be, a company that could have been Cannon if only it had been run by the famous Cannon cousins, Menahem Golan and Yoram Globus, the so-called "Go-Go Boys" who pioneered the art of the video back-end deal. Golan and Globus would go to Cannes and announce titles of movies that didn't exist, featuring stars who had yet to be contacted, then finance the deals by selling future video rights to the foreign market. Deals were scribbled hurriedly on bar napkins and matchbooks; that is the famous story of how Tarantino hero Jean-Luc Godard got his deal for the experimental *King Lear*, a 1988 movie starring Woody Allen and Molly Ringwald which nevertheless had no official list of credits. Knowing this, Quentin added *King Lear* to his résumé; a motivated employer would have trouble checking it, journalists were too lazy, and anyway, Quentin figured no one would want to admit they hadn't seen it.

Imperial's players may not have had the charisma of the Cannon cousins, but they managed to churn out a respectable volume of exploitation flicks of a certain kind—ninja, Sho Koshugi–type vehicles. They picked up foreign genre pieces and repackaged them for the U.S. video market. The trouble was in trying to sell these untested B-movies to video stores, so they hired a staff of salesmen whose job it was to call the stores, pretending they were customers hot to rent specific titles. The U.S. video business at that time was still driven by the mom-and-pop store, but the clock was ticking and they knew it. Naive owners would fall for the salesman scam and order a copy rather than risk losing a "customer" to the better-stocked chain-store competition that would drive them out of the business within the next few years anyway.

It was 1990, and Quentin was perfect for the salesman job at Imperial in a number of ways. For one thing, he had already worked in a mom-and-pop video store himself. For another, he had acting skills. He could do impressions, he could improvise scenes. He'd call a store and pretend he was a black dude, a housewife from Dubuque. Best of all, he really had an affection for the product; he was forever sampling the merchandise.

In one of his more inspired moments, he actually called up the store he had worked at, Video Archives. One of his buddies, Russ Vossler, answered the phone, and not recognizing Quentin's voice, fell for the stunt and wound up ordering some crappy kung-fu flick. "Maybe I was a little upset at the time," Russ would recall later after he figured out the ruse. "For a video store that had to watch its budget, it was really kinda sneaky in a way. I'd much rather have seen us get something else, like a classic rather than some dopey vampire movie or ninja thing or something."

The Imperial job was good for kicks, but it really paid off when Sheldon Lettich began using the editing room across the hall. Sheldon was a walking conduit to the outside world of low-budget indies. He was the Dr. Frankenstein behind Jean-Claude Van Damme, writing *Bloodsport* and then writing and directing *Lionheart* and *Double Impact*. When Sheldon made *Lionheart* at Imperial, Scott Spiegel had played a "pool fight bookie," Lawrence Bender had played a "garage fight heckler." Later, Scotty produced a screenplay co-written with Sheldon, *Thou Shalt Not Kill Except . . .* , "a Marines-versus-the-Manson-family kind of movie," recalls Scotty. "Quentin, being the video watchdog–video freak that he is and was, knew about that movie. It was a $50,000 quickie. Quentin ran into Sheldon, and he knew that Sheldon knew me and Sam Raimi, and of course Quentin was pining away to make a low-budget feature. So Sheldon calls me up and tells me Quentin knows my work! He had seen *Intruder*—nothing gets by that boy—not once, but four times, and remembers every line! I thought, this guy is scary."

Scotty was suspicious. "I go to those Fangoria conventions and you meet every Tom, Dick and Harry with a screenplay. I was going into production on *The Rookie*"—he and pal Boaz Yakin had sold their screenplay to Clint Eastwood and were about to make some very major bucks—"and I didn't have time."

But Scotty's a nice guy, and Quentin when he wants something is like a battering ram. "He was so energetic and vivacious, I thought if his script is half as energetic as he is in person, cool!" They met at a Hamburger Hamlet.

"I knew Lawrence was trying to get something going, so I told Quentin to send *Natural Born Killers* over to him. And Bill Lustig and a few other people were calling me to do rewrites, so

I turned Quentin on to Bill, and that's when Lustig went and said, 'I'm gonna buy *True Romance* from you!' Quentin sold it to him, but you have to remember, Quentin had no car, no money, no nuttin'! Just a couple of unproduced screenplays and a lot of hopes and dreams."

The Bill Lustig connection proved fruitful. Lustig took the screenplay of *True Romance* over to CineTel, and while setting up a deal to direct it, pitched them on Quentin as a guy who would make a great script doctor.

A script doctor is someone who comes in and does triage on a script full of holes. What CineTel really needed was more than a script doctor, more like a script surgeon—someone to do what they call a "page one rewrite," meaning reworking the entire script. What helped Quentin's case was Catalaine Knell, whose boss Paul Hertzberg had handed her the script for *True Romance*. Hertzberg liked Lustig and trusted Cat Knell's opinion. "Because of my incredibly high opinion of Bill," sarcastically recalls Cat, now the vice president of creative affairs at CineTel and one of the anti-Lustig faction, "I was really sour on the whole idea that my boss made me read anything this guy would bring me."

Cat started to read, holding the manuscript as far away as possible, her body language conveying her opinion. By page 10, Cat was dancing through the office, reading dialogue to anyone who would listen. "I just thought it was the most incredible stuff I'd ever seen. And I want to tell the world this—there's only one Quentin Tarantino."

Cat was sold on Quentin, and while CineTel attempted to set up *True Romance* with Bill Lustig—a deal that ended in agonizing litigation—Quentin was hired on December 18, 1990, to do a page one rewrite of *Past Midnight*, a grade-B thriller set in Oregon whose existing script was lagging far behind the talents of stars Rutger Hauer and Natasha Richardson. "It was and it always will be a *Jagged Edge* ripoff," is how Quentin describes it today.

Hauer was to play an ex-con who, having served time for killing his pregnant wife, has to report to parole officer Natasha Richardson. Richardson senses that Hauer could indeed be innocent, and against the better judgment of co-workers, tries to solve the case herself while carrying on a passionate affair with the convicted murderer.

Quentin was in one of his down-and-out, no-car phases. In the morning he would take the bus in from Glendale, where he was living rent-free in his mom's house, trying to write scripts and get *Natural Born Killers* off the ground with his producing pal Rand Vossler. At night, he would either take the bus home again or Cat would give him a lift. "We were paying him such a pathetic sum, something horrible like $5000," recalls Knell. ("It was $7000," says Quentin.) "And he was a doll. He rewrote and rewrote and rewrote, and that's why he never writes for anyone else now. The director at the time didn't 'get' Quentin. Some of his most wonderful scenes are not in the movie. Quentin is a wild guy, and they were shooting in Seattle and getting conservative up there. Some of the craziest scenes had to be turned around, and Quentin was really quite generous about it."

"I kept the whole structure of the mystery and everything, but I wrote in a retarded boy, and I wrote a ton of stuff in there," says Quentin. "And then Rutger Hauer comes in and says, 'I don't like that script. I like the one that I said yes to.' And so basically the script kind of became a mix between that first one and mine. Most of Rutger's stuff is from the original script, and most of Natasha's and Clancy Brown's stuff is my stuff."

There was no money, but Quentin had the sense that he was on the move. He had sold Lustig the option on *True Romance* "for about five cents," but on the bright side, *Past Midnight* was a screenplay that was guaranteed to see the light of day. And he was feeling free to inject all the trademark Tarantinia. For example, there's a line about an office worker who has switched from regular to decaffeinated (the Coffee Thing—Quentin says he associates coffee with work; going to make a cup of coffee is always a good way to get out of doing any). And there's a character pining for an absent dad (the Father Figure Thing). One character offers Natasha Richardson a choice between a dead-baby joke and a sexist joke; she chooses the sexist joke. "What's the difference between a whore and a bitch? A whore will sleep with anybody. A bitch will sleep with anybody but me."

Rutger Hauer is disappointed that his IQ is four points less than Ted Bundy's; one character comments that maybe Hauer "just isn't a natural born killer." Another character comments on Hauer, "For a serial killer, he's a damn fine-lookin' guy."

Quentin was particularly proud of a scene he wrote where the father of the slain pregnant woman gives Natasha Richardson a really insinuating foot massage. As Vincent Vega would say about foot massages a few years later in *Pulp Fiction*, "Is it as bad as eatin' her out? No, but you're in the same fuckin' ballpark." The way the older man was to touch and manipulate Natasha's toes was so personal, so provocative, it bordered on molestation. "That's actually kinda interesting about foot massage, it's almost kinda like a first move somebody could make," says Quentin.

Up in Seattle, director Jan Eliasberg hit the roof. What was this crap with the feet? "I wrote it thinking that would be really creepy for him to do to her," says Quentin. "And they didn't have the guts to go into it. They turned it into a back rub, which isn't the same thing."

The director also hated the line about the rock star biting his date's butt, and the reference to natural born killers . . . well, she would just have the actors do very straight line readings and hope for the best.

During this time, Scott Spiegel was off to see a double-feature of *House of Wax* and a Three Stooges short, *Spooks*, both being shown in their original 3-D—not with those flimsy red-and-blue cardboard glasses, either, but shown on a dual-projector system on an ultra-silver screen, with Polaroid 3-D glasses, the way 3-D was meant to be. He invited Quentin along, with his friend Rand Vossler. He also invited Lawrence Bender, figuring it was high time for Lawrence and Quentin to meet.

Lawrence—don't call him Larry—has the delicate features of a dancer and the cold ambition of a hit man. In Hollywood, both are a virtue.

He was born in the Bronx and later moved to South Jersey before his parents divorced when he was eleven. He had no idea what he wanted to do with his life. "My grandfather was a civil engineer," he says. "I was close to him, and I was good in math and science." So Lawrence got a degree at the University of Maine in civil engineering. He has never worked a day in his life as a civil engineer.

"It's beautiful country up there by the school, but there's not really a lot to do unless you go skiing and sailing," says Lawrence. "I was searching in my life for what to do. I tried many different things. I was going to open a dojo. I was going to become a potter. I almost quit college to go to chef's school."

He found yet another calling when his then-girlfriend urged him to join her dance class. "The first day I felt so uncoordinated, really awkward. But dance to me was like a drug, the most amazing high. We did the snake dance, undulating like in a trance. I had found ultimately what I wanted to do with my life."

Lawrence returned to New York on a scholarship with the Louis Falco company, and earned his living dancing flamenco. But his dance career was not to do the grand jeté he had imagined. "What happened was, I started getting injured—back problems, knee problems." Now he was depressed during the day, waiting tables at night. And like a lot of young people in that situation, he took acting classes, first with Sandra Seacat, whose floor he swept in return for tuition when the money was low. In his class were Jessica Lange, Frances Fisher, Lance Henriksen, and a pre-*Diner* Mickey Rourke. "What I was doing was searching to find myself, and Sandra, a big part of what she teaches is that you have to know yourself first. In acting, I found my ultimate form of expression. Although in my heart, I'm a dancer."

For the next few years, Lawrence danced when his tendons would allow and took acting classes when the money would allow. As an observer at the Actors Studio, he was permitted to do a scene with a partner in front of Eli Wallach. "What were you working on?" Wallach asked, genuinely puzzled, when Lawrence finished his scene. "Breathing," said Lawrence.

At Ellen Burstyn's sprawling grounds in Sneden's Landing, New York, where every year she and her friends put on a play, Lawrence took part in a production of *A Midsummer Night's Dream* with Christopher Walken. Years later when Lawrence and Quentin were on their way to the Sitges Fantasy Film Festival in Spain with *Reservoir Dogs*, Ellen Burstyn was sitting behind them, and it turned out she was to be a judge. (*Reservoir Dogs* did indeed take home a prize.) In Hollywood, Lawrence would run into former acting classmate Jessica Lange. He reminded Walken on the set of *Pulp Fiction* that they had been in *A Midsummer Night's Dream* together at Sneden's Landing. "I've come into my own in a different kind of way," says Lawrence, explaining his fascination with being a player in Hollywood, even if he never made it as a dancer or actor. "I'm reconnecting with people who had a lot of meaning for me in my life, but reconnecting in a different way." As an equal, that is. Not as the kid who hoped only to breathe properly through a scene.

It took a long time and a lot of heartache to meet those people on an equal footing. He flew to L.A. for "pilot season," the early part of the year when television pilot episodes are cast, and out of his $1000 stake he bought a $400 car roomy enough in case he'd need to live in it. He supplemented his pilot hunt with a catering job, where at the end of the night he might score a few bottles of leftover champagne that would make great gifts to friends on whose couches he crashed.

Catering was paying off better than acting. He landed only one *General Hospital* episode. He couldn't even get a job in the mailroom of the William Morris Agency—the agency that would later clamor to represent him and Quentin—because he couldn't type. Briefly he was a salesman for an educational company in San Francisco. By the time he was down to his last fifty dollars, he offered to work for free on the set of an American Film Institute (AFI) movie; at least he'd be on a real set. The script supervisor let him use her couch for a year.

"On another AFI movie, they asked me what I wanted to do," recalls Lawrence. " I told them I wanted to be a producer.

They said, what do you do now? I told them I'm an actor, just tell me what to do, I'll get coffee, whatever. I didn't realize I was saying something naive. They thought I was being stupid. I was naive and energetic. I had no savvy. I figured if I couldn't be an actor, I might as well be a producer—isn't he the one who runs the show?"

Lawrence's civil engineering degree had made him good at problem solving; certainly producers have been created out of a lot less. Meanwhile, Lawrence grabbed odd jobs as production assistant, dolly grip, whatever he could cadge. "The bottom line was that after a few years of this, I thought, this is not exactly what I want to do. I wanted to produce a movie for myself to act in. I was really missing acting."

His friend Boaz Yakin took pity on Lawrence and told him about Scott Spiegel, with whom Yakin would later write *The Rookie*. Spiegel was financing movies for $50,000 and selling video rights at film markets. Lawrence realized that what he needed was a low-budget horror movie, the chief point of entry into Hollywood for anyone who didn't have money or contacts. Scotty Spiegel had an idea for a slasher movie that took place in a grocery store. "We pitched it to a guy in October 1987 who said, 'Great, I love the idea, we shoot in January.' Well, we didn't have a script, so Scotty wrote it fast, and we went into preproduction on $7000. We got Sam Raimi to do a part, and two weeks before shooting was to start, I found a bankrupt grocery store where the manager said we could have it for six weeks for $2000. And we stocked it with spoiled food from a Ralph's warehouse."

The movie became *Intruder*, also known as *Night Crew: The Final Checkout*, a horror thriller that barely limped to home video a year after shooting began in March 1988.

Maybe Quentin Tarantino was the only one who ever saw *Intruder*—the only one who saw it four times, anyway—but Spiegel and Bender remember the shoot fondly. Scotty had never directed; Lawrence had never produced. "I didn't have a computer," says Lawrence, "so I did budgets by hand. I'd tape paper up on the wall, writing in the line items each week. I decided I couldn't act in my own movie, it was too complicated to produce and act at the same time. I was doing accounting work, and I didn't know anything about accounting. I had a big wad of cash in my pocket; that was how I paid people."

Charles Band, a producer who has helped many people get their start in Hollywood, put up the final production money, then made a video output deal with Paramount. "Because of that, our movie never opened in a theater, although we had this beautiful 35-mm print and a theater lined up in Detroit and other cities," says Lawrence. "The movie cost $125,000 to make. Charlie made $600,000. Scotty and I only got $10,000 each and no points. I didn't know any better. I didn't know I should be getting a back-end. But it was a really great experience."

As for Scotty Spiegel, once he became friends with Quentin he knew that *Intruder* had not achieved the benchmark that Quentin believed in for all first-time directors: that your first film has to shoot itself out of a cannon. Instead, Scotty had achieved a personal goal, and Lawrence Bender was now a bona fide producer.

But that wasn't enough for Lawrence; he was hungry. He still didn't know anyone in Hollywood, he still had no money, he was still working on AFI sets as a production assistant. Scotty invited him out one night to see a midnight 3-D double feature. He figured Lawrence needed a little fun in his life, and he also needed to meet Quentin, a screenwriter in search of a producer.

Lawrence arrived and found Scotty standing patiently on line. Lawrence didn't have that kind of patience. It had been a long day, and he shifted from one foot to the other. "It was a really long line. It was really late. It was half an hour past the time the doors were supposed to open and the line wasn't moving. So I left," says Lawrence. "The other guys stuck it out." The other guys were Scotty, Rand Vossler, and Quentin Tarantino.

The next time Lawrence ran into Quentin and Rand was at a Memorial Day party for *The Rookie*. Scotty had just gotten a half-million-dollar payday after years of struggle. Lawrence knew tangentially of Quentin, not only because of the midnight movie line, but because the script for *True Romance* had recently come his way when he was trying to put together a production company with Swiss financing. "I had read the script and thought it was really cool," says Lawrence.

"Of course it's obvious now, but when I met him back then, what was obvious is that he was a filmmaker," says Lawrence. "He may not have made any films yet, but he had made them in his head, over and over again. He had a kind of visual and audio memory. We decided to try to work together. He'd been trying to raise money on these two scripts for so long, he was tired of them."

"I'm going to write another script," Quentin told Lawrence. "It's about a bunch of guys, see, who pull a jewelry heist and go back to this garage. One guy's been shot, one guy's been killed, there's an undercover cop in their midst."

Lawrence was intrigued. Maybe there'd be a part in it for him.

"Oh, and you never see the jewelry heist," added Quentin. "It's a low-budget movie, so you don't have to worry about that."

Quentin was writing and rewriting *Past Midnight*, but no matter what he did, the director Jan Eliasberg wasn't buying it. Personally, Quentin thought Jan was intimidated by his presence.

Catalaine Knell drove him home one night and Quentin was particularly pumped up over all the possibilities that Hollywood had to offer. He jumped up and down on his mini-trampoline—not that he was big on exercise, but at least the trampoline was reminiscent of kindergarten, the only part of school he had ever liked. As he rose and fell amid the pop-culture explosion that was his bedroom, he regaled Cat with one of his favorite riffs, about how *Top Gun* was a subversive movie with a homosexual subtext about entreating Tom Cruise to go "the gay way." It was originally Roger Avary's idea, but it had become a running gag between them. Cat was a good audience because she had once worked for *Top Gun* director Tony Scott. In fact, she was planning to bring Quentin to Tony's Christmas party as her date.

It made dramatic sense that the director whose work Quentin was always parodying would wind up directing *True Romance*, and if Quentin didn't make as much money as he should have, neither did the movie. "Quentin was really naive and kidlike," says Cat. "In that whole period, you're talking about someone who was incredibly naive about business. He was into being happy and supportive of his friends, but he made some incredibly bad deals for himself in the process. He got taken advantage of. He wanted to give these people these things, not realizing they were going to make millions off of him. A lot of this started out as best intentions and went downhill from there. It was very messy."

Nevertheless, Quentin's check from *True Romance* paid for a Geo Metro and provided seed money for *Reservoir Dogs*. Cat brought Quentin over to the set of *The Last Boy Scout* while Tony was shooting, where Tony let Quentin "blow up a few things." In 1995, Quentin would be one of the script doctors on Tony's megabudget *Crimson Tide*. He thanked Tony in the end credits of *Reservoir Dogs*.

In those days, as the career clock was ticking—Quentin had a neurosis about becoming famous before age thirty, and he was already twenty-eight—Cat was a good friend to have. Not only did she love Quentin's writing, not only did she introduce Quentin to Tony Scott, but best of all, Cat was actually personal friends with Brigitte Nielsen! Brigitte—Gitte to her intimates—was an Amazon, long and strong, lean and mean, with endless legs. Quentin had an idea for a scenario in which Gitte could be a gun moll, a gangster's wife who is too dangerous to mess with but too seductive to pass up. Gitte, known mostly for her failed marriage to Sylvester Stallone and her fetishized tough-gal role in *Red Sonja*, had never shown the kind of acting range that maybe Quentin should have been evaluating in his haste to cast her in his as-yet-unwritten scenario. But she sure looked the part.

"This was the first indication of Quentin being an idiot," explains Catalaine Knell today with affection. "He didn't sort of question whether she could pull off the role. He had me bring

Gitte to the Formosa Café, a hot little bar, where he would meet us to have drinks so he could size her up for what became the part of Mia in *Pulp Fiction*. I'm sitting there with her, and sitting there, and he never shows up. I was like, I can't believe he would have me bring her down here and drink martinis and then not show up."

Much later, Quentin called Cat with what he considered a good excuse. His longtime girlfriend from the video store, Grace Lovelace, had dumped him just as he was on the verge of fame ("Bad timing, that girl," clucks Cat.) Grace decided to go back to school in Orange County for her master's in literature, and Quentin didn't have that Geo Metro just yet. So he took up with a new girlfriend, Stacey Sher of Jersey Films, and the night he was supposed to check out Gitte, he and Stacey had gone to see *Beauty and the Beast*. He was so smitten with Stacey at that point it was all he could talk about—besides movies, of course. "He was so incredibly in love at that moment, I had to forgive him," says Cat.

Anyway, it's not as if Quentin came away empty-handed from standing up his pal. He took from Catalaine Knell what Tony Scott had taken from Cat before him—her hair. For years, she had worn it in an interesting bob, straight and dark with bangs, falling just below the chin. Some people thought she was trying to be Louise Brooks, but Cat's real inspiration was Helmut Newton. Tony Scott had asked Gitte to wear a wig modeled on Cat's hair for *Beverly Hills Cop 2*. And Quentin, fusing Cat and Gitte perhaps subconsciously, put the same hair on Mia in *Pulp Fiction*. Quentin and Uma Thurman both insist the hair was Uma's idea, but any photo of Cat will confirm that Mia is a dead ringer for her.

Quentin brought his pal and writing partner Roger Avary around to meet the folks at CineTel. Roger was using *Pandemonium Reigned* as his calling card, a script he wrote about a boxer who doesn't go down like he promised, then has to evade gangsters while returning home for a precious heirloom watch his girlfriend accidentally left behind. The boxer gets into escalating trouble trying to escape the gangster he double-crossed and a pair of sadomasochists who get in their way.

CineTel was very pleased with Roger, and threw some rewrite work his way. Later, they'd set up a movie deal with him.

Past Midnight was almost in the can, and a new problem arose—the original writer, Frank Norwood, didn't want to share screenplay credit. To share credit, according to the rules of the Writers Guild of America, you have to have rewritten more than 50 percent of the script and created new characters. Quentin could have won in arbitration—"this was no mere dialogue polish," says Cat—but there was no time; the credits had to be slapped on and the movie, which never made it to theaters, was nevertheless due for a 1991 cable TV run. Advertised as "past passion, past terror, past murder," the movie gave associate producer status to Cat and Quentin. It was Quentin's first official movie credit, and it left a bitter taste—as the characters in *Pulp Fiction* would say, like freeze-dried Taster's Choice, not the gourmet expensive stuff.

CHAPTER 9

Reservoir Dogs: The Backstory

Mr. Brown:	*Mr. Brown, that's a little too close to Mr. Shit.*
Mr. Pink:	*Well, Mr. Pink sounds like Mr. Pussy. How about if I'm Mr. Purple? I mean, that sounds good to me. I'll be Mr. Purple.*
Joe:	*You're not Mr. Purple. Some guy on some other job is Mr. Purple. You're Mr. Pink.*
Mr. White:	*Who cares what your name is?*
Mr. Pink:	*Yeah, that's easy for you to say. You're Mr. White. You have a cool-sounding name.*

—Reservoir Dogs, 1992

"I feel like a director who has not directed, therefore I don't exist," said Quentin as Lawrence Bender hovered over the typewriter, reading a freshly minted section of *Reservoir Dogs.*

If it had been a few years before—even a few months before—Quentin would gladly have given Lawrence all the time he needed to come up with the cash to make his movie. But Quentin was frustrated, distracted, exhibiting all the signs that in grade school had made his teacher want to dose him with the sedative Ritalin. As an adult, however, the symptoms manifested themselves as decisiveness.

"Give me a year," pleaded Lawrence. .

"You get two months with an option to extend for another month," said Quentin. "At the end of October you can do a shot list, and if you haven't raised the money, we'll do it on 16-mm."

It had been three years since Lawrence produced *Intruder,* and he couldn't bear the thought of going back to doing odd jobs on other people's sets. So he took *Reservoir Dogs* and went into a frenzy of phone calls and networking as if his life depended on it. He originally entertained the notion that he would play the character of Nice Guy Eddie, but from the moment Lawrence got the option on *Reservoir Dogs* he barely had a moment to breathe.

Lawrence managed to interest the producer/director Monte Hellman, who had been in the business since the early sixties, making movies with Roger Corman and Jack Nicholson. Monte liked the script so much he wanted to direct it himself. Lawrence cringed at the thought of how Quentin, who had seen *True Romance* and *Natural Born Killers* slip away from him, would react to that. "You'll see, Quentin is the guy who should direct this," Lawrence assured Monte.

"One of the things that I was the proudest of was the fact that this film of mine that got produced was one that I directed. So I felt real great about that because I was so scared that if something of mine got produced that I didn't direct, it would take me forever to become a director, cause I would just be, oh, a writer trying to be a director," says Quentin now.

Once Monte met Quentin and got an Arctic blast of his enthusiasm, he agreed. The plan was for Monte to mortgage his house along with some land he owned in Texas in order to scrape together a few hundred thousand dollars. Quentin was a little queasy because he remembered the last time someone mortgaged a house to help him out—Stanley Margolis on *True Romance*. Stanley no longer lives in that house.

Then, like Butch looking around the pawn shop of *Pulp Fiction* for successively bigger and more effective weapons, Lawrence began to find better deals. "I found a video company with half a million dollars, and then another investor up in Canada with half a million dollars—but only if his girlfriend could play Mister Blonde," shades of the Hun Brothers scene that was forced on *Natural Born Killers*. "It was such a wacky idea that we actually considered it for a couple of hours; I mean, it was 180 degrees off the wall!"

"I see this movie as a comedy, a dark comedy," said the Canadian. "I see it like *Raising Arizona*. I don't think they should really die at the end. At the end, they should live." The guy offered $1.6 million that the dogs should live, but Quentin and Lawrence wouldn't bite. They were desperate, but not *that* desperate. They were now coming from a position of relative strength because there was still money left over from the *True Romance* deal, and they were perfectly willing to shoot it guerrilla style the way Quentin had done years ago with *My Best Friend's Birthday*.

"It's an interesting dynamic when you can walk into an office like that with a feeling of equalness," says Lawrence, who was always driven to get on equal footing with those in power. "You're in a different space, not in a really needy place, like, give me the money or else I'm gonna die. More like, it would be great if we could use your money, but if you don't we'll make this movie the way we want to make it anyway. We were a powerful unit."

The way Quentin and Rand Vossler had once developed a method of teamwork on *Natural Born Killers*, now Quentin and Lawrence were working out their modus operandus. "In other people's eyes, the producer's the parent and the director's the child," says Lawrence. "When a parent says something, he's Mister Responsible. When the child says something, he's Mister Irresponsible. Of course, Quentin is the most responsible direc- tor I've ever met. He takes pride in coming in on budget and on time." But they played the game for potential investors, with Quentin as the happy kid and Lawrence as the stern papa.

Lawrence was still taking acting classes on the side with Peter Flood, who was divorced from acting teacher Lily Parker. Lawrence told Peter that he and Quentin wanted more than anything to get Harvey Keitel into this movie, so Peter gave the script to Lily, who knew Harvey from the Actors Studio. When Lawrence got home one night after a day of heartache and despair, there was a light blinking on his message machine.

"Hello, Lawrence? This is Harvey Keitel calling." Lawrence recalls the message verbatim, and still giggles like a schoolkid when he repeats Harvey's name. "I read *Reservoir Dogs* and I would love to talk to you about it."

Lawrence forgot all he had learned in acting class about controlling his breathing. Hearing Keitel's voice on his answering machine made him perspire and hyperventilate. "One, Harvey Keitel is like god. He's not only a star, but an actor's actor. Not just a personality. Two, the fact that Harvey was going to be in the movie, I knew that was the thing that would help us get this movie made. His presence gave us more weight. It was really an amazing moment in my life."

"Lily Parker called me with the script," is Keitel's memory of how it happened. "I read it, and I was very stirred that here was a new way of seeing these ancient themes of betrayal, camaraderie, trust and redemption. I then called Lawrence and told him I'd like to help the movie to get made."

Harvey was motivated by more than just an interest in the script. "Let me just say this, if there is one thing I regret not doing as a young actor it is that I didn't make my own films," Harvey confided later at the Toronto Film Festival. "I grew up with a bunch of talented people and we didn't take best advantage of the talents we all had, the actors, the writers, the directors. We were struggling to make a living ourselves, to get work, to get agents, that whole thing. But in retrospect I'm sorry me and my group didn't make our own films early on. So I encourage that, I support it. I would do anything I could to help someone get their first films off the ground and not wait for Fox, Paramount, Universal to bestow upon you their good graces."

In 1989, Monte Hellman had directed *Silent Night, Deadly Night 3: Better Watch Out!*, the third in a slasher series about a Santa Claus killer. He and Richard Gladstein had worked up the story and Gladstein had done some producing work on it.

Now Gladstein was the vice president of production at LIVE Entertainment, a video company known at the time for financing small films; they later invested in *Light Sleeper* and *Bob Roberts*. Monte dropped the script of *Reservoir Dogs* off at his pal Richard's house, and Richard leafed through it idly on his way from the mailbox up to his front door. "That diatribe at the beginning, it immediately grabbed my interest," says Richard, who today is executive vice president of production at Miramax. "I laughed my way through the opening pretitle scene. Then I ended up sitting down and actually reading most of the thing right there. I've never been that drawn in by a script; I think I left my front door open. I was just shocked that it actually obtained that level of suspense and interest, that the drive of the characters continued at such a fervent rate."

The next day, Quentin and Monte came over to Richard's office in Van Nuys. He had been apprised by Monte that Quentin would never give up his idea of directing it himself, and Richard went along on that assumption. "I just took the approach of, 'I am making this film unless this guy is a complete idiot.' I figured he couldn't be a complete idiot if he had written that script. In fact, the title page said 'Written and directed by Quentin Tarantino.' You don't get that very often."

Richard was impressed by Quentin's air of certainty. Still, he asked him if he had ever directed before. "He told me that he had been directing some things for himself that he'd shot in his backyard. I asked to see these things and he said no. So I said, '*Ho*-kay.'"

Quentin thought outtakes from *My Best Friend's Birthday* were no way to clinch this deal. Anyway, he didn't need them—

Richard Gladstein and his partner Ronna B. Wallace offered to finance the movie through the video company for $1.3 million. It was the first time LIVE had offered full financing; usually they would line up half the money from foreign presales.

"Here's the thing, Richard," Lawrence told him two weeks later at their first budgeting meeting, still coming from that feeling of take-it-or-leave-it equality. "I can finish the movie on that money, but here's what we can do if you give us $1.5 million." Gladstein agreed. In fact, he eventually ponied up $1.6 million.

Lawrence, Richard and Harvey Keitel were having coffee to discuss casting. Harvey was still vacillating over whether to play Mr. White or Mr. Pink, or maybe even Mr. Blonde. Fortunately, Quentin had only described the characters by their actions, not by their physical appearance, so really anyone could fit into any role, another unusual aspect of the *Reservoir Dogs* script.

That initial casting meeting was a little uncomfortable because it was the first time Richard was meeting Harvey, who was in the middle of shooting *Bugsy*. "I walked in and he's been a sort of icon to me and I was really looking forward to meeting him," says Richard. "We went into his kitchen and he was sitting there in a sort of cut-off T-shirt and he had this weird makeup on and a guy either taking it off or putting it on him. In an attempt to make small talk, I commented on the makeup and asked what it was for."

"*See the movie*," replied Harvey tersely.

"So it didn't start off exactly as I wanted it," says Richard.

At least Harvey was dressed for the meeting. At a preliminary casting session, an actor came in to read for a role and was so nonplussed that Harvey was sitting on the couch cleaning his toes that he blew his audition.

Although they couldn't pay anyone until the deal came through, a casting agent agreed to get started with no money down. The casting agent had a bungalow on the Fox lot through her connections with *L.A. Law*, so Quentin, Lawrence, Harvey, Monte and Richard moved in there to start auditions. They would all read with the actors, twenty minutes apiece, doing several scenes and a few improvisations. "At the end of the day, we were exhausted and sweating like a gym," says Lawrence.

Toward the end of the process, Harvey told Quentin he owed it to himself to go to New York—Harvey's home turf—and take a look at the actors out there.

"Um, we don't have any money," said Lawrence. Indeed, no one had been paid yet.

"That's okay, I'll get you guys out there," said Harvey, one of many generous offers he made them.

The boys were flown to New York and put up at the Mayflower Hotel. It was during these subsequent auditions that they found Steve Buscemi. "He didn't even give the best audition, but something about him was so right for the part," says Lawrence.

Harvey took the boys out to the Russian Tea Room; it was like taking kids to the circus. Quentin tried caviar for the first time.

"Harvey, you've done so much for us," said Lawrence, feeling mellow and happy. "I want to make you co-producer."

"Lawrence," said Harvey, breaking into a rare smile, "it's about time."

"What do you think, Blonde or Pink?"

In his casting office on the Twentieth Century Fox lot, Quentin was offering the British actor Tim Roth a choice of roles in *Reservoir Dogs* the way you might ask someone to pick a couple of playing cards for a magic trick. "Blonde or Pink?"

"Orange," said Tim.

"*Orange?*" Quentin was incredulous.

All the characters in *Dogs* were given the names of colors so that they wouldn't identify each other in case something went wrong with the job they were pulling. The idea of the color names came from *The Taking of Pelham One Two Three*—subconsciously, says Quentin—but in any case Quentin had taken the conceit a step further, with the men arguing over who gets to be called what. "Mr. Brown, that's a little too close to Mr. Shit," says Mr. Brown.

The roles Quentin was offering Tim Roth were Mr. Blonde, the sadist who will cut off the ear of a policeman, or Mr. Pink, the role Quentin originally wanted to play. He later wrote in Mr. Brown for himself and appropriated a chunk of Mr. Pink's dialogue, mainly the opening bit about the true meaning of Madonna's "Like a Virgin" (*"Dick, dick, dick, dick, dick, dick, dick, dick, dick."*).

The role of Mr. Orange was a different kind of challenge. Mr. Orange spends most of the movie dying in a pool of his own blood from being gut-shot during the botched robbery.

"I liked the idea of being a fiction within a fiction," says Tim about the role that calls for an undercover cop to rehearse his lines like an actor in order to infiltrate the gang. "I'm a liar. I'm creating my own fiction within a fiction, a lie within a lie."

It was spring 1991, and Tim had one caveat. He had to know whether the part was truly his, because he was going up to the Sundance Institute lab in Utah to help another director streamline a movie, and Quentin was going to be up there too, learning how to work with cameras. "Because if you're gonna be there and I'm gonna be there and I haven't got the job, I'm gonna be rather pissed off," explained Tim.

Before Quentin could decide whether Tim could have Mr. Orange, he wanted the actor to read for him, not an unusual request. But Tim Roth doesn't read for parts. It's not arrogance, "I'm just very bad at it. The way I look at it is you can lose work by reading for it and you can also lose work by reading and not doing it well. I think it balances out. My choice is just not to do it."

Harvey Keitel was insistent, and perhaps to make Tim more comfortable, they tried to do it over lunch at Katz's Deli, down the road from the Fox lot. Tim continued to resist the reading until Harvey finally left and Tim and Quentin continued the discussion at a bar. "We started getting drunk and having fun," says Tim. "Once you start talking with Quentin it can be hours and hours. We also had a lot of passions in common. At about 11:30 I decided, oh, I'll read, I have enough beer in me. So we went to my place and I think we read every scene, every part, until about three in the morning. It was the best time I ever had reading."

*   *   *

Michael Madsen was looking for something different. He had just played Susan Sarandon's dim, barely committed boyfriend in *Thelma & Louise*, and he liked to change off after each project and go in an entirely different direction so the spirit of his last character wouldn't cling to him like stale cologne. "I was looking for a project to put together for myself and I was a little disgusted with a lot of the material I had been getting and most of the things I was being cast in," says Michael.

Steve Sachs, a mutual acquaintance who ran a messenger service, used his service to drop off a copy of *True Romance* to Michael. "I thought it was one of the best things I had ever read in my life, and I took it around to most of the producers and studios and people that I had known to try and get it made. Nobody wanted to have anything to do with it," says Michael. "Nobody wanted to touch it."

Soon thereafter, Steve Sachs used his messenger service to drop off another package for Michael, this time with the *Natural Born Killers* screenplay in it. "I read that one and I was, like, oh my god, I couldn't believe it was written by the same guy! Usually a writer like that has one thing and he never ever surpasses it."

Again Michael made inquiries and again no one would touch the stuff.

A few months later, Steve Sachs came by with more than a package; he had a message as well—Quentin Tarantino had written yet another script, and there was a part in it for Michael. But there was a catch: "He's gonna shoot it in his backyard with a fuckin' camcorder."

The scene in which the Dogs argue over the colors they're assigned turned out to be prescient, because although Quentin wanted Michael for Mr. Blonde, Michael preferred Mr. Pink. And he assumed Harvey Keitel, with whom he had made *Thelma & Louise*, was going to play Joe, the mastermind of the crime (Keitel ended up as Mr. White). "Finally they were like a week or two away from shooting and I still hadn't committed to the thing because I still had this idea in my head that I was

Hawthorne Christian School, the expensive South Bay private school Quentin hated. Contrary to the hillbilly-childhood myth, he had to wear a uniform. *(Photo by Stephen Schaefer)*

The most famous video store in America stands permanently shuttered after failing to survive the move to Hermosa Beach. *(Photo by Stephen Schaefer)*

A sign still hangs in the Video Archives store window, trumpeting past glories. *(Photo by Stephen Schaefer)*

Some of the Video Archives gang at Rowland Wafford's wedding. *Seated:* Stevo Polyi, Rowland. *Standing:* Jerry Martinez, Quentin, Russell Vossler. *(Photo courtesy Rowland Wafford)*

Quentin and Rand Vossler at the Christmas 1992 tamale party, the last time the two friends have horsed around since the *Natural Born Killers* debacle. *(Photo courtesy Rand Vossler and Jerry Martinez)*

The gang at the 1992 Sundance premiere of *Reservoir Dogs*. From left: Tom Merino, Rand Vossler, Stacy Sher, Quentin, Quentin's mother, Connie Zastoupil, Jerry Martinez. *(Photo courtesy Rand Vossler and Jerry Martinez)*

All the "Reservoir Dogs." *From left:* Michael Madsen, Quentin, Harvey Keitel, Chris Penn, Lawrence Tierney, Tim Roth, Steve Buscemi and Eddie Bunker. This photo was used to demonstrate similarities to a shot in Ringo Lam's *City on Fire,* but the shot never actually appeared in the movie; it was just a publicity still taken by a photographer on the set. *(Photo courtesy Miramax)*

Quentin Tarantino directs himself and Harvey Keitel in *Reservoir Dogs;* a director who knows what he wants and how to get it. *(Photo courtesy Miramax)*

Quentin fades to white from his usual all-black *Reservoir Dogs* look at the Disney party for the premiere of *Ed Wood*, September 1994. *(Photo courtesy Albert Ferreira/DMI)*

Three of the most individual directors around at the star-studded *Ed Wood* party, September 1994. *From left:* John Waters, Quentin, Tim Burton. *(Photo courtesy David Allocca/DMI)*

Hair Apparent: This publicity still from *Pulp Fiction* features Samuel L. Jackson *(left)* without his Jheri-Curls, plus Uma Thurman, John Travolta and Bruce Willis. Notice the similarity between the wig on Uma and the natural hair on old Quentin buddy and CineTel veep Catalaine Knell *(inset). (Photo by Firooz Zahedi, courtesy Miramax; inset photo courtesy Peter McAlevey)*

Quentin, John Travolta and Bruce Willis in high spirits before the opening night screening of *Pulp Fiction* at the New York Film Festival, September 1994. *(Photo courtesy Albert Ferreira/DMI)*

Uma Thurman, with "the best feet in the business," and her director, Quentin, on the opening night of the New York Film Festival. *(Photo courtesy Albert Ferreira/DMI)*

"Pushing each other power." Quentin Tarantino and producer Lawrence Bender, yin and yang, on the set of *Pulp Fiction. (Photo by Linda Chen; courtesy Miramax)*

Quentin and former best friend and writing partner Roger Avary, reunited to accept the Independent Spirit Award for the *Pulp Fiction* screenplay, March 1995, three days before winning an Oscar together on Quentin's birthday. *(Photo courtesy Alan Weissman)*

going to play Mr. Pink. He had the most interesting dialogue. I thought Mr. Blonde was a kinda boring character."

Michael marched over to Quentin's office on the Fox lot. Producers Lawrence Bender and Richard Gladstein were there, and Harvey for some reason was barefoot; the guy who had auditioned right before him had been too intimidated by Keitel's devotion to hygiene to make the grade. Michael had never met Quentin and he wasn't sure which one he was. When he figured it out, "I was surprised at how young he was. He seemed like a big kid, ya know? He seemed like a big happy kid who had suddenly been given a gift certificate to Toys 'R' Us."

He was kidlike, but he was firm. Michael was not going to get the role of Pink, he was getting Blonde. Steve Buscemi was getting Pink, and that was that.

Not since kindergarten had Quentin enjoyed school so much.

The Sundance film lab is a highly competitive, monthlong intensive workshop at the Sundance Institute in Park City, Utah. Every January, Sundance sponsors a film festival featuring the best and brightest of American independent films. And every June, seven to ten lucky young filmmakers get chosen out of about a thousand applicants to come to the film lab and work on their projects. Sometimes it's a screenwriter who needs to have actors perform in order to fine-tune the dialogue; sometimes it's a novice director who isn't sure how to handle a camera or work with actors.

In January, the chosen few work with screenwriters for four days, all expenses paid. In June, they attend the filmmakers lab under the stewardship of a handful of professionals who volunteer their time. The novice filmmakers get room, board, free advice and access to equipment. Some of them wind up shooting three or four scenes from their screenplays. "It's a place about process and not about product," says Michelle Satter, the director of the feature-film program who has been with the institute since its inception in 1981. "They shoot on video, edit on video, use very low production values. We're just trying to see if they can tell a story filmically. They get an incredible amount of input, because everyone who is a creative advisor has in-depth one-on-one meetings with the filmmakers. Our job is to help the filmmakers articulate what they want to say, not about telling them how to do it."

Quentin had been recommended to the program by Monte Hellman. "I met Quentin in my office in February 1991 and I loved him," says Satter. "He had enormous energy, a passion for filmmaking. I find his writing kind of stunning. We're always looking for new material and to discover new writers at Sundance but you rarely read something that sort of jumps off the page. He just has such a great ear for dialogue and great character. He could talk about any scene and how he visualized that scene." Satter considers for a moment. "He was nonstop talking, of course. But it was great."

Quentin was in good company that June. The seven other filmmakers included Alison Maclean, who made the female doppelganger movie *Crush*, which premiered at Cannes. Tom Noonan was there with *What Happened Was . . .*, the first-date movie that went on to win a prize a few years later at the Sundance festival. Quentin arrived on a Friday in June 1991 and left ten days later with the bathroom scene shot, the scene where Messrs. Pink and White discuss what could have gone wrong. Although Tim Roth was there simultaneously, he was working on someone else's movie. But Steve Buscemi came along, and he played Pink while Quentin played White.

"This was to give him an opportunity to find confidence on his feet," says Satter. "To allow him the time to explore for himself what his own issues were for this particular project."

Quentin did something that was a first for the Sundance lab—although he had come in with two scenes he wanted to shoot, he quickly discarded one of them and decided to write a whole new scene right then and there because the movie needed it. "It was my sense that he wanted to challenge himself in terms of getting on his feet," says Satter.

The scene Quentin added at Sundance never made it into the finished film, but Satter describes it as "quintessentially Quentin." It was between Joe and Mr. Pink, in which Joe says his girlfriend wants him to read Sylvia Plath's *The Bell Jar* and then discuss it with him. The subtext of the scene is the relationship between Joe and Pink, and how they relate to the women in their lives.

Later, Quentin actually shot that scene for the real movie; all references to Joe's girlfriend and *The Bell Jar* were cut out. "We couldn't get the rights," says Quentin. "The Sylvia Plath estate was just having a thing where they weren't letting any-one use *The Bell Jar*. But also, Lawrence Tierney didn't do it that well, to tell you the truth. That's not really what he does."

The institute has a large cafeteria building with skylights, used for filmmaker brunches and the like. When students are filming their scenes, the diners have to finish their meals and move out while the building is broken up into thirds. Quentin shot his new scene in a third of the cafeteria, and used the lobby of the institute's screening room to shoot the bathroom scene.

Every week there are different advisors on hand. Quentin had access to the help and opinions of directors Ulu Grosbard, Jon Amiel, Terry Gilliam, and Volker Schlöndorff. He also worked with actress Carlin Glynn, who helped him in the area of working with actors. For the *Bell Jar* scene, he used Buscemi to play Mr. Pink and a local Utah-based actor named Dave Jensen to play Joe.

"He just seemed like the happiest person I'd ever met," says Carlin Glynn, a creative advisor with the lab since its inception. "He was absolutely gracious, he thought it was the greatest opportunity to be there, and he was receptive to any questions. I found him easy as pie to work with. He had very definite ideas about what he wanted to do, but he listened to what everybody had to say."

The first night at dinner, Quentin was handed a specific schedule. It mapped out rehearsal and filming times, and meet-ings with creative advisors who would watch the progress of his work in the screening room and discuss it with the other advisors. Every day at lunch, another advisor would sit down with him.

Some things Quentin wanted to try out at Sundance before unleashing them on a real-life movie set were avant-garde, experimental things to do with the camera. "He had ideas that weren't conventional," says Glynn diplomatically. Some of these ideas worked; most were quickly discarded. One that worked Quentin kept in the final movie—shooting the bathroom scene at first from way down the hall so that it seems you're spying on the robbers as they have an intimate talk.

The experience at Sundance was undoubtedly of great value to Quentin as a filmmaker, yet he is circumspect in doling out credit. "The two most important things I learned there were very specific," he says. "One was from Ulu Grosbard, whose brother is totally involved in the diamond business, and he told me everything about how the cases of diamonds are shipped and all that stuff. You know, I had a reasonable facsimile for everything, but he just gave me a bunch of information that I didn't have which I put into that scene between Lawrence Tierney and Harvey Keitel, when they talk about shipping in 'boxes.'"

The other thing he learned seems self-evident; it has to do with delegating authority. "I asked Terry Gilliam about his films, they all have a very specific vision. And I wanted to know, how do you get the vision from film to film? And he told me you don't just do it, you hire people to do it. You hire a production designer and tell them what you want, and they come and give it to you. You get a costume designer and you tell her what you want and she comes back with something and you bring it down from there. You just hire really talented people and tell them what you want, and they get it for you. So all of a sudden it wasn't so hard, because I can totally articulate what I want. I know what I want and I can definitely describe it. I just don't know how to make the costumes or how to build the sets. But I don't have to. It's not my job, all right? So all of a sudden, this big mystical thing seemed doable. Easy. I mean, not easy, but it seemed I had a handle on it."

Unlike most of the people who attend the lab, Quentin's finance deal was shaping up simultaneously back home. He was out of the lab in June and down in the trenches by the summer. In the end credits of *Reservoir Dogs* he thanked a few of his advisors—Satter, Grosbard and Gilliam. After the film debuted in January 1992 at the Sundance festival, Quentin Tarantino became the most famous person ever to come out of the filmmaking lab. "He's just full of life and energy and opinions and ideas and stuff and there's a kind of innocence, a sheer wonder," says Satter. "You could see it in the first draft of the script—his talent is undeniable."

Cathryn Jaymes had been Quentin's manager since around 1983 or 1984, when Quentin's former acting-class scene partner Craig Hamann brought him around to meet her. Cathryn saw in Quentin "a combination of Elvis and Charles Manson, with an unusual and amazing energy," and sent him out on dozens of casting calls over the years. "I fought for him like mad," she says, although the only gig he actually landed was a cameo as a singing Elvis impersonator on a *Golden Girls* episode that aired November 19, 1988. This event was immortalized in *True Romance* when Michael Rapaport gets a cameo from his agent "Cathryn" on a *T. J. Hooker* episode.

Now that Quentin was on the cusp of stardom, he needed more than just a manager to line things up for him. What he needed was an agent to look after his business interests and cut deals for him. Someone with clout.

"I took him to the William Morris Agency," says Cathryn, "but part of my reason was to protect him from himself." Against Cathryn's advice, Quentin had made an oral agreement with another agency—"I'd have bound him with duct tape if I knew he was doing that"—and there was much scrambling to undo the mess.

As lucky as Quentin was to sign with the William Morris Agency, they were just as lucky to get Quentin. It was right at a time when the once glorious agency was trying to shake off a funk. The very fact that it was considered so venerable and had represented so many stars of the Golden Age gave the company an old-fogey taint. They were seeking fresh blood, and they were finding it in the new crop of indie filmmakers. The minute the *Reservoir Dogs* script hit the street for casting purposes, actor Matt Dillon got it over to his agent at William Morris, and agent Lee Stollman brought it to the attention of his department head, Mike Simpson.

"Well, it better be great if you want me to read it tonight," Simpson said testily.

That night, Simpson took the script home and put it off until after midnight when he was soaking in the tub. "Sure enough, I couldn't put it down. I read it and read it again the same night," getting bath bubbles all over it. "It's hard to read bad scripts, but a good script you can read really fast. I couldn't get it out of my head. I was obsessed with the idea that I had to meet Quentin and be involved with him."

Mike met Quentin in a William Morris conference room one night at around 8:30 P.M. What Mike brought to the table was his agency's interest in hip, young independent filmmakers, "and the raw enthusiasm we had to represent him and be involved with him."

No current William Morris clients made it into *Reservoir Dogs*, but ten days after that meeting, Quentin himself was a client, and the agency began to crank up the star-making machinery.

Michael Madsen couldn't believe the contrast between Quentin Tarantino as a person and the kind of material he was writing. "There's a very strange duality there," says Michael. "If you met him and had never read anything that he wrote you'd be very hard-pressed to put him together with that material. Just the insight into the darkness and the insight into those characters. After you spend a lot of time with him and work with him, all these things kinda come out and it all comes together, but in the beginning, it's very disconcerting. I think there's a tension that's created when you have a duality in your personality. And I think that tension is the source of creativity."

Although he loves talking about himself, Quentin is not very inward-looking, as if careful not to disturb the demons. "I don't necessarily see a duality," he says, although he seems to equate "duality" with "irony." "Because to me, I'm all over my stuff. You know, I'm soaked through with it. It's all really personal and I'm positive after I've finished a screenplay and someone reads it I won't be able to show my face because I've just told too many of my secrets. You know, is Elmore Leonard living a duality because he writes about killing people in Detroit and everything? Is *he* killing people in Detroit? I don't know, but I don't think so, all right? And before he was writing crime films he was writing westerns. Is there a duality about a guy who was born in Michigan, you know, and writes westerns?"

As to why some of his material is dark and he seems so happy: "I live a pretty good life now, so I'm in that kind of situation that allows me to be like that. I'm not living in oppressive poverty in a horrible neighborhood where you gotta look everybody three times over. Now I look at everybody one time over. But I've *been* in that kind of situation, and I've *lived* in those kind of places, and although my spirit didn't get crushed it does something to you, all right."

Eventually he touches on something that must be true for him since it is so clearly defined in his movies. "I guess my biggest demons have to do with boyhood masculine pride. Like, if I'm pushed into a situation I will totally respond with violence or something like that. Which I wish I didn't. I used to fight at the drop of a hat through my early twenties. And I stopped doing that, basically because I got older and I realized it's not what mature people, thinking people, do. But the thing is, now I can get into an argument with somebody and I can be really mad, I mean, really really fucking pissed off, and it'll never occur to me to lay hands on them or to threaten them. Because I just don't have the right to do that. Unless they have done something horrific, really crossed the line, you know. If they do cross that line, and either lay hands on me or something like that, then it's just like . . ." Quentin forces air out of his mouth like a hurricane. "You know, then I'm just like eighteen years old all over again. Although I was lucky, I won most of my fights."

There were two weeks of rehearsals for *Reservoir Dogs*, then five weeks of filming. Not to mention the preparation time required by Tim Roth, who spent hours with Quentin watching *Speed Racer* and *Gigantor* cartoons just to get in the mood.

The first day of actual filming, they did the scene in Joe's office when Vic Vega, the brother of *Pulp Fiction*'s Vincent Vega and known as Mr. Blonde for the purposes of the jewelry heist, gets out of prison. He and Joe's son, Eddie, are supposed to have a mock fight to show that they go way back. "Chris and I had such a great working relationship," says Michael Madsen of Chris Penn, who played Nice Guy Eddie. "We just really fought. We just really beat the shit out of each other and I remember Quentin just laughing. But what happened was we wrecked the office and kept going out of frame. So Quentin realized he had to choreograph it so we could stay in the parameters of where the camera was pointed. What you see in the movie is about the third or fourth fight of the day."

Joe was played by Lawrence Tierney, who became a late-1940s B-movie star as John Dillinger, and was wildly unpredictable. "Quentin was very, very excited about Tierney," says Michael. "I didn't know who the fuck he was. I had never even heard of him. But Quentin is like a walking human bibliography of old movies and characters. So I became educated about Lawrence Tierney. He's an incredibly complex man. He'd just tell stories and jokes endlessly and constantly all day on the set. One minute you were in love with the guy and at the same time he would drive everybody just crazy."

Tierney came up with an all-purpose response to the oft-asked question about the origins of the title *Reservoir Dogs*. Quentin always refuses to answer that question, "it's more of a mood title than anything else," he explained a month before the movie opened theatrically. "It just sums up the movie, don't ask me why. It did come from somewhere but it's not supposed to be a literal thing. The main reason I don't like to go on record for it is I just really believe that movies are an art form, and 20 percent of that art form is supplied by what the audience brings to the movie. I am constantly astounded by their creativity and their ingenuity. As far as I'm concerned, whatever they come up with is 100 percent right. I want to keep that coming. Otherwise, the minute I say whatever I'm gonna say it becomes official and then all that stops."

During filming, a journalist from Germany came to the set to interview Lawrence Tierney. *"So vat ees zee meaning of Reservoir Dog, vat ees a Reservoir Dog?"* asked the writer.

"Well, as you know," replied Tierney, "Reservoir Dogs is a very famous expression in America . . . for . . . dogs . . . who . . . hang around the reservoir."

Actually, several people from Quentin's life—including his mother, Lawrence Bender and co-workers from Video Archives—concur that *Reservoir Dogs* is what Quentin, the world's worst speller and pronouncer of French titles, called the Louis Malle movie *Au Revoir les Enfants.* Customers would ask to rent it and Quentin tried and tried to say it right, until finally he said, "Fuck it, I'm just calling it the Reservoir Dogs movie from now on."

CHAPTER 10

Reservoir Dogs: The Movie

I don't really give a good fuck what you know or don't know, but I'm gonna torture you anyway, regardless. Not to get information. It's so amusing to me to torture a cop. All you can do is pray for a quick death, which you ain't gonna get.
—*Mr. Blonde in* Reservoir Dogs, *1992*

Michael Madsen was having trouble with the torture scene, the one in which he slices off the cop's ear, then douses him with gasoline and threatens to ignite him. For one thing, he thought the scene was too tame; it didn't jump off the page. "In the script, it says Mr. Blonde maniacally dances around the cop and then decides to cut off his ear. But you know, as far as talking into the ear or the way that I danced or the way that I interpreted it, those kinda things are not in the script. Those are things you have to come up with on your own. That's your job. But I never really figured it out until we were actually doing it. If I'm not on the set with the other actor and doing it, it's very hard for me to arrive at what it is I'm going to do. I can't do it in a room sitting in a chair with my lines in my fucking hand. It's impossible. And we were up on our feet in the rehearsals for this and I didn't really connect with it yet."

Kirk Baltz, the actor who was playing the cop, was also having trouble with the scene. He ad-libbed a few lines to try to get things moving. "Oh, please don't burn me up, I've got little children at home."

Quentin loved that touch, but Michael had a problem with it. "I'm not going to set this fucking guy on fire if he starts talking about kids," said Michael. "It's one thing to shoot people, but you bring women and children into it, it's a little different. You're really going to have to ask yourself where you want to go with Mr. Blonde. You're really crossing over into another area if he's going to go as far as to be somebody who is gonna cook somebody who starts talking about children. That's a little rough. That's a little too far for me."

Ultimately, Michael Madsen would reach deep inside and find the sociopath within, and the man who would help him do it was Kirk Baltz, the actor playing the cop. Michael was asleep on the floor in the production office waiting to shoot the ear scene when Kirk came in and gently shook him awake with a request.

"Uh, Michael, would you mind putting me in the trunk of your car? I'd like to see what it feels like to be your hostage."

There was no money in the budget to give Mr. Blonde a car, so Michael had brought along his own '65 yellow Cadillac. Later he would flatbed it up to his sister in Wisconsin because he felt he shouldn't sell the "Dogs Car," and that's where it still sits, in her garage. It had a nice, roomy trunk, perfect for taking a hostage. Michael popped the hood and Kirk climbed in. Quentin rushed over, but as soon as he heard what his Method actors were up to, he started laughing his Woody Woodpecker laugh, *hehhehheh*. The plan was for Michael to drive around the block with Kirk in the trunk.

But once Michael was in the driver's seat, he felt a surge of power. "I suddenly realized that not only would it be advantageous for Kirk to know what it would be like to be in the trunk, it was also good for me because now *I* could get a feeling of what it was like to have somebody in my trunk. So I just took a drive, you know, I just started driving all around. I drove around for about half an hour. I went up and down these bumpy alleys and I had the radio on and I was fully into my character. I think that's when it all came together for me. It was a reality that paralleled the character's reality."

One of Michael's favorite films as a boy was *White Heat*, with James Cagney. "There was a scene where he puts a guy in the trunk and he asks the guy if he needs some air. He shoots a couple of holes through the top. At the same time he's eating a piece of chicken. It gave a little normalcy to what he was doing, but it was a bizarre contradiction. It kinda stuck in my mind my whole life."

Which is probably why he nonchalantly stopped off at a Taco Bell to pick up a Coke while his scene partner was still locked in the trunk. When he got back to the set and pulled into the parking lot, "I had been gone for quite some time and Quentin as I recall was a little concerned."

Word had gotten around the set that Michael had driven off with another cast member, so everyone was standing in the parking lot waiting to see what would happen. Michael released his hostage and "poor Kirk was in really bad shape. He was all sweaty and I had all this junk in the trunk that had been banging around back there, banging him in the head and all. He just didn't look too good."

They proceeded to rehearse the scene while Michael continued to sip his soda. Quentin realized what a great thing that was for the character—Mr. Blonde was so cool he actually stopped off on the way to the rendezvous to buy a drink!—that they left the bit in, although they substituted an anonymous cup in case Taco Bell didn't appreciate the notoriety.

Shooting the ear scene took about five hours. They tried it three different ways, one where Michael played the whole thing right into the lens of the camera, another where you see him slice the ear off, and the one Quentin wound up using, a wide shot moving in and then switching between the cop and Mr. Blonde. When the ear-slicing begins, the camera discreetly moves up and to the left while the soundtrack continues. "That's when I finally sit on his lap," says Michael. "I hadn't leaped into his lap on the other two tries, it just kinda happened by the time we were doing the third one. I felt like a wild animal pouncing on him."

That evening, driving home, a very strange thing happened to Michael Madsen. He was getting onto the freeway when he absently turned on the radio and of all things, it was playing *Stuck in the Middle with You*, the Stealers Wheel song that had been blaring all day for the ear-slicing scene. "For it to come on the radio at that time at the end of that particular day, I thought someone was fuckin' with me. I thought it was a joke, maybe somebody had rigged up a tape on my dashboard."

He pulled off the freeway and stuck his head under the dashboard to look, then just sat there, dazed. "It was a very bizarre moment."

Quentin, the full-service director, often gives his actors career advice. "I was approached to play Mickey Knox in the Oliver Stone movie," says Michael. "But Quentin and I came to the conclusion that without him directing it, it was not going to be what it should have been. He advised me to stay away from it and not do it. Of course he had had a falling out with Oliver over the rewriting and restructuring of the script. But in the long run, looking back at it, I think it's a damn good thing I didn't do it. I might have ended up being the Norman Bates of the nineties. Woody Harrelson can get away with it. He's always been playing this hokie-dokie kinda guy. And he can go play Mickey Knox and everybody goes, oh wow. If I had done it, first of all my interpretation would have been completely and totally different. If Quentin had directed then he would have been able to slip the humor in there, and we would have made something very bizarre and really memorable. Oliver is a great filmmaker but it wasn't the *Natural Born Killers* it would have been if Quentin and I had done it together."

In retrospect, Michael Madsen ranks *Reservoir Dogs* among the two movies he had the most fun making—the other was *The Getaway*. He had never wanted to be Mr. Blonde in the first place. "And you know what? For the rest of my life, I'm going to be known as Mr. Blonde, the guy from the garage scene in *Reservoir Dogs*."

Tim Roth spends most of his time in *Reservoir Dogs* as Mr. Orange mired in a pool of his own blood, doubled over in pain. Because of that, he's had to field many of the questions the public raises about violence in movies.

"Violence in most movies doesn't affect you," he says. "They're comic books. This wasn't. This one put you on a journey and it was relentless. It made you, as an audience member, it made you guilty too. You were tapping your foot to the music and getting involved with the characters and laughing at what they're saying and then they hit you with something."

Like the rest of the cast, he doesn't see it as a particularly violent movie, but one about loyalty and betrayal. "Who's a tough guy?" says Mr. White (Keitel) as he tries to comfort Mr. Orange and take his mind off the fear of dying. "I'm a tough guy," Mr. Orange sputters weakly.

In flashbacks, we see Mr. Orange, an undercover cop, prepare for his "role" as a gang member by rehearsing a four-page anecdote he's been handed that will give him some credence. He rehearses it so well that we actually see it played out in a white-tiled bathroom as if it had really happened.

"We set it up for a voice-over, and it was going to be a 360-degree track shot going around and around me," says Tim. "We were racing to get it done and we had already sent the sound crew home and I was still working on the narration. It was late, but we all realized what we were doing was better than the narration, so somebody was sent off to hunt down the sound crew.

And we got them back and we shot it the new way, with me talking to the cops as well as talking to the guys at the bar. Those things happen and Quentin has always got the balls to make those last-minute decisions."

The only fight Tim had with Quentin was over the dailies, when actors traditionally watch a replay of work they shot that day. Quentin made a hard and fast rule that no actors were allowed at the dailies. Tim, who hates auditioning, also hates watching himself; even so, he fought Quentin if only on behalf of Steve Buscemi, who wanted the right to tailor his performance day by day.

"I will defend anybody's rights to go to dailies, because some actors really benefit by it," says Tim. "I understand Quentin's point that some actors get very self-conscious. They start doing bits that they think are good that they've seen in dailies just over and over again, and it can be distracting. But it doesn't always have to be that way and if you see that happening to an actor, you can take it up with them. So we had this big kinda battle about it and I won."

Reservoir Dogs opens with a 360-degree pan around eight men in a diner arguing over the true meaning of the Madonna song "Like a Virgin" and whether it is incumbent upon customers to tip when there haven't been enough refills on coffee (the Coffee Thing). Originally, there was a waitress in the scene—actress Nina Siemaszko, whom Quentin later dated. Her entire part remained on the cutting-room floor. ("Her scene just didn't work," says Quentin.)

After the galvanizing opening credits—with the eight men striding purposefully in their black jackets, skinny ties and sunglasses—the audience is treated to the direct aftermath of a jewelry heist gone bad. Mr. Orange is bleeding to death and screaming in the back seat of a car. Mr. White is trying to console him while driving to the appointed rendezvous, an empty warehouse. Over the course of the movie, the surviving robbers show up at the warehouse and try to piece together what went wrong, who is left and who is to blame. Through the use of flashbacks, the audience gradually learns how the men got together for the job, how they masked their identities from each other with names of colors, and how one of them is the under-cover cop who set them up.

Near the end is a Mexican standoff of epic proportions, which became the subject of a thriving ongoing dialogue on the Internet concerning just who shot whom and whether there is still one bullet or body unaccounted for.

"What I did was I applied a novelistic structure to the screenplay, which I've always thought if you use it in cinematic terms it would be extremely cinematic but when they transfer novels to movies it's one of the first things that goes," says Quentin of the architecture of *Reservoir Dogs*, in which compre-hension of the central action is supplemented by flashbacks to different characters, giving the movie a *Rashomon* texture. "When you read a book the writer thinks nothing of starting in the middle of the story. In chapter four or something it goes into a character's childhood for a while. Is that a flashback? No, it's just the way the narrator is telling the story. I like using that structure and applying it to film. Not just for the sake of doing it. If the film would have been more dramatically engaging by telling it in a beginning-middle-end situation, I would have done that. I actually think the kinda 'answers first, questions later' structure has made it better, made it more involving."

Martin Scorsese maintains a film library in midtown Manhattan that employs a full-time archivist who is ready at a moment's notice to cue up a film so Il Maestro can see how another director handled a certain shot. Quentin Tarantino has the low-rent version of the same thing—he can pop in a video-cassette any time he likes. Or, he can simply browse through his computerlike memory of movies that impressed him.

He doesn't deny that there are elements of other movies in *Reservoir Dogs*. Nor does he feel he has stolen or remade them.

"I didn't really lift anything from *The Killing*, like people brought up the fact that the story goes back and forth like *The*

Killing does. A big difference is that *The Killing* uses a newsreel structure as a framework, whereas I tried to adopt a novelistic structure. While I was making the movie, I was kinda like sorta saying, 'This is gonna be my *The Killing*. I didn't mean I'm gonna remake it or anything. What I meant was, if I were going to do a World War II movie than it would be my *Where Eagles Dare*. Or a western, it would be my *One-Eyed Jacks*. So it's just the way I was thinking, that this would be my *The Killing*."

It was not always Quentin's intention to leave out the jewelry heist altogether. At the earliest stages of the screenplay, he thought of putting in tiny flashbacks. "Maybe like a little flash, *pooft!*" he says, waving one arm. *"Phisst! Pooft!"* He waves each arm in succession. "So you are not really seeing anything but you just get a sense of the mayhem, but not like an actual scene or anything you can even get a handle on. I think in the first half of the movie it generates a great deal of suspense because you keep waiting to see what everyone is talking about. By the second half of the movie, when you realize you're probably not going to see it, it doesn't matter anymore anyway because the movie has become about something else."

Later, Quentin and Steve Buscemi would joke about how they "got into character"—as Jules and Vincent might say in *Pulp Fiction*—to create the feeling of having committed a robbery. "We knocked over a fruit stand," says Buscemi. "I put a quarter in a newspaper machine and, like, took out a bunch of 'em as opposed to one, ya know?" says Quentin. "We got that living-on-the-edge feel."

But they did stage the robbery during the two weeks of rehearsal just so the actors would have the "sense memory" of having botched it.

Although Quentin wrote in the part of Mr. Brown for himself after he gave up his coveted role of Mr. Pink to Buscemi, he's adamant that it's an ensemble where all Dogs are created equal. "I didn't want it to be a movie where it's, like, okay, here's the people we care about and here's the people we don't care about so much anymore, so don't pay so much attention to them anymore. In that opening scene these guys don't know they're peripheral characters. As far as they're concerned they're the star of the movie. They're all talking and doing things and I wanted it to be a vital thing that they were people. They're wondering where Mr. Blue is all the time. *Where is Mr. Blue?* Was he killed? Did he get away? Does he possibly have the diamonds, or do the cops have him, sweating him down at the stationhouse? I wanted us always to be thinking, making us big enough so that we could be walking through the door at any moment."

By the way, the answer to the Mexican standoff mystery is this: Joe shoots Mr. Orange; Mr. White shoots Joe; Nice Guy Eddie shoots Mr. White, who has meanwhile shifted slightly so he can shoot Nice Guy Eddie. They all go down, but Mr. White is still breathing long enough to discover the identity of the traitor. Mr. Pink gets away with the diamonds just as the police show up, so he is probably arrested.

The last time Lawrence Bender had produced a movie, he paid people from a wad of bills in his pocket and wrote line-item expenditures on a sheet tacked to the wall of the set. This time he had help from his executive producers, longtime professionals Monte Hellman and Richard Gladstein. And by this time, Lawrence had smartened up.

"We looked at how we were going to shoot the movie," says Lawrence. "When you're with a company, the last thing you want to do is tell them the first shot is weird, quirky stuff with no 'coverage.' But if you start the movie with the more conservative shots, they start to become enrolled in your process. They're not as worried about you. Quentin wanted to start out conservative; he was scared of getting fired off his own movie."

During the five-week shoot, Quentin and Lawrence started out playing safe. They'd go for the tough stuff later.

Richard Gladstein from LIVE Entertainment, which was funding the movie, hung around the set and went to dailies each night religiously. Lawrence even got some tips on producing from Harvey Keitel, who continued to act as a sort of godfather for the whole production. "It's not that anyone deferred to me," says Harvey modestly. "I just think I had something to contribute in terms of the process. I'm not sure I'd call that deferring to me, because that implies they would be giving something up of their own. No, I think there was an openness on Quentin's part to work with me and take what I had to offer in terms of my experience."

On the day Quentin was to shoot the ear-slicing scene, which was hard for the actors to work out emotionally and hard for cameraman Andrzej Sekula to work out logistically, Harvey Keitel took Lawrence aside for a little chat. "Now, Lawrence," he said, "this is a very important scene, and Quentin is under a lot of pressure here. So maybe you should give him some extra time in this scene." From that, Lawrence learned to fine-tune his expectations according to the needs of his director.

"To handle eight actors like this for anyone would be a task," says Harvey. "For a first-time director, an enormous one. Quentin as a first-time director had enormous energy and enthusiasm, intensity and intelligence, vulnerability, and a great willingness to learn, to want to be very open to the input the actors had in terms of their process to arrive at the characters he wrote."

Lawrence and Quentin continued to work on their relationship as producer and director, oftentimes switching roles. "Quentin would say, no, I don't want to do this shot, it's too much money and takes too much time," recalls Lawrence. "It was the opposite dynamic from the ordinary stereotype. We worked really well together. What's great is this idea of 'pushing power'—we push each other a lot of power, we protect each other. If you push somebody power, it comes back to you. We support each other, we know each other's intricacies. We trust each other. There's chemistry."

Reservoir Dogs wrapped production in the fall of 1991, and had a finished print still wet from the lab just in time for its first public screening in January at the Sundance Film Festival.

At Sundance, filmmakers have no choice as to where their films are screened. The first showing of *Reservoir Dogs* took place at the Holiday Village Cinema, "a theater I don't particularly like," says Richard Gladstein.

The projection was a disaster. Quentin had shot in widescreen, carefully composing each scene so that there was relevant cinematic information on both sides of the frame. To show a film that is shot in widescreen, the projectionist requires an anamorphic lens to "unsqueeze" the images, plus the appropriate aperture plate to make sure the image fits the dimensions of the screen, plus the proper masking on the screen so that the picture doesn't spill out onto the sides of the curtain. That night, the projectionist didn't have the right aperture plate, and a third of the movie bled right and left into the curtain. "I remember there were scenes when Michael Madsen had lines of dialogue and you couldn't even see him," says Gladstein. "So I was having a fit."

"Half the characters were out of focus and off the screen," says filmmaker Alexandre Rockwell, who was in the audience that night; he too had a film in competition. "Quentin was freaking out in the background, he was screaming and yelling and walking down the aisle yelling: 'Stop! I can't take this! This is the first public screening of the only film I've ever made! You don't understand, this is horrible!' He was really agonizing over it, angst-ridden and freaking out."

The majority of the audience enjoyed the film. The few walkouts were caused by the ear-slicing scene. "Even *I* wanted to leave at that point," says Rockwell. "But everyone was really excited about the film. You already got this feeling that Hollywood had found a new voice. Everyone was talking about *Reservoir Dogs* and how it was really violent, but that it really delivered the goods."

Gladstein was furious and went to festival director Geoffrey Gillmore. "Aside from the fact that we are just not presenting the film as the director intends it to be seen, this is the first time we are showing it, and we are not showing it properly," he told him. "We also have a lot of distributors here and I can't show the film like this, I just can't."

Gillmore was receptive to Gladstein's plea and made sure

the projection booth was properly equipped for subsequent screenings.

Although the faulty projection may have hurt the movie in the short run—it didn't win any prizes from the jury—it certainly didn't hurt it in the long run. There was a buzz even before that first screening. And where there is a buzz, there is Miramax.

Miramax is the 800-pound gorilla of the independent film world. Founded by the brothers Weinstein—behind-the-scenes Bob and outspoken Harvey—and named after their parents, Miriam and Max of Queens, New York, Miramax as an entity has the uncanny ability to ferret out and exploit new talent. They welcome controversy, like the ratings squabbles over Pedro Almodovar's *Tie Me Up! Tie Me Down!* or the "big secret" of *The Crying Game*. They made an art-house hit out of the Mexican *Like Water for Chocolate* and fine-tuned *The Piano* to a three-Oscar win. When Disney acquired the company in May 1993, it gave the indie some maxi advantages in terms of money and distribution machinery; now Miramax could actually fund movies at their inception and be involved in their development as long as they stayed on the short side of $10 million.

In the audience that first night were Trea Hoving and Mark Tusk, two youthful go-getters from the Miramax acquisitions department who can smell a movie's potential like skilled parfumiers.

The scouts were enthralled and couldn't wait until Bob and Harvey returned from Los Angeles to their Tribeca office in Lower Manhattan; instead they shipped a print to them the next day.

Although some say Harvey needed some initial prompting, Harvey has a way of casting a golden glow over his memories. "Bob and I saw it with four friends, and we just kept cracking up in the theater, six people making the laughter of six hundred," says Harvey. "It was a blow-away movie, I couldn't believe it. It was a movie that said hooray! Here is filmmaking the way we grew up with it as kids watching Bogart movies, yet it was an original voice, contemporary, not afraid to be politically incorrect, because it echoed the truth. It was like a wakeup call."

Miramax held a special staff screening, "and we were all, like, if you don't buy this movie we're all gonna quit!" remembers publicity veep Cynthia Swartz. "It was the first time in years that everyone on the staff really wanted a particular movie."

Richard Gladstein and Ronna Wallace of LIVE opened discussions with various theatrical distributors to buy rights to the movie. They negotiated with Bob Weinstein for Miramax to distribute *Reservoir Dogs* in North America. LIVE's sister company, Carolco Pictures, would take care of foreign rights, where they sold the movie territory by territory.

While securing a deal with France, they screened the movie for a scout from Cannes, the most prestigious of all the international film festivals. *Reservoir Dogs* was accepted as an official selection playing out of competition—which meant it was not eligible for the Palme d'Or, yet would have a high-profile, journalist-packed screening in the Palais alongside all the major films.

When Miramax bought *Reservoir Dogs*, they were investing not only in a hot little movie, but in Quentin himself. Quentin was all the Weinstein brothers could have hoped for in a new talent—he was smart, committed, energetic, able to charm the press. He had an infallible memory for the names and tastes of film critics, and he genuinely enjoyed talking with them. "I was impressed with his incredible enthusiasm for movies and moviemaking. I never saw anything like that, such a buoyant spirit," says Harvey. "Not only did he like his own movie in a purely nonegotistical sense, but he was a cheerleader for everyone else's movies."

If Harvey had any doubts at the beginning, they had to do with the ear scene. "I knew we were down to one thing," says Harvey. "If you cut out the ear scene, you have a popular hit. If you leave it in, you lose the women. Thirty seconds would change the movie in the American marketplace."

Business instincts aside, Harvey based this calculation on the behavior of Eve, his wife. Eve doesn't like violence, and has been known to turn down $500 bribes rather than see a Steven Seagal movie. "I bring Eve and my sister-in-law Maude to a screening," says Harvey. "When the ear scene comes on, they're out of their seats like jumping jacks. I said forget it, there go the women."

Harvey does not go gentle into that good night, or into any business deal. Once Quentin was in the Miramax stable, Harvey told him, in a way that has intimidated many a more seasoned director, to slice the ear scene. "You cut that out, we've got a home run," said Harvey. But Quentin, who as a toddler wouldn't abandon the word *bullshit* just because his mother washed his mouth out with soap, had spent his life going single-mindedly after what he wants. Quentin and Harvey, both equally bull-headed, squared off. "And that was the last conversation we had about cutting the movie," says Harvey, not easily defeated.

There are no overnight successes. Quentin toiled in the video store for years, went out on endless casting calls, wrote screenplay after screenplay in hopes of making his directorial debut. Even once he had made *Reservoir Dogs* and was hailed by the critics, there was still no overnight success. By the time Quentin was invited to Cannes, he was at the center of a huge piece of well-oiled machinery, which became as much a contributing factor to Quentin's "overnight success" as his talent and force of personality.

There was Lawrence Bender, his producer, with whom he formed the production company A Band Apart—named after his favorite Jean-Luc Godard movie, *Bande à Part*—with their office overhead covered by Miramax and the security of a two-year, first-look deal. Together and separately, Quentin and Lawrence already had plenty of projects in the pipeline.

There were the Weinstein brothers, famous for paying premium prices for premium talent and then protecting their investment like a lioness protecting her cubs. The Weinsteins had big plans for Quentin.

Then there was Bumble Ward, Quentin's personal publicist, a cheerful but deceptively sturdy British import who would later accompany Quentin on his publicity tours through foreign countries and whose job it was to make Quentin visible while protecting his flanks. "He's a special challenge," says Bumble of her star client. "You have to completely adore him, otherwise you can't be doing the work. He drives me completely bananas, I'm just about ready to kill him, then he'll call me up and be lovely and sweet and wonderful. He has that effect on people. He's so brilliant sometimes that it's worth that challenge. He has his own time frame. He chooses to deal with things when he wants to deal with them. He doesn't have a bourgeois point of view, he is never ever rude to anyone, but he has his own time frame. Another thing, once he makes his mind up, that's the way he's going to go on it. He doesn't second-guess himself ever, *ever*. He has his own voice. He doesn't let people sway him from it. He has strong opinions and he stands by them. That's a wonderful attribute, very rare."

And there were the resources of the powerful William Morris Agency, for whom Quentin would become the jewel in the crown. "It's unusual for someone so young to have very concrete short-term, mid-term and long-term goals," says agent Mike Simpson. "Quentin has a tenacity to stick with those plans while retaining flexibility to deal with situations as they come along. He has a game plan and he is executing it, whereas most people just go around and let events drive them. It makes it terrific to work with him, because on a personal level, I have a similar orientation. I've tried to be very strategic about career planning for important clients. I have a lot of respect for somebody else who has that same philosophy, and not only sticks to it but gets results from it. You start from ground zero, a great foundation, then layer on top. If there's no plan to begin with, you wind up spending time and energy assimilating the situation without being able to exploit it."

Like a military campaign, all these people in the Quentin camp confer and move forward on different fronts at different rates. "We talk on the phone every other day, we work as a real team," says Simpson. "There's a constant flow of information among all of us. If one person didn't get a piece of information, someone will call and make sure he does."

Actor Tim Roth says it was very clever of Quentin's people

to market the movie not through its cast, but through its director. "They called it 'a film by Quentin Tarantino,' which is unheard of for a new director," says Tim. "You can put that on your film if you want, but nobody would really care who you are, they just want to know who's in it. What they did was put a machine around the movie very early on because they knew they had something different. People get very bored because they're spoon-fed, as far as films are concerned."

This well-oiled machine took *Reservoir Dogs* to Cannes, where Quentin was promoted as a major new American talent alongside people like actor Tim Robbins, who was making his directorial debut the same year with the political satire *Bob Roberts*. Unfortunately, *Reservoir Dogs* was screened the same day as Abel Ferrara's gritty *Bad Lieutenant*, and because the journalists first encountered those movies as a double-bill they also linked them in their reports from the festival.

"The American journalists in Cannes weren't talking about the humor of the movie at all," Quentin notes. "They were just hammering in on the violence, the violence, the violence. But the critics"—a separate breed from entertainment writers—"they actually weren't doing that. They got it. They got the humor in it too. I've watched the movie with audiences that didn't know they were supposed to laugh, which is hard for me because I'm hearing the laughs, I'm hearing the beats. When they don't get it you're like, 'Oh, they're bored, man, this is like the most grueling movie ever made.' By the time they see the handing-out-the-colors scene they realize they can laugh at that. No matter what, that always gets laughs. Eventually they catch on by the last half hour of the movie. They've heard what a really tough movie it is and they heard that it's a gut-wrenching experience, so they're not expecting to laugh, so they're not letting it out when they want to laugh."

After Cannes, word trickled out that, yes, you can laugh. But the ear scene still caused problems for the marketers and distributors. "It's a problem if they're expecting it to be a *Pretty Woman*," said Quentin. "This movie was never meant to be everything for everybody. And I don't mean that as a slam. I'm just saying that I made this movie for myself and everybody else is invited."

Riding on the success of Cannes, *Reservoir Dogs* played the tiny Telluride festival at the end of August, then moved to the mammoth Toronto Festival of Festivals in early September. Toronto offers a choice of hundreds of movies playing over ten days, yet it is a very relaxed, filmmaker-friendly festival, where stars and press mingle freely at cocktail parties and screenings. At that time, most of the players were staying at the Sutton Place Hotel—in later years some of the press were moved to cheaper lodgings—so that you could run into Quentin in the elevator, where he might slip you a cassette of the *Dogs* sound-track. By the end of the festival, Quentin could greet by name just about every major critic in North America.

Festival director Piers Handling, who at the time was artis-tic director, remembers welcoming *Reservoir Dogs* as "one of those films which just galvanized people right away." He had seen the movie at Sundance and was in Cannes where enthusi-asm for it was growing. "The French love the kineticism of American cinema and the more often I go to Cannes and see the films that participate you really get the sense of the Europeans looking for the sheer energy and visceral powers that American cinema gives them," says Piers. "Their own cinema tends to be much more intellectual, much smaller in terms of its concerns. It deals with life in a more realistic way generally and it doesn't deal with the large gestures, the larger-than-life image that American cinema gives them."

In the less frenzied atmosphere of the Toronto festival, Quentin dropped by the staff party and hung out with the vol-unteers. "He had this kind of motormouth which was really appealing," says Piers. "There was this energy spilling out of him. Of course at festivals we're all charged up and full of adrenaline, so it's nice to run into that kind of person. He was the way I would imagine Orson Welles would have been around the time of *Citizen Kane*. There was this kind of incredible delight he had in playing with this tool; such a big train set for him."

Not having a taste for violent movies can be a drawback for a festival programmer, but Piers nevertheless loved *Reservoir Dogs*. He thinks the way Quentin handles violence is up there with the best of them. "I think he may be one of the first directors who has achieved with his work what Arthur Penn and Francis Coppola and Sam Peckinpah did with their work in the late sixties and seventies, just in terms of incorporating violence into the actual work itself. The ear-cutting scene is like in *The Godfather* with the horse in the bed, those moments of a movie you remember and take away and tell your friends about. I think Quentin has found a form within which to contain his violence."

It was the ear scene that Piers believes "pushed the film over the boundary into what some people would perceive as bad taste, or just extreme violence. That may be one of the reasons why the film was not that commercially successful."

In the years since *Reservoir Dogs*, Piers has been sent any number of imitations for inclusion in the festival. "I don't think they have the skill, the insight, the sheer ability to play with words and scenes that Quentin has."

Or, as Cat Knell said two years before at CineTel, "There is only one Quentin Tarantino."

Miramax opened *Reservoir Dogs* in New York and Los Angeles on October 23, 1992. The critics went wild, but Harvey Weinstein was right about the ear scene. Every review contained a warning like the kind you get on the side of a pack of cigarettes. "I'd call up Quentin and read him the reviews," says Harvey. "They all said, 'Warning: Don't see it unless your stomach is made of iron. Caution: This movie will kill you.' We sold it as entertaining as we could, as fun as we could, but ultimately, people read the critics and were afraid it was too violent."

The movie did a disappointing $3 million or so in its domestic theater release. Later it would sell a whopping

900,000 videocassettes, more than twice as many as you'd expect for a movie that withered at the box office. In England, where it was banned on video for its violence, it retained a huge cult following and has continued to play in theaters, grossing over $6 million.

"It cost so little to make that it had to do well," says Quentin. "Before the movie even opened the people who came up with the money for the movie had made their money back three times over by selling it around the world. As far as I'm concerned, the movie is a smash because the people who took the chance on me have been paid back in spades."

It was around then that Harvey Weinstein became fond of saying that Miramax was "in the Quentin Tarantino business." He packed Quentin off for an extended press tour of Europe and Asia, doing all the film festivals, meeting all the foreign journalists, promoting himself as an identifiable celebrity as much as he promoted the movie.

"I remember my very first interview, it was a feature story for *The New York Times* on the making of *Reservoir Dogs*, a location interview," says Quentin. "It was so exciting to do an interview. Since then, I've done a million. But the way I did them was like an actor would do a scene, not just answer the questions, but engage the journalist in a conversation, just sit and talk to them about whatever, keep it on a personal level, try to find answers and articulate them, get it across, sound witty and everything. Now you do another interview, what are you gonna do to do it differently, be *in*articulate?"

It was the start of a grueling process in which the joy of discovery that is the essence of the interview process became the challenge of keeping it fresh. "At Toronto, I was sitting in a bar talking to one of the directors of *Man Bites Dog*," a Belgian black comedy about documentary makers getting overinvolved with their serial-killer subject, "and all of a sudden while I was talking to him I felt I was in another interview. It had ruined it now for me to talk about my movie. It's like I've given it all away. I had all this stuff, and I've given it all away, and this was another filmmaker, and I would have liked to share, but there was nothing left to share. Since then I've tried to hold onto something about the movie for myself."

That is why Quentin won't answer questions about how to interpret his movies, turning it back on the audience to force them to grapple with their own opinions.

Meanwhile, Quentin got to travel, the one thing he had told his mother he regretted never having done as a child. And while he was traveling, he began to work on another idea he was toying with, "three stories about one story," as he described it to his friend Stacey Sher at Jersey Films. He was calling the new screenplay *Pulp Fiction*.

"Let me tell you what "Like a Virgin" is about," says Mr. Brown, played by Quentin, in the opening scene of *Reservoir Dogs*. "It's all about a girl who digs a guy with a big dick. It's a metaphor for big dicks. *Dick dick dick dick dick dick dick dick dick.*"

The Madonna riff, written for Mr. Pink but appropriated for Mr. Brown so that Quentin would have some juicy dialogue, was one of numerous monologues he had cooked up for his acting classes. "When you're an actor you have different things you can just like whip out from your sleeve on a moment's notice, things you can do, and that was one of mine, I wrote it for myself," says Quentin.

Before Madonna had seen it, Quentin speculated on what her reaction would be. "She knows of it," said Quentin. "She's very aware of it. Her lawyers are very aware of it. My lawyers are very aware that her lawyers are very aware of it." The Madonna riff was not only an actor's exercise; like the I-don't-tip riff, Quentin actually believed in what he was saying. "I'm positive it's the case. I have no doubt in my mind she is going to come to me and say, 'Quentin, you're 100 percent right, that's exactly what the song's about. And I was laughing my ass off when all these fourteen-year-old girls were singing it. Because that is what it was.'"

Quentin finally got to meet Madonna when he visited her

at her Maverick office. Madonna gave him a copy of her album *Erotica* and inscribed it with what any of those fourteen-year-old girls could have told Quentin, what he could have known himself if only the reservoir dogs in his life had included more females: "To Quentin—it's about love, not dick."

CHAPTER 11

Reservoir Dogs: The Barking Continues

Being loyal is very important.
> —John Travolta as Vincent, reminding himself
> in the mirror, Pulp Fiction, Quentin Tarantino

Jean-Hugues Anglade: *You can no longer be in our club. You forfeit your cut of the pie.*
Eric Stoltz: *I guess this means our friendship is in trouble.*
> —Former boyhood friends whose true colors show
> during a bank heist, Killing Zoe, Roger Avary

This is an excellent example of why you can trust nobody. Zero. The big zero. You let yourself trust one person and bang! The

169

equation results in zero. You know, I grew up with Quinn. On the streets . . . When he was stuck in that minimum wage, nowhere cycle, always askin' me for money, I let it slide. Told myself that I owed him . . . And I've been floating him ever since. Truth is . . . that motherfucker owes me!

    —*The boxer in* Pandemonium Reigned,
    Roger Avary

There is no mistaking one of the ongoing themes in all of Quentin Tarantino's screenplays—loyalty between friends, and its flip side, betrayal.

In *Reservoir Dogs*, the gang is sold down the river by the traitor among them, who in turn tries to make it up to the man who tends his wounds by offering him the truth of his identity. The truth, of course, is guaranteed to get him killed, but that is the fair price for betraying your buddy.

In *Pulp Fiction*, the specter of Tony Rocky Horror being thrown out a window for touching the feet of the boss's wife hangs over the entire second act, where John Travolta is having too fine a time with Uma Thurman to hold on to his allegiance. "I'm of the opinion that Marsellus can live his whole life and never ever hear of this incident," Travolta tells Thurman, and they shake on it, sealing an agreement to lie to the man who pays their rent.

Even as early as *My Best Friend's Birthday,* no good deed for a pal goes unpunished—everything the Quentin character does just makes life worse for the Craig character.

Quentin's war with himself over issues of loyalty and betrayal may have started early in life when a succession of father figures came and went through the revolving door. His biological father has never shown any interest in him. His adoptive father abandoned the role when the mood hit. Connie's third husband's interest in Quentin seems rooted in a desire to be near the power and glory of the movie industry. None of the male authority figures in Quentin's life has hung around to show the kind of unselfish, indestructible love that would lead a character like the father in *True Romance* to welcome death rather than rat on his son.

Quentin prefers not to self-analyze—there's danger in them thar hills! But there is no end of former (and current!) friends, buddies, helpmates and colleagues who all agree that Quentin has a problem in this area. For all his brilliance, sweetness and sudden bouts of kindness, he is also selfish, grandiose, unreliable. An only child, he doesn't share his toys.

"This is going to sound like the lamest thing to say to you," says Quentin, "but you know, I almost feel compelled to go on record as saying that I'm a real nice guy, all right. And I haven't ever done anything to anybody that I can think of that was maliciously meant to fuck with them, to hurt them."

Here then are the Quentin Controversies, pro and con, mostly having to do with his reluctance to give credit where credit is due:

The Roger Thing

Roger Avary and Quentin have known each other since 1984, when they both worked at Video Archives, first as rivals, then as friends. The competitive edge cut into the friendship, but they were as close as brothers—or, as Tony Scott likes to say, "thick as thieves"—collaborating on screenplays, tossing ideas back and forth, and fusing in such a way that it is difficult to separate who contributed what to the early screenplays. Roger handed Quentin something he'd written called *The Open Road*, which Quentin expanded into *True Romance* and *Natural Born Killers*. "Quentin read it and thought it was great and wanted to rewrite it," says Roger. "He said, 'This is so good, with just a little bit of work this could be a great script.'"

Granted, Roger's contribution was by no means equal on *True Romance* and *Natural Born Killers*. And, judging by Roger's own script that he later directed, *Killing Zoe*, Roger is no Quentin Tarantino. But a full third of *Pulp Fiction* consists of a screenplay

Roger wrote years ago called *Pandemonium Reigned*, which Quentin bought from him to create the Bruce Willis segment.

There is no question that what Quentin did with *Pandemonium Reigned* improved it tenfold; Roger's script was coarse (one character suggests taking a shit on a woman before she is murdered) where Quentin's was funny; Roger's was nihilistic (everyone dies at the end) where Quentin's ended on an unexpected note of redemption. But Quentin did not create something out of nothing—the boxer's story was laid out in detail, including the anal rape, the "gimp" on the chain, the sacred watch and the girlfriend who eats pie for breakfast. People who talk trash about Quentin may in fact be every bit as jealous as they sound, but they have a point—Quentin is an excellent writer of dialogue and architect of story structure, but his plots tend to come from other sources.

Is that a crime? No. Some of the best movies are collaborations between people who find in a partner the qualities they themselves lack. But some say Quentin has been less than gracious about sharing credit.

Roger was originally supposed to receive a shared screenplay credit on *Pulp*, but he settled for a "story by" credit and Writers Guild minimum because, say his friends, he was broke and badly needed the money upfront, and this was the deal his friend offered him.

"Oh, *no no no no*. That is not the truth," says Quentin when told that the perception has been that he robbed Roger of his due. "The situation that happened with Roger is that I had purchased the rights to a screenplay that he'd written a long time ago, and what I was going to do was adapt it into the world that I was creating for *Pulp Fiction*, like you would adapt a novel into a screenplay. And what I proposed to Roger at the beginning was that I'd finish the script, and when I got to the end of it, let's me and you sit down and do a rewrite on it, you know, we'll put our heads together and just really make it better. You have to understand that at that time, Roger had never sold anything, he didn't have a screenplay credit to his name. He had written *Killing Zoe,* but he hadn't sold anything yet. And then what ended up happening was I went to Europe to write it, and in the course of time it just became my baby, and I didn't want to write it with him. I had like a 500-page thing, like a novel, and I had to condense it. And by the time I got to the end of that journey, I didn't want to do it with anybody else. I didn't want somebody else to come in and make decisions. I had lived with it, I had written this novel and I wanted to do it on my own. So that was how it changed. He was disappointed about it and everything, but ultimately I think he understood."

Perhaps. But Roger's wife, Gretchen, isn't quite so understanding. At the Golden Globe awards, when Quentin didn't mention Roger during his acceptance speech for the screenplay award, Gretchen Avary headed Quentin off from visiting their table by yelling, "Fuck you!"

"I wish he'd give Roger more credit, even though he took the material and made it his," says Jerry Martinez, a mutual buddy from Video Archives who is intensely loyal to Quentin. "I would have liked Quentin to give more of a nod to Roger. He complains about Oliver Stone taking his stuff, but Quentin's as guilty as anybody of taking Roger's stuff. Quentin is a sweet guy, a nice guy. But this was an only child. He can be kind of self-absorbed."

Quentin compounded the insult by appropriating Roger's *Top Gun* theory—about the Tom Cruise movie's subversive homosexual subtext—as a monologue for his cameo in Rory Kelly's 1994 pastiche *Sleep with Me.* Quentin plays a guest at a party, and Rory simply wrote in the script "Quentin does his thing here." Quentin showed up that day wearing his Psychotronic T-shirt and began doing this hilarious riff, which everyone assumed he had improvised on the spot. In fact, it had been Roger's idea, and he and Roger had rehearsed it for years until neither one of them truly owned it.

"What is *Top Gun*? You think it's the story about a bunch of fighter pilots? It is a story about a man struggling with his own homosexuality. That's what *Top Gun* is about, man. You've got Maverick. He's on the edge, man. He's right on the fuckin' line.

And they're saying, 'Come, go the gay way, go the gay way.'"

Quentin never told Roger he had used the *Top Gun* riff. Roger discovered it during casual conversation with Eric Stoltz, who was in both *Sleep with Me* and Roger's movie *Killing Zoe*. He had to buy a ticket to the movie in order to see what Quentin had done with his idea. Roger may have made his peace with Quentin, but mutual friends say he was crushed and angry.

"It wasn't something from one of Roger's screenplays or anything," says Rand Vossler, who had his own falling out with Quentin over the aftermath of *Natural Born Killers*. "It was actually one of those things where, like, a friend of yours tells you a real good joke but you can tell it better so you repeat it a lot and that becomes your favorite joke. Eventually people will know you for that joke and when people think of that joke they think of you."

"Roger never wrote that down, all right?" says Quentin defensively. "Roger came up with the basic idea of the *Top Gun* theory. But I didn't even rip it off, I did it as an improv in a movie. It's not like I even wrote it down in a script. You know, I just did it as an improv. The script said, 'Quentin is at a party and he says something funny.' So I showed up on the set, and we were trying to come up with things to do, and if you ask a Groundling performer to come up with something, they'll come up with something they've done in one of their improvs or something before. So Roger came up with the idea, and then we did it together at a party, and then the two of us proceeded to turn it into a routine. See, it was just a cockamamie theory of Roger's when he first said it, all right. Then the two of us started expounding on it, and then doing it for people, and performing it for people, you know. Anyway, the bottom line is, we just turned it into a routine between the two of us. And then I ended up doing it in the movie."

Rand says the rhythm and cadences of all the riffs in Quentin's work echo the atmosphere at the old Video Archives. "It's just the banter and the chat from all of us being together all the time," he says. "The tipping speech in *Dogs*, all those speeches, those are the exact conversations I've had with him.

After *Dogs* was made it was like everybody grasping at things and taking credit for this thing, that song."

"I can tell you where just about everything from *Reservoir Dogs* came from," says Jerry Martinez. "But, you know, if we're sitting around joking and he remembers the joke, is that taking stuff?"

Quentin thinks of himself as a good friend to his friends, which is why he agreed to lend his name to *Killing Zoe* when Roger was set to make his directorial debut. Quentin and producer Lawrence Bender as a team had clout now that *Reservoir Dogs* was critically acclaimed.

According to some people who worked on *Killing Zoe*, in combination with published reports in *Variety*, Quentin and Lawrence had nothing to do with the physical production, they were just there to lend their famous names. But they balked even at that when they held out for $100,000 and didn't get what they wanted.

No way, say both Quentin and Lawrence. "We never took a fee," says Lawrence. "And I would never storm out of a meeting, that's not my style."

Lawrence says there was discussion of salary but they deferred it because "Roger needed all the money to put it up on the screen, and we did want to help him."

It's true that at one point late in the game, the duo removed their names from *Killing Zoe*, and the William Morris Agency's legal department sent out a letter warning that their clients could not be connected with the movie in any way. But Quentin says this was to keep the movie's producer, Samuel Hadida— who also produced *True Romance*—in line.

"We didn't know how much we were going to be able to make the movie for, so we didn't put in a salary for us, we left that blank," says Quentin. "If it was going to be a $700,000 movie, then we weren't going to give ourselves big salaries. And basically, we know Sammy—he's an exploitation distributor. What he was going to do was throw our names all over the fucking thing, which, one, wouldn't be good for the movie to begin with, and two, you can't do that. You can't say 'From the makers of *Reservoir Dogs*,' you know, have our names in there big, and pound that over everyone's head, and if you are, you're going to fucking pay us for it. But it had nothing to do with me and Roger. If Roger could have had our names off of that movie by the time it was released, he'd have done it. He had to put up with all this *Reservoir Dogs* shit and when the film came out, all these comparisons and everything."

Hadida eventually agreed to their request for $100,000, but since it was a back-end deal and the movie never made any money, "we haven't received dime one," says Quentin. "And the only reason we did that is so we could protect Roger if things went sour in the editing room and Roger needed help, so we would have the power to help him."

The Cathryn Thing

Cathryn Jaymes was Quentin's manager from 1984 or so until January 1994, when the William Morris agents she helped land him a contract with called to let her know her services were no longer required.

"It was the day after the Los Angeles earthquake, and I was in the middle of rubble, my desk broken in half and computers smashed. Only the phone lines were working," says Cathryn. "I left a message for him on his answering machine telling him I was angry and annoyed and wanted to have a conversation, and he calls that afternoon asking me to do him a favor. He hadn't gotten my message. Then he wondered why I was upset, because I was a wonderful manager and my job had been to launch his career, which I had done, so there was no reason to employ me anymore. I explained to him that I knew where he was coming from and how he could justify his behavior, but I had invested ten years of money, time and faith in him, and that I made that investment hoping I would start seeing a return. He said he loved me but didn't see any reason why he should pay me. He wasn't being heartless; he felt he was being genuine and truthful."

Over the years, Cathryn had sent Quentin out on hundreds

of casting calls, which yielded only one job—an Elvis impersonator stint on a *Golden Girls* episode during which he wore his own Elvis outfit and had to sing, inexplicably, Don Ho's "Hawaiian Love Chant."

During *Reservoir Dogs,* Quentin's first big payday, Cathryn swallowed her pride and accepted the conditions Quentin offered her—5 percent instead of her usual 15. By the time she was let go after *Pulp Fiction,* she says she had made a grand total of $40,000 from Quentin after ten years' investment.

Quentin agrees with most of those facts but rejects the interpretation. "I know Cathryn," he says. "She's a fuckin' drama queen. She feels betrayed because the thing that she said when I left was, 'You said you would never ever leave me.'"

To which Quentin is said to have replied, "What is this, the devil calling in a contract?"

"A director doesn't need a manager," says Quentin of why he dropped Cathryn. "That's the bottom line. Directors have managers when their career is doing badly, or when they're trying to change their image. The thing is, Cathryn was my manager when I was trying to get work as an actor, she would send me out and everything. She didn't have anything to do with *Reservoir Dogs* getting set up or anything. I did that all myself, me and Lawrence. And when I got William Morris, I decided not to get rid of Cathryn, 'cause she had a small company, she wasn't powerful, and my prestige was helping her out. And Cathryn was fiercely loyal, so my thoughts were that she could help keep William Morris in line at the very very beginning. And, so, basically, after I didn't need Cathryn anymore, I stayed with her for two more years. She got paid on *True Romance, Reservoir Dogs, Pulp Fiction*. It wasn't that she was doing a bad job, I just don't need her to turn around a perception of me, because I like the perception of me. You know, it's like, I didn't need her, so I said I'm going to leave. I don't need a manager."

Quentin is matter-of-fact when he discusses this, but he goes ballistic when he hears that the conventional wisdom is that Cathryn helped pay his rent when he was down and out.

"She never paid my rent! She never gave me money!" he says, outraged. "She couldn't pay her *own* fucking rent! That's bull- shit, unless she counts taking me out to lunch, which she did from time to time. Unless she counts, like, not charging me for a postage stamp when she sent something out for me. I might have said at one time, Cathryn, do you have five bucks? But it's not like she was feeding me money or slipping me money or anything. And she *never* paid my fucking *rent!*"

Cathryn isn't the only one who makes the rent claim. At least four other people independently mention in conversation that Cathryn bailed Quentin out on numerous occasions.

"He didn't have money for meals or rent or copies of his scripts," says Cathryn. "I needed to cover those expenses for our mutual interest. You can't work with somebody if they can't feed themselves or don't have materials. I absorbed his expenses as much as I could over the years. Quentin is always the first one to forget his wallet. People say isn't it cute that he's made all this money and barely dipped into it, but he probably keeps it in a sock under his bed."

Like most people who come in contact with Quentin, whether they feel ill or well used by him, Cathryn still adores him; he has what his detractors call "a salesman's manipulative charm," and what his admirers call a Svengali-like effect. "I know him inside and out and exactly how he operates and how unpredictable he is. That unpredictability is what makes him great and exciting, but it is also challenging for any representa- tive because he runs his own show and then comes over later and says can you fix this. He lives in his own universe," says Cathryn. "My heart would break for him because he's a roman- tic at heart and he'd fall in love with a gal and she wouldn't return his affection and he'd be heartbroken. He was kind of a big galoot, totally unaware of his appearance. He'd never take any interest in the way he dressed."

Cathryn seems more upset that when Quentin left, he took with him the assistant she had nurtured. Victoria Lucai was an ingenue from Detroit who had just been fired from her bartending job when Cathryn took her in. She lent Victoria to Quentin part-time when he needed help finding an apartment—she's the one who found him the West Hollywood apartment in the complex where John Travolta had once lived—and they got along so well Quentin offered Victoria a full-time job without telling Cathryn. "That was my deepest hurt," says Cathryn. "He could have called and asked if I minded if he raided my staff."

People who move on when they get famous is an old story in Hollywood. "At least I know my instincts are good," says Cathryn. "God definitely broke the mold when he made Quentin."

The Craig Thing

Craig Hamann is Quentin's former acting-class partner who got Quentin his first manager, provided Quentin with his first screenplay (*My Best Friend's Birthday*), typed Quentin's notes into formatted screenplays, helped Quentin with the drug scenes in *Pulp Fiction*, and co-wrote an unfinished screenplay with Quentin called *The Criminal Mind*.

"I think it could be one of the best things he's done, but Quentin's not prepared to finish it because it's got Craig's name on it, and he won't release it to Craig," says Stanley Margolis, the producer who nearly got to make *True Romance* but got stuck with a lawsuit instead.

The Criminal Mind is an outline for a story about a serial killer who stops killing, thus baffling the police. "It's not anything that he has against Craig," says Stanley. "It's just that he doesn't like to share credit. It's too bad, because it's a great idea. I could sell this tomorrow if Quentin would release it to Craig to finish."

But Craig won't say anything bad about his former friend. "He's a very encyclopedic filmmaker," he says. "It is possible he borrows without knowing he's borrowing."

"Craig is so loyal it's eerie," says Cathryn. "Quentin would call him at three in the morning and wake him up to come get him and drive him home from Manhattan Beach, and Craig would get up and put on his shoes and socks and go get him. I was hoping Quentin would eventually develop a conscience."

The Barry Levinson Thing

The story goes that Quentin agreed to direct an episode of Barry Levinson's *Homicide* TV series, then backed out at the last minute. Then, Levinson wrote in a cameo for Quentin to play in *Jimmy Hollywood*, and when the day came to film, Quentin canceled with only two hours' notice, claiming he was too busy and anyway, he wanted to go catch a particular movie at a theater.

"I did back out at the last minute," Quentin confirms, "but I didn't leave him in the lurch. It was like one of those things where it sounded like a really good idea at the time and everything, and then I realized I just couldn't handle it."

Levinson, though contacted repeatedly, did not care to comment.

This echoes several other accusations—that Quentin in his enthusiasm makes oral commitments (and sometimes written ones, too), then backs out when he finds he's too busy, without regard to the inconvenience he has caused others. Again, this is not unusual for Hollywood, where half the things that get talked about never get off the ground. Still, a new wariness has been in play ever since Kim Basinger was successfully sued for backing out of her oral commitment to *Boxing Helena*, and people are generally more sensitive about reneging these days.

In addition to the Barry Levinson Thing, there is the Showtime *Rock All Night* Thing, the Doug Lindeman *Five Rooms* Thing (which would become Quentin's *Four Rooms* movie), the VH-1 Thing, and others. In some cases, legal settlements prohibit the parties from discussing the particulars.

The Ringo Lam Thing

It was a 1994 letter to the editor of a small magazine called *Asian Trash Cinema* that lit a match to *City on Fire*.

Diana Bowman wrote: "The reason I'm writing is to get

something off my chest. As you know, Quentin Tarantino has gotten a lot of attention for his movie *Reservoir Dogs*, and rightly so. I enjoyed it very much—until I saw a 1987 Ringo Lam film, *City on Fire*. . . . It's a blatant ripoff of *City on Fire*. Without question, they are one and the same. Sure, *Dogs* is set up differently and told from the robbers' point of view rather than the undercover cop's. But there are just too many similarities to be ignored. . . . With the growing popularity of Hong Kong films in this country, it's just a matter of time before Tarantino is found out! I feel much better now."

The alarm was picked up by *Empire* magazine in England and *Film Threat* in the U.S., with comparison photos to show how closely *Reservoir Dogs* stacks up to the last twenty minutes of the Lam movie. There is no doubt that, along with *The Taking of Pelham One Two Three*, *The Killing* and other movies that Quentin has verbally credited, *City on Fire* was, if not on his mind, then at least in his subconscious when making his directorial debut. The jewelry heist gone bad, the doomed retreat to the warehouse, the undercover cop who gets wounded, the Mexican standoff, the declaration of truth between friends—these are all present in both films.

"This is what's called being a writer," says Quentin, who makes several valid points on his own behalf, including that *Reservoir Dogs* has been compared to so many movies that it cannot be a remake of any one of them. "Why don't they make up their minds just what the hell it is I'm ripping off? They talk about *City on Fire*, well, you know, it's about an undercover cop who's inside of a robbery. Well, I didn't realize *City on Fire* had the copyright on *that* storyline. Neither did five thousand other movies that have done that storyline either."

Quentin agrees that *City on Fire* was "a total influential movie all right," but says that his critics leave out the details that don't make their case. One example of this is in *Film Threat*, which ran a still of both movies side by side to show the similarities. Yet the photo from *Reservoir Dogs* was actually a publicity still taken on the set; that shot does not appear in the movie.

"I steal from every single movie ever made," Quentin told *Empire* in November 1994. "I love it—if my work has anything it's that I'm taking this from this and that from that and mixing them together. If people don't like that, then tough titty, don't go and see it, all right? I steal from everything. Great artists steal, they don't do homages."

Samuel L. Jackson has noted that Quentin is "a film sponge" who knows which shots he wants by referring in his memory to the way he's seen it done before. "He even describes scenes as shots from other films, and he will take which shot from which film and go on with this shot from this film."

In a bit of film-geek enterprise Quentin might appreciate, Mike White, then a twenty-two-year-old manager of a Blockbuster video outlet in Riverview, Michigan, rented the Lam video and made a clever twelve-minute short called *Who Do You Think You're Fooling?* by splicing together footage from both movies to highlight the similarities. The video might have simply continued to circulate in the underground, were it not that Mike entered it in short-film festivals, and suddenly it was the high point of the New York Underground Film Festival in March 1995, playing to the public (and undermining Quentin's reputation) just before the Oscars.

Like many of the people who don't appreciate Quentin's manners, Mike nonetheless is a die-hard Quentin fan. What gets him riled is what he calls the Great Poster Defense. "Quentin tells people, yeah, I saw *City on Fire*, I've got the poster at home, it's great!" says Mike. "So, what does that mean? It's like, I have the poster of, you know, *The Black Shampoo* down in my base-ment, does that mean I can just go out and make *Black Shampoo 2* or just rip it off and not say anything about it?"

Mike sums up the Great Poster Defense in the fanzine he writes, *Cashiers du Cinemart*, as: "I have the poster, that over-rides copyright law."

It's not a matter of copyright, says Lawrence Bender. "The thing that is so great about Quentin is that he's an artist with a unique voice who has been influenced by other movies. Cinema is a medium that he works in. He is influenced by many other people, but he doesn't copy; he's an originator."

Quentin understands the impetus for the Mike White video. "It's a film-geek thing to do. I remember when I was younger, me and all my film-geek friends would say shit like, 'Oh man, Ridley Scott on *Aliens* totally ripped off Mario Bava's *Planet of the Vampires*. Okay, yeah, they're similar, there are similar touches, but you know, you watch *Aliens* and you watch *Planet of the Vampires* and you're seeing two totally different movies. But it empowers you to make the case because Ridley Scott has prestige and is in the mainstream, whereas Mario Bava was denied that, so you make a stronger case by building him up and putting the other down. That's just a total film-geek thing to do."

The important thing about film geeks, says Quentin, is that they have to "show a high regard for their own opinion . . . He with the most point of view wins. When I walk into a room, I always have the most point of view."

The Violence Thing

"Violence is one of the most fun things to watch," Quentin said while he was in Cannes with *Pulp Fiction,* summing up his attitude toward screen violence.

It is a subject that filmmakers have trouble discussing, because in their eyes, anything they decide to include in their movies must be discussed only in the context of their art. Portraying violence in a movie is not the same thing as condoning violence, although many people in the audience (or on the ratings boards) may believe otherwise.

"The ratings people like Quentin, they really like him," says Miramax's Harvey Weinstein, who lets Quentin plead his own case to the MPAA when necessary. "They know he's a real cinema boy."

"I'll tell you, me and Quentin are really different, I get really offended with Quentin, I'll be honest with you, I get turned off by a lot of what Quentin does and I get into arguments with him about violence," says filmmaker and friend Alex Rockwell. "I don't want to be like a cliché—it disturbs me a lot, the treatment, the way he treats people at times. And we used to argue about it. But I'll tell you, I really get inspired by Quentin, too. When I'm jammed up on a story he's the only person on the planet that I would ever go to to collaborate with. And he's the only person I know who can actually write a sentence or a line of dialogue that I can fit right into my film without seeming that somebody else had tagged something on. I get very inspired by that, and we really have a lot of fun together that way. We'll just sit and talk for hours and hours about stories and about character. And it's really great, we really see eye-to-eye nine times out of ten. I guess that one-tenth that we don't see eye-to-eye on stands out sometimes."

Bruce Willis hates when there's an outcry over violence in movies. "I don't think anybody goes out and commits a violent act because they saw a violent act on the screen," he says. "And my thesis is that there is no way that any film could be as frightening as the things you see on the news."

Actor Dennis Hopper totally defends Quentin's use of violence. "I don't think that any movie makes anyone violent," he says. "Unless somebody already has a real problem already. I'm tired of the questions about violence, but in point of fact I live on a street in Venice, California, where drugs are sold in the alley, where people are killed once a week. Now, that's where I live, and these things don't have anything to do with the violence that these people are seeing in the movies. *Nothing.*"

Quentin himself draws a distinction between the cartoon violence of most movies and real violence. "In *Reservoir Dogs,* I want it to hurt," he says of the ear scene. "The lightness, the catchiness, the frothiness, it makes it harder not to watch. That song can never be heard the same way again. Real violence is a couple laughing one minute and the next minute there is blood on the walls."

The Gay Thing

Quentin is amused that, on the Internet, there have been lengthy discussions about whether he is a closet gay. "I find that very interesting," he says, laughing and wanting to hear every little detail of what people have said about him.

Village Voice writer Lisa Kennedy's lover told Quentin that his movies seem to say that "he wants to get butt-fucked by a black man."

"Do I?" asks Quentin rhetorically. "No. But it's a very provocative statement. I took it with a sense of humor. There was a piece written about the homosexual subtext of *Reservoir Dogs*, but what was really funny was Jerry Martinez and I were saying, you know what? If he's really going to go down this road, he left out a lot of things."

Quentin does a variety of his distinctive, rapid-fire laughs—*"ha-ha-ha-ha, huh-huh-huh-huh"*—when told that one of the reasons people think he's gay is the tight tracking shot of Bruce Willis's butt as he climbs over the fence to retrieve his father's watch in *Pulp Fiction*. "Oh, like only a gay man can appreciate Bruce's butt in just that way, him in those jeans."

But Quentin is delighted that people are speculating about him. "Are there other things like that, you know, weird stuff? Groups that are claiming me?" he asks. "I heard that there is a lesbian community in the Northeast who just love *Reservoir Dogs*, and have totally adopted the movie and everything, and you know I work on the assumption that lesbians have better taste than anybody else, so that's the highest compliment to me."

The John Woo Thing

At the 1992 Toronto Film Festival, Quentin Tarantino and his Asian cinema hero, John Woo, announced that they would be doing a movie together. Quentin would write the script, John would direct, with Chow Yun-Fat making his American film debut. The movie never materialized.

"I hope it's going to happen, but I don't know," says Terence Chang, Woo's longtime producer. "We like Quentin so much. We think he's a genius."

The feeling is mutual. "John Woo is such a hero of mine," says Quentin. "As far as I'm concerned he's making the best action films since Sergio Leone. He is reinventing the genre there in Hong Kong. Writing like a lunk-headed action movie would be really hard work and it wouldn't be worth my time and I would be doing a disservice to John Woo. But I actually came up with a good story, all right? And good stories are easy to write, they more or less write themselves. To tell you the truth, I was just excited about the idea of the collaboration. I think I have a few things I can give him and he's got a ton, a mother lode to give me. I also like the responsibility of it, of putting John Woo out in the American market unfiltered. All the way, no holds barred."

The kidnapping thriller that Quentin pitched Woo never made it into script form, possibly for the same reason that so many other Quentin projects have fallen apart—he bites off more than he can chew. "We tried to say to him if you're busy and you can't write it can we buy the story from you?" says Terence. "But he said no, he wanted to write it himself."

"I never had the time to write it," says Quentin.

Another theory, propounded by people who overheard some of Quentin's conversations with the Asian director, was that John Woo was secretly mortified by Quentin's scenario. "There's this whole generation of nerd boys like Quentin who think that all the action in John's films is so amazing, when really the violence and all these deaths are like metaphors for what's going on in the relationships," says a source who prefers to remain anonymous. "Quentin's interest is in sensation and shock value, not emotion. That's completely the opposite of what John Woo's work is all about. And Chow manages to project this amazing goodness, he's not some crazed Asian killer. I heard that Quentin's opening scene had Chow mowing down women and children and so forth to establish him as a purely ruthless killing machine. But John's work is about these incredibly deep and powerful relationships between his characters that has meaning that transcends everything else, an emotional exchange."

John Woo was, however, set to direct a script by Roger Avary, after he makes *Broken Arrow* with Quentin alumni John Travolta and Christian Slater. Roger's script had been called

Hatchetman, but was undergoing a name change. Also a scene change—Roger had to delete one of his original scenes, something about *Top Gun,* "for obvious reasons."

The Language Thing

In *Pulp Fiction,* the word *nigger* is used thirteen times by black characters, seven by white. There are those who believe Quentin has liberated the language from the straitjacket of "political correctness," that he defuses the negative power of the words by exposing them to the light. And there are those who think he is racist.

"The minute any word has that much power, everyone on the planet should scream it. No word deserves that much power," Quentin told writer Manohla Dargis.

"Tarantino is deeply intrigued by the artistic challenges of the many miscegenations that shape the goulash of American culture and by how powerfully the influence of the Negro helps define even those whites who freely assert their racism," writes social commentator Stanley Crouch.

"Quite honestly, he didn't need to use the word that often," says actor Ving Rhames, who plays the crime boss whose wrath everyone fears in *Pulp Fiction.* "But personally I think Quentin really captures the way people talk, white people and black people. His character Jimmie talks in the movie about 'dead nigger storage' but in the flashback you see he has a black wife, so there's some irony, there's reality. But I do know many African-American friends of mine who have a problem with that word being used like that. I can understand their perception of it. Here's a white boy using the word nigger like, you know, I'm asking you about the weather."

"Uh, that's such a boring thing, you know, I have so absolutely little to say about that," says Quentin. "I'd almost rather just not talk about it than blow it off and just say, well, that's what the characters are saying."

Quentin says that the majority of the people who complain about his use of the forbidden word are "white liberals, the most sensitive human beings on the planet," but that when he meets members of his huge black following who have a problem with it, "not because they think they should have a problem, but because they actually have a problem with it, in every case it's been my view that they are of unpure heart. That they are racist, basically. That they have a problem because where they are coming from isn't pure. And they're projecting their own baggage onto me. Now, this is just my judgment, I'm not naming names or anything, but that's just what I have seen. Because basically I am coming at it with a pure heart. And people with a pure heart recognize it. In a weird way, when you do the kind of stuff that I do, you just get used to being misunderstood. It becomes part and parcel of everything, and that's the way it is."

The "I'll Beat You Like a Woman" Thing

Quentin jokes that in his Video Archives days, he would occasionally indulge his self-doubts in an all-night "Quentin Detest-fest," in which he would examine his life to see how truly fucked up it was. In Hollywood today, there is an actual Quentin Detest-fest in the form of a circulating underground list that catalogues all the heinous things Quentin has allegedly done. Some of the items appear to check out but prove not to be all that heinous; others are things that people would confirm only off the record, bearing out Danny DeVito's letter to *The Hollywood Reporter* in which he said Quentin's detractors are sour-grapes cases who secretly would love to work with him.

One of the items involves a phone call he made to one Stephen Sachs, a friend of Lawrence Bender who was instrumental in getting Michael Madsen interested in *Reservoir Dogs*. It is said that Quentin called Steve and left a message on his answering machine in which he threatened to "beat you like a woman!"

Steve himself is cagey on the subject and will not confirm or deny the story; he says he'll "think about" playing the message tape for an interested party. He never calls back. But Quentin admits that it's true; "It's the eighteen-year-old boy in me that comes out sometimes," the part of him that used to come out swinging at the slightest provocation but now is controlled enough to keep those fights verbal.

"It's not like some dark skeleton for me. He got me mad, he ignored me, he was rude to me in a public place and I got mad and stewed about it, and I contemplated dragging him out by his hair, all right, and then decided to forget about it and went home," says Quentin. "It was at a time when I was really happy, too. He really bummed me out. I got home and thought I would forget about it and I didn't forget about it and I left that nasty message on his machine. But actually, if someone left a message like that to me, I wouldn't be telling people about it. To me it would be kind of humiliating. I wouldn't be bragging about it if I were him."

"Now that he's famous, people are trying to expose Quentin's rotten side," says Alex Rockwell. "They're looking for something to say about Quentin being an asshole or a megalomaniac. The truth is, Quentin is different from most of us, he's a guy on a mission. He's very sure of the fact that he wants to succeed at being a director. He already sees himself as Alfred Hitchcock or Orson Welles. So that's sometimes off-putting, it freaks people out, and they go, who is the arrogant young guy who's acting like this? But the more I know Quentin, the more I realize it's just natural for him. It's not at the expense of anybody else. It's not superficial, either. He wants to start a film library, for instance, like Martin Scorsese. And he wants to start collecting prints now of obscure films from the seventies. And he wants to distribute films. I guess what I'm trying to say is, his vision is large, and it's a generous one, it's not just like some selfish trivial idea. He really wants to affect film in many ways, and he's got a very ambitious agenda."

Quentin is concerned about the ways in which truths and half truths take on a life of their own, depending on the agenda of the person telling the anecdote. But he revels in the limelight of being controversial. "I could listen to this kind of stuff all day," he says. "I actually like the idea that people are, you know, talking *about* me and *gossiping* about me. I watch *The Gossip Show* hoping to see myself."

CHAPTER 12

Pulp Fiction

Don't be telling me about foot massages. I'm the foot fucking master!
>   —Samuel L. Jackson as Jules in Pulp Fiction, 1994

Travolta: *Pulp Fiction is just everything that Quentin loves.*
Tarantino: *It's a Quentin world!*
>   —John Travolta and Quentin Tarantino on MTV

Uma Thurman's feet are considered the finest in the business. "You're kidding, is that what they say?" says Quentin, less alarmed by what they say than by the idea that there may be other foot fetishists in the business besides him.

"He's a real feet guy," says his longtime friend Steve Martinez, who was put on the *Pulp Fiction* payroll to render Uma's portrait, all digits included, in oils.

There were other actresses who tested for the role of Mia, the mysterious wife of crime boss Marsellus. Rosanna Arquette tested for the role and wound up as Eric Stoltz's wife. Holly Hunter was up for the part. But when Quentin had dinner with Uma at the Ivy restaurant in L.A., he felt that he had met the Mia of his subconscious, the only character he had ever written that flowed from his fingers to the page with no particular real-life person in mind—except, perhaps, Brigitte Nielsen.

Uma's agent had put her up for the part of Honey Bunny, the role that eventually went to Amanda Plummer. It was a sensitive period for Uma, who had a miserable time on the set of *Mad Dog and Glory*, where crew members had ogled her nude scenes and she had felt like a slab of beef. Further, she had been "terrified" of *Reservoir Dogs*, even though she liked the movie. She just didn't know what to expect from Quentin.

"I was totally astounded by the script for *Pulp Fiction*, but not knowing Quentin, I found some of the imagery was so completely open to interpretation, and I didn't know what was intended," says Uma. "I found it rather terrifying. But I was just overwhelmed by his incredible energy and personableness and enthusiasm, and our first dinner together was like a dinner of two close friends. It was really wild. He met me and thought he had met Mia."

The two made plans to hang out for the weekend, and Uma went back to her hotel for a swim, during which she contracted conjunctivitis, or pinkeye. "I locked myself in my room and never called Quentin because I was too ashamed and too contagious to be seen."

Later, back in New York, they had dinner at a Mexican restaurant and Uma confessed why she hadn't called him. Quentin had actually been hurt by the snub. But he forgave her when she consented to do his favorite thing—they went back to her hotel and read aloud. Uma played Mia, and Quentin played the other parts, "which he loves doing."

Still, Uma wasn't convinced she was right for the role. "I was really shy about doing it, I was really nervous, and I was in a weird place in my life. And he convinced me, he made me feel fearless again. He restored a kind of un-self-consciousness that had just simply been overshadowed by other experiences."

Quentin, who had not shown any great facility with female characters up till then, was particularly proud of Mia. "He really invented the character," says Uma. "You know, Quentin always says that all of his characters come from somebody he knows, or somebody he's met or something that he's seen. And he's always been led by that in casting and designing it. And my character was one of the few that came purely from his imagination. He didn't have a preconceived notion, he just knew he'd know her when he saw her."

Uma turned down the role. But Quentin, persistent as always out of a need to make things conform to his worldview, kept after her. He telephoned her and begged her to explain her reasons in detail. During the conversation, he gradually turned her around—mostly by making her trust him to do right by her. And he did.

"Oh, it was incredible," says Uma. "I mean, from the very beginning, from creating the character together physically through costuming and rehearsals, then running the lines and working with them, me and Quentin together and then me and John Travolta. We spent several days in that room at Jersey Films, a studio like a huge garage, we sat there at a card table in the middle of the room and worked and worked and loved it. You know, sometimes great things come out of unpleasantness and suffering. But this came out of joy. Pure joy. Every day we'd have some new adventure, some new mountain to climb, and we'd just climb it together and it was great."

For the big needle scene, in which the overdosing Uma is stabbed with adrenaline through the heart, the script called for her to rise with her arms forward like *Dawn of the Dead* or *Dracula*. But Uma recalled hearing about an overtranquilized tiger that was revived with adrenaline and "just went ballistic"; she insisted that Quentin let her try it that way.

"The rehearsal was really a scream," she says. "At first, Quentin wasn't too into this idea, and he said, well, just show it to me. So they carried me into the rehearsal hall at Jersey Films, and John punched an imaginary needle through my chest, and I just flew across the room like the Tasmanian Devil, just like it is in the movie! I scraped my knees up and I think I cracked Rosanna Arquette in the chin with my knee. When I did that, they all just scattered."

Steve Martinez, who had once painted Quentin's girlfriend asleep on the couch while the gang was watching Sonny Chiba on TV, was paid $1500 to paint a portrait of Uma that would hang in Mia's white-on-white townhouse. Quentin wasn't too specific about how he wanted the portrait, except that he wanted Uma, like Grace before her, curled up on a sofa with bare feet. He specified that the feet had to be bare, and that she had to look "beguiling, ethereal."

Steve doesn't work from photographs, so Uma was promised to him for two portrait sittings. She wound up doing only one, which is probably why no one in the end really liked the painting, even though it was used in the movie, and Quentin kindly has the camera linger on it.

"She was wearing her favorite dress, kind of like a cloth or cotton body thing, really kind of form-fitting with stripes. She looked like a Life Saver," says Steve. "She's real gangly and double-jointed, she does things most people can't, and this turns into wonderful poses. Although she was a little apprehensive—I don't know, she saw this huge canvas I had and probably thought I was gonna do this kind of strange, abstract performance art/self-mutilation thing or something."

While sitting for the portrait, the subject of Uma's hands and feet came up. "She said, 'Look how big my hands are!' And she held them up for me to place my hands against hers," says Steve. "And her hands are at least as large as mine and, uh, yeah, she has great hands and feet. And I wanted to get all that in."

When Uma didn't return for a second sitting, Steve had to paint Uma's spectacular hands and feet from memory.

"Her arms can, like, shoot up from her elbows," rhapsodizes Quentin. "And her hands are, like, at the end of the wrist like a completely separate entity on their own." He laughs. "She's got this kind of total praying mantis kind of body language. And Steve captured that really well in the painting."

The question naturally arises—did Quentin ever give Uma Thurman a foot massage?

"What?" he cries, as alarmed as if someone had read his diary. "Oh, oh, I, I cannot say! But she definitely has both the wildest fingers and feet in the business. 'Cause, like, they're so big! And it's really funny, because most people don't think of big feet on women as a sexy thing, but with her they are. Actually, I think with most they are. And her hands, her fingers are so damned long! It was funny, cause at one point I had to do something with her hands, and she was off in another room, unavailable, and they go, 'We'll use her stand-in,' and I go, 'No, you can't use anybody's hands except Uma's hands!' They're too distinctive."

Quentin was also instrumental in having the character wear those black pants that stop short of the ankle, to further accentuate her bare feet—her feet are the first we see of the character after the lips and the nose. "She looked really cool. When we found that outfit, she was just over the moon. She was like, 'I am going to look cooler in this movie than I've ever looked in any movie I've ever done!'"

Uma says the whole foot-massage conversation between Vincent and Jules is "hysterically funny and completely true. I think with a non-blood-related, non-eunuch member of the opposite sex, you know, foot massages are definitely, you know, raising the stakes slightly. It's the pleasure zone."

Some say that Quentin and Uma were in fact dating during the movie. All Uma will say on that is, "if he weren't my great friend, I'm sure I'd be, you know, banging down his door like the rest of female-kind."

In the hash bars of Amsterdam and fast-food joints of Paris, wherever he went to publicize *Reservoir Dogs* or wherever the spirit moved him, Quentin Tarantino refined his script for *Pulp Fiction*, weaving together stories and characters the way Mario

Bava did in the 1963 horror film *Black Sabbath* and J. D. Salinger did with his Glass family stories. "Characters float in and out," is how he described the voluminous 500-page manuscript, written with felt markers in a series of notebooks. "I'd get the opportunity to weave the characters—but not in a 'Hey, look at me, I'm so clever' kind of way—but very much like the way novelists do, in a way that filmmakers don't get a chance to do."

In Europe, he didn't lack for company. Filmmaker Alex Rockwell accompanied him to Amsterdam, Paris and various film festivals. "We went to a festival in Avignon where I was on the jury," says Alex. "I felt so guilty since I'd gotten the prize at Sundance, so you better believe there was a prize for Quentin in there, man. He won $10,000 worth of film to make a movie."

Tim Roth saw him in Spain, where Quentin would call his hotel at 3 A.M. to read him handwritten pages of *Pulp Fiction* in progress. "I didn't know which part I was going to play until later," says Tim. "I had done a student film with Amanda Plummer and I told Quentin I wanted to do a film with her, as a team, but she has to have a gun in her hand. And that's how Pumpkin and Honey Bunny came about."

Reservoir Dogs was a big hit in Europe, so finding women was no problem—Quentin later joked to pal Allison Anders that he should write a "guide to getting laid at film festivals." Even with language problems, he'd simply trot them over to a newsstand, show them his picture in some magazine, and the rest was accomplished with body language.

Mostly Quentin stayed in Amsterdam, where a Howard Hawks festival was in progress. He spent his time watching movies, buying European posters of *Reservoir Dogs* at cult video stores, writing *Pulp Fiction*, and visiting hash bars like Betty Boop. "I think that Amsterdam has this kind of ring to it for him," says Alex. "You know, you can smoke pot legally, and it's a cool place to hang out. Here's an opportunity to see the world, it's almost like a surfboard, you jump on your movie and let the film take you around the world."

*   *   *

Pulp Fiction was set up as a development deal at Jersey Films by Quentin's former girlfriend, Stacey Sher, with a first-look agreement at TriStar. But TriStar nervously passed on the script and Miramax agreed in mid-1993 to fund it for a little over $8 million. All the actors were paid scale—$1400 per week—but were offered the catnip of "points" on the back end; if the film made any money, so would they.

Richard Gladstein, the executive from LIVE who had shepherded *Reservoir Dogs*, was now head of production at Miramax. Richard sent the script to Harvey Weinstein, who started reading it on a plane and kept calling Richard begging him to reveal the ending. "It's the greatest opening scene I've ever read," Harvey shouted above the airplane static. "Is it this good throughout? Does Vincent Vega come back?"

Because of the circular nature of the fractured narrative, Vincent Vega did indeed come back. The character of Vincent was designed to be the brother of Vic Vega from *Reservoir Dogs*, part of Quentin's overall idea of creating a community of characters who travel between stories and among movies. Quentin even discussed the role with Michael Madsen, who had played Vic. But Madsen, after some soul-searching, went off to do *Wyatt Earp*. Deep in his heart, Quentin really wanted John Travolta—if only because he wanted to meet his hero and have an excuse to play the *Grease; Welcome Back, Kotter* and *Saturday Night Fever* board games with him. Like a rich kid who can make the servants play with him, a director with a love of pop-culture board games can get actors to humor him if there's a possible role hanging in the balance.

Although usually Quentin takes the parts of Danny, Vinnie and Tony in those games, he deferred to Travolta, who won all three matches over the course of twelve hours. "The deal was, on occasion I would slip into the character," says John. "So that was the fantasy, you know, that we're just two guys playing this movie game or something, and then I would like slip out into the actual character. That's how he wanted it. I totally understand that obsession."

After dinner, when Quentin and John were really getting along, Quentin let him have it with both barrels for making movies like *Look Who's Talking* and wasting the promise of having once been the biggest star of the seventies. "I was kind of moved and hurt at the same time," says John. "He took me off guard. I saw that he cared about me and my career, and that I wasn't at a place that he felt was where I should be. So I left that meeting kind of baffled. He had quoted Pauline Kael, François Truffaut, Bertolucci and De Palma, he said I was these guys' favorite actor, why aren't I choosing better vehicles? I didn't know what to say. So I went home and kinda stewed in my thoughts and realized that this is a guy who cared. He cares more about me than anyone has ever cared about me professionally in my life, and I had some very serious people care about me professionally. I have never seen anything like it, the totality of my film career matters to him. I don't know how to classify it, other than that at a pivotal point in his upbringing, I meant something to him onscreen, the way as a kid Jimmy Cagney meant a lot to me. At any rate, it woke me up a little bit."

Six months later Quentin offered him the Vincent part, even though everyone around him was against it, from Lawrence Bender to Harvey Weinstein, who was pushing Daniel Day-Lewis. Daniel had worked with Miramax on *My Left Foot* and really wanted this role, putting Harvey in an awkward position. And when Harvey pushes for something, it registers on the Richter scale.

Nevertheless, Quentin stood firm, even going so far as to say that unless he could use Travolta, he wouldn't make the film. "And to his credit, he used Travolta and reinvented his career," says Harvey.

"Once again, he moved me," says John, "because I felt that sort of thing was said or done only in novels or fiction, not really in life. He really put himself out on a limb for me. I worried, what if I don't come through? What if I'm not what he thinks I am? So I made it a point when I got the part to pull out all the stops, and do the best I could."

From the long stringy hair (with extensions to make it thicker) to the extra avoirdupois to the almost African-American way of talking, John carefully crafted a character who would be memorable, lovable and funny. He kept his doubts to himself about some of the violence in the movie, but later he got Quentin to change certain things that were giving him trouble. "Initially the character of Marvin was going to be shot in the throat, and you were going to see him suffer, and then I was going to put him out of his misery with a second shot which then blew his head off," says John. "Well, that looked a little vindictive and mean-spirited." It was John's idea to make it look more like a sudden accident. "I changed the line from 'Oh, I shot him,' to 'Oh, I just shot Marvin in the face,' which made it funny. Using the word 'face' and using his name, Marvin, made it personal, like I had just stepped on his toe. And I knew it would be funny just from my comedy background."

Quentin allowed the actors plenty of leeway, except when it came to the rhythms and cadences of the dialogue. There he had a specific vision of how he wanted it to play.

"In the opening scene where I'm describing the hash bars and the cops, he wanted a clarity to it, like, bada bada bada BAH, bada bada bada BAH. I think I was the only one who ever asked him to rewrite. If I ran into a little area that I couldn't make work, I'd have him do it, and then he'd see that there was a word or something that wasn't quite right, and he'd rewrite it. The thing is that he's a good actor, and he knows what he's doing."

The hardest part for John was the long take in which he and Samuel L. Jackson argue about foot massages. "It was like eight pages of dialogue, and I'm so used to movies now, not theater," says John. "Years ago I used to be better at memorizing long sections of dialogue, but movies it's so much cut-em-up and shoot-em-up, so it was not what I was used to. It took us all day to get a half-dozen usable masters. Over and over again. And then finally about four or five o'clock we got the ultimate perfect take. The last time I did such a long take was for *Saturday Night Fever*, the dance solo. I did that all in one shot, but it was something I had rehearsed for six months and something I knew like the back of my hand. The only problem there was the exhaustion factor. This was the first time in a long time such a demand had been put on me."

Another big scene to film was the twist contest at Jack Rabbit Slim's, in which Vincent and Mia make like the cool cats in Quentin's favorite Godard movie, *Bande à part*.

"It never ceases to amaze me that for whatever reason, the audience gets so excited when I dance," says John. "There must be something with me and that form that communicates, you know, it's just a kick. There's a lot of fun going on, because the audience gets to interpret it however they want, and as an actor I get to dance in character, someone who's on heroin, who's a little overweight, who refers to the novelty dances of the sixties when he grew up. There was one moment where I have a little gut and I lift up the pants and I thought, 'That's hysterical,' you know what I mean? That's why I get a kick, because it doesn't matter what dance I do, here I am, this heroin addict hitman with a gut, dancing, and it still kind of gets everyone going."

Quentin showed John what he wanted. "He did a twist for me," says John. "It was like watching a twelve-year-old at his first dance. Then he shows me this Billy Jack move, where he takes off his shoes before dancing. And me with a gut, that's an exciting way to do the twist."

Uma felt a little left out because John and Quentin knew more about this kind of dancing than she did. "They showed me some of the dances and we picked a few of them, the general sort of order that we would do them in. Quentin was pretty clear about the kind of attitude he wanted from me in the dance, you know, that very cool kind of Top Cat shake. We would dance and Quentin would call out the styles, now do the Catwoman, now do the Swim, whatever. And of course there was the take where Quentin wanted to hold the handheld camera but he was dancing along with us because he was so excited by it, so it was hysterical with me and John sort of bebopping along and Quentin with this camera going up and down and up and down."

John had a nightmare shortly after shooting that scene. "I dreamed we had finished shooting at Jack Rabbit Slim's, and everyone went home except me, and I'm left there with all the other icons."

Bruce Willis hadn't been approached to be in *Pulp Fiction*, but he has a daughter who plays with Harvey Keitel's daughter. "One day, Harvey came over to my house at the beach to pick up his little girl, and I hadn't seen him in a while, and I was talking with him about what he was doing, and he told me about *Reservoir Dogs* and *Bad Lieutenant*. Then he told me Quentin was doing a new film, and it had a lot of good parts in it."

The next day, Bruce was invited to a barbecue Harvey was throwing; "meanwhile I got the script from my agent and I met Quentin at the barbecue and we talked. I didn't ask for any particular role, I left it up to him. I said whatever you want me to do, I'll do. I didn't flex. How much I was paid wasn't a consideration."

Bruce sees Quentin as a figure of Greek mythology, sprung on Hollywood fully formed from the head of Zeus, "no knocking around doing student movies, no working your way up the ranks, you know. Quentin came out of the box already on fire. He's a very gifted storyteller, and he gets noticed on two levels—on the critical level, and also on the corporate level, because this movie only cost $8 million and it's going to gross $120 million."

Bruce was already in shape because he had just done the nude scenes in *Color of Night*; "there's nothing that will get you in shape faster than having to appear nude in front of a camera. But I also work out a lot, too. There's no actual boxing in this movie, but if there had been, I would have gotten in shape for it."

When his character rides off into the sunset on a chopper named Grace, it ties in with the general themes of honor and redemption that run through the movie. "We never discussed it at the time, but I found out afterwards that he was dating a woman named Grace, but it sounds much more dramatic to say it was about redemption; it certainly worked on that metaphoric level."

The scene Bruce likes the best is when he's in a hurry to get out of town but he has to console Maria de Medeiros, who has big tears welling in her baby-doll eyes. "It's such an American thing," he says. "I'm a guy on a Harley, very practical, we gotta go, come on, do this. And she is like, 'Your nose is broken.' So I take a moment and say, 'How were your blueberry pancakes?' Everybody gets it instantly."

Samuel L. Jackson's first experience with Quentin wasn't a very good one. He was one of the batch of New York actors who tested for parts in *Reservoir Dogs* after Harvey Keitel convinced Quentin and producer Lawrence Bender that they needed to widen their horizons beyond L.A.

Sam came in to test at a midtown office on a Sunday, under the impression that he would be reading with Harvey, but Harvey didn't show up that day. Instead, Sam was alone with Quentin and Lawrence. "That was very strange to me, not only being on a Sunday, but if I'm going to read, where are the other actors?" says Sam. "Quentin was very enthusiastic and, you know, talkative, and I was like, uh, just shut up and let me audition, okay?"

The next time he saw Quentin was at the initial Sundance screening for *Reservoir Dogs*. "I committed the lamest fuckin' faux pas," admits Quentin. "I asked Sam what he thought of the actor who got his role."

"I told him he would have had a better film with me in it," says Sam.

After making *Jungle Fever*, Sam heard that Quentin had written a role for him in a new movie. They met for dinner at a fancy restaurant on Sunset Boulevard. "He told me he'd written Jules with me in mind and hoped I'd like it, and he'd make sure I got it when he finished, and I was like, cool. Then we ended up having this great conversation about Hong Kong films and blaxploitation."

Sam thought little about their conversation again until he got the script. "I just couldn't believe somebody had written a part like this and that they wanted me to play it," he says. "I had to read it again to make sure I hadn't been fooling myself. It was a great marriage of theater and film."

He was called in to read the part so they could get a sense of Jules's voice, and Sam did this in a workmanlike way because, after all, the part had been written for him. Then he went off to make the movie *Fresh*, the directorial debut of Lawrence Bender's old pal Boaz Yakin. Lawrence was producing.

While making *Fresh*, Sam heard that another actor had gone in, read for the role of Jules, and blew them all away. "All of a sudden they were getting ready to cast this guy and I was like, *what*? Nobody told me I had to audition! They can't do that! And suddenly I was in an acting contest with this guy."

The other actor was Paul Tatagliarone, and Quentin was now leaning toward casting him. Harvey Weinstein of Miramax, which was making *Fresh*, called Sam and argued with him. "Yes, you gave an audition, but you didn't knock his block off," Harvey told Sam, whose pride was wounded.

"But I thought I had the part!" sulked Sam.

"I guess we all learn in this life that nothing's for certain until you nail it down," said Harvey. "Now I want you to do something for me. I want you to reaudition, and I want you to blow his balls off."

A tall order. But Sam was up to the challenge. "I had to fly from New York to L.A. to go into this meeting on a Sunday." Sam chuckles because all his difficult meetings with Quentin seem to take place on Sundays. "This time I prepared myself, and I went in and I kind of rocked the house."

Sam got the part of Jules, and Paul got the consolation prize of the bartender cameo. It didn't completely cure Sam of his anxiety, because some of his scenes were shot so far apart that he would have time to "think about it," as they say in sports. But the crew gave him a standing ovation after he delivered the first Ezekiel speech, when he blows away the yuppies—he told

Playboy that the mysterious briefcase he recovers from them contained two lights and a battery—and witnesses the miracle that saves him from the fate awaiting his nonbelieving partner, Vincent.

"The voice of redemption flows throughout the whole film," says Sam. "I mean, Mia gets it when she comes back to life after OD'ing, Butch gets it, Marsellus gets it, and I'm the person who actually voices it."

One of the people on the set hearing him voice it was the actor whose TV series had inspired that noble speech in the first place—Sonny Chiba, whose *Shadow Warriors* character always denounced the tyranny of evil before putting a sword through the heart of the bad guy at the end of each episode.

Sonny had visited the set the day before to have lunch with Quentin. It was Harvey Keitel's last day on the set, and Sonny went totally unrecognized, except by Jerry Martinez from Video Archives, who did the biggest double take of his life when he saw his hero sitting there.

"All the black guys in the fucking movie, none of them were working that day, you know, *they'd* know who Sonny Chiba is," complains Quentin. "*There were no fucking black guys to appreciate that a god was visiting the set!* Everybody else was white, they didn't know who the fuck he is!"

Sonny returned to watch Sam Jackson deliver the Ezekiel prophecy against the Philistines. "And it was like so cool," says Quentin, "because Sam is always real cool, nothing affects him or anything like that. He was *affected* by seeing Sonny Chiba. He was just, 'Mr. Chiba, I just want you to know that I am a great admirer of your work for many years.'"

When Quentin would visit Sam in his trailer between takes, Sam would be watching "some karate kamikaze in the nude."

After the first rough cut of the movie, Harvey Weinstein turned to Quentin and said, "I am so happy I convinced you to use Travolta in this film."

And Quentin turned to Harvey and said, "And me with Sam Jackson, you know what I mean? I had to push you for that, Harv."

*   *   *

Eric Stoltz and Quentin had an ongoing debate about whose bathrobe was filthier and more repulsive. Each of them wore their bathrobes for days on end to give them that lived-in feeling before appearing onscreen. "I did everything in that bathrobe," Quentin told *Vanity Fair*. "I ate. I drank. I masturbated in that bathrobe." His former and future girlfriend, Grace Lovelace, had once told Quentin she liked his smell, and perhaps he was planning to bottle it.

For the role of Jimmie, Quentin wore an *Orbit* magazine T-shirt under his bathrobe; the T-shirt had been given to him by Paul Zimmerman, who later became the executive editor of *Film Threat* when the magazine accused Quentin of stealing from *City on Fire*.

Meanwhile, Eric wore a Speed Racer T-shirt under his bathrobe. "I did spend a great deal of time in that lovely robe," says Eric. "The whole outfit, as a matter of fact, was fairly well lived in by me. I wanted to make sure I was totally comfortable in it and that it looked like an extension of me. It certainly wasn't a pleasant time for my loved ones, but it was only a month or so. Quentin and I would often ponder which of us had the better robe in the film. I still think my lime green robe was the most tremendous."

Eric first met Quentin at the Sundance festival in 1992, when Tim Roth introduced them. "I turned and saw this wild and woolly young maniac with a laugh that turned heads," says Eric. "He was totally different from what I'd imagined. From *Reservoir Dogs*, I thought he'd be an old grizzled Sam Fuller, Sam Peckinpah type guy. But I was happy to see that he was my age. I told him his film had disturbed my sleep; I had weird dreams about it, which is rare for me."

Eric was walking down the street on the Upper West Side of Manhattan one day months later when "a blustery looking fellow in a black leather jacket and a bright orange *Toxic Avenger* watch came toward me. Before I could move to the other side of the street I heard him yell my name."

It was Quentin, telling Eric about *Killing Zoe*, the screenplay his friend Roger Avary had written with Eric in mind. Eric went on to play the role of Zed in January 1993. Then in August, Eric was producing and starring in *Sleep with Me*, "and we wanted to create an ensemble of people we liked and who were fun to make films with. Naturally Quentin came to mind." That's when Quentin showed up and did Roger Avary's *Top Gun* riff for the party scene.

After *Sleep* was in the can, Eric met Quentin for dinner at a Thai restaurant to talk about *Pulp Fiction*, and the next day he was cast as the drug dealer Lance. "That year was truly a case of running into people you like at the right time and ending up working with them."

The needle scene was a night shoot, "which is always kind of cool and kind of a drag, too," says Eric. "The crew always gets tired, but I always feel like we're a bunch of criminals doing vaguely illegal things, so I'm wide awake. We did most of it in one take, one long handheld take, something like five pages of dialogue. We had a few minor screwups. When John's car crashes into my house"—the car was played by Quentin's actual car, a red Chevy Malibu that he keeps in storage while he drives his Geo Metro—"the front-door window was supposed to explode, but special effects had some problems making that work, so Quentin just had me jump a little as though the house rocked. During one take I threw something that ended up breaking a window in the bedroom, for which I was given a great deal of guff from the crew. But generally we were all in good spirits and had a good time. The needle that I prepared was the real thing, and then we did an insert shot backwards of John with a prop needle in Uma's chest."

Working with Quentin as a director, says Eric, is like being with "Steve McQueen on speed."

Rosanna Arquette, whose younger sister Patricia had played Alabama in *True Romance*, tested for the part of Mia. On her birthday, she got a call saying she had gotten a different part—the wife of the drug dealer, the woman who has nearly every body part pierced—including her tongue—for maximum sexual stimulation.

"I was really excited," says Rosanna. "It was fun just to be a part of the movie. I like ensemble pieces and the set was very much like a Scorsese set, the feel of kind of a big family and everybody's there having a good time, including the crew. That's an art in itself."

Quentin based the character on someone he overheard at a diner talking about piercing; he was fascinated by the conversation and jotted it down.

"It was a month before my wedding and Quentin and I were gonna go get our noses pierced together," says Rosanna. "He said I'll do it if you'll do it. One of the things that a lot of people told me was that your nose can get infected, and with my wedding coming up ... well, anyway, I did get it pierced and it did get infected, so I let the hole close up after three days. Then it was like it had never been pierced."

Quentin had wanted to score the anal-rape scene with "My Sharona," a 1979 song by The Knack. "It's got a good butt-fucking beat to it," he told *Movieline*. But he couldn't secure the rights to it; instead the song was used for a mild convenience-store scene in *Reality Bites*, a look at Generation X from another side of the prism entirely.

"We did about ten takes of the rape scene, and nine of them I did crying," says Ving Rhames, the actor who played Marsellus. "What I liked about the character was that he is the most powerful man who is then put in the most horrible position. That was my acting challenge, my acting task. But Quentin wound up using the take where I did not cry, although personally, I thought he should cry to show the vulnerability of the character."

Ving had auditioned previously for *Reservoir Dogs* for the part of the cop who trains Tim Roth to go undercover, the same role Samuel L. Jackson auditioned for and also didn't get.

Ving was offered the role of Marsellus, but he had already

been offered a role in *Renaissance Man* for twice the bucks. All the actors were being paid scale for *Pulp*, "but the good thing was everyone got one percent of the net gross of the film. Who would have thought it was going to make this kind of money? Miramax didn't think that, or they wouldn't have given us points."

The role in *Pulp Fiction* was too juicy to pass up. "Quentin as a writer gives you what I call people-talk. There's actor-talk, and there's people-talk. He writes in a way that sounds like the way people talk. So there's no need for improvisation, because he does half of your work for you by dialogue. And so if you're just real and honest as an actor, you'll come across very well."

Ving secretly wished there would be fewer scenes between Bruce Willis and his baby-doll girlfriend Maria de Medeiros— "You know, those scenes didn't really add much to the piece, in my opinion"—and more between his character and trophy wife Uma Thurman. "Quentin said he wanted to leave it kind of mysterious," says Ving. "Here was this white woman, who a lot of America perceives as very attractive, and here's this black man who's been oppressed, suppressed, depressed by white society. You know, here's the big, black, bald-headed fuck, with the white man's most prized possession. And Quentin just loved the mystery there as to what exactly is their relationship. He's had a guy thrown out the window supposedly for massaging her feet. Yet you don't necessarily see the two of them very intimate. And I don't even know, quite honestly, if white America would be ready for them getting intimate."

Instead, there is the graphic anal-rape scene. The most uncomfortable thing about the scene, however, was the part where Bruce and Ving are tied up with orange rubber balls stuffed in their mouths, held there by bondage-fetish straps. "It was completely uncomfortable," says Bruce. "Ving and I chose to have it strapped up exactly as tight as the bad guys would have done. That was a toughie, several intense days of shooting the rape scenes."

"He doesn't get in your way," says Ving of Quentin as a director. "Except one time in the rape scene, right after where I shoot the guy in the groin. The actor wasn't there, and Quentin was lying on the ground under the camera, acting as if he was that character. I had to say, look, cut. Uh, Quentin, don't do that, you're destroying my concentration. I don't think he's the best actor in the world, you know."

Quentin told *Rolling Stone* he had high standards to live up to with those scenes. "*Deliverance* did it. *American Me* did it, too. There's like three butt-fucking scenes in *American Me*. That's definitely the one to beat in that particular category."

Richard Gladstein had the final cut on *Reservoir Dogs*, and although he didn't use his power to intimidate Quentin, there was always that unspoken threat hanging over the director's head. On *Pulp Fiction*, Quentin had final cut. But Richard still voiced his concerns.

For instance, the middle section between Bruce Willis and Maria de Medeiros with all the sugar-pop endearments seemed to lag. Lawrence Bender had dated Maria when they were both down at the Sarasota French Film Festival, but Lawrence insists Maria was Quentin's choice for the role. She made the Fabienne character similar to her own personality—very sweet in a retro sort of way that usually doesn't play well in America.

"I thought that there was such a momentum in the piece that I was afraid that there were really very long sections of dialogue the film wouldn't be able to sustain," says Richard. "We talked about that and about what he was trying to achieve there, the intimacy he was going to create. Quentin told me later that he knew in his back pocket that he had final cut, which made him a little bit more relaxed talking about it, although we still related the same way. Psychologically and philosophically, he was able to hear things and deal with them differently because he wasn't under the threat of someone actually doing it to him."

The sequence stayed put, and Miramax took the whole cast over to the 1994 Cannes Film Festival in May with a movie in competition that was running 2 hours, 40 minutes, and hadn't been seen yet by anyone. Even so, fans made a fuss over him wherever he went; *Reservoir Dogs* had been a huge hit in France.

While Bruce and Uma stayed at the exclusive Hôtel du Cap some miles away, Quentin stayed at the Carlton Hotel, closer to the action. "The first thing he did when he checked into the room was he took off those spreads that are on the bed," says Miramax publicist Cynthia Swartz.

"Helpful tip for traveling," he told her. "Whenever you travel, the first thing you do when you get into a room is take these spreads off and put them in the corner and get rid of them, cause they're really really unhygienic and you can get, like, terrible diseases from them."

This from a guy who never cleaned up his room in his life.

Miramax held an early screening at the Olympia theater for selected critics because they were nervous that *Pulp Fiction* would get lost in its late-in-the-festival screening slot. "That's when we knew it was going to be a hit," says Cynthia, although they didn't realize it would make so much money until a market research screening months later in New Jersey, when someone in the audience yelled out: "Tarantino is God!"

At the Olympia screening, Quentin got up in front of the audience to preface his movie. "Give me a show of hands, who liked *Reservoir Dogs*?" he asked to wild applause. "Who liked *True Romance*?" he asked, to more applause. Then he asked, "Who liked *The Remains of the Day*?" When a few people clapped, he said, "Get the fuck out of this theater!"

"You don't merely enter a theater to see *Pulp Fiction*, you go down a rabbit hole," Janet Maslin wrote in *The New York Times* after that early screening.

Miramax arranged a highly unusual, informal lunch for Quentin, John, Bruce and Sam at the Hôtel du Cap with a handful of the most powerful American film critics. Quentin wore a Flintstones T-shirt that sopped up spills from the table as he leaned forward eagerly to chat with the people who were about to spread the word about *Pulp Fiction*. In his nervous energy he hardly touched his sea bass and asparagus; Bruce Willis ordered two helpings and was more relaxed than he'd ever been around the press. It was probably the first time the *Die Hard* star had been treated with this much cumulative critical respect.

The day of the awards, festival programmer Gilles Jacob called Harvey Weinstein and told him to come, he'd enjoy the evening. Quentin had told Harvey he woudn't go if he wasn't going to win anything; after the disappointment at Sundance with *Reservoir Dogs*, he never wanted to go through the humiliation again. But Gilles assured Harvey that it would be worth their while.

"We figured we'd get screenplay or director, some prize like that," says Harvey. "So they go through all the prizes, and I look at Quentin and say, 'I think we're going to get the big one,' and I'm bouncing up and down in my seat, and Quentin just looks at me like, *nah*, and then, bang! Clint Eastwood gets up on the stage and gives the Palme d'Or to *Pulp Fiction*. Thank god Bruce Willis was there to keep me cool and calm."

Someone in the audience jeered when Quentin jumped up to accept the award, and Quentin gave him the finger. "My films don't usually bring people together," he said. "They usually split them apart."

After the awards, Bruce organized the victory party at the Hôtel du Cap and put it on his tab—about $100,000 worth. He was now in the hole more than John Travolta, who figured that what with flying his own jet and bringing his wife and baby, he wound up paying $30,000 out of pocket for the privilege of appearing in *Pulp Fiction*.

A source from the post–Palme d'Or party who wishes to be anonymous claims that Clint Eastwood admitted that John Travolta had really won the best actor award, but that Clint had been pressured in an unmistakably French way to make sure the prizes were divvied up so that not too many Americans won. On the second jury poll, John Travolta was no longer the winner.

*   *   *

Travolta got to repay Quentin for standing up for him for the role of Vincent Vega. *Pulp Fiction* was expected to open as a big summer movie, right opposite Oliver Stone's *Natural Born Killers*.

"Don't do it," John told Harvey Weinstein, who is famously difficult to argue with. "You can't fuck around with this movie. Regardless of what Quentin says or what Bruce says, you do *not* release this in the summer. He protected me by putting me in this movie, he showed me more love than anyone has, ever, and I'm going to show him more love now by telling you you must protect him. You've won at Cannes, you saw those critics, I know those critics, this is bigger than you even know. You have to release this in October."

The fall is the time to release prestige films, the ones that will compete for the Oscars. "I really respect your balls for this," Harvey told John. "That's a very ballsy call you're making."

Several meetings and shouting matches later, Miramax revised its marketing plan. Instead of a splashy, feel-good summer movie, *Pulp* was going out as a prestige art-house product. Further, it would open the New York Film Festival in September.

"That's right, let the intellectuals run the show, let the top ten critics in the country tell everyone about it," said John. "The hardest group to get is this intellectual group. Give them the respect of loving this movie as an art film, and you'll get a big commercial success out of it."

Cynthia Swartz figures the movie ultimately made an extra $10 to 15 million by cashing in on Academy Awards season.

"There was a certain amount of trepidation on all our parts that maybe this wasn't the right slot for it," says Richard Peña, director of the New York Film Festival. "The violence of the film or the subject matter could work against it. But in fact, in the end it worked brilliantly."

Peña had admired *Reservoir Dogs*, "but this was just such a quantum leap over almost anything happening in American independent cinema. His early promise had been fulfilled three times over. I remember that opening night screening well, because you really thought you were in the presence of the beginning of something very important."

He describes Quentin as "a second-generation movie brat whose range of influence now goes beyond old Hollywood and European outré cinema to include Hong Kong and a lot of other references, including television, which is obviously a very major reference for him, whereas it wasn't at all with the earlier generation of people like Scorsese. And his films are playful in a way that invites the audience to come along and play. He has a very infectious quality. I mean, you're with him, and you find yourself pretty soon mimicking his hand gestures and stuff like that just 'cause he has that sort of very overwhelming quality. And I think the films have that, too. You know, they're bright, they're colorful. He's someone who has great faith in characters, and has the ability to create really full-blooded, three-dimensional, very contradictory people, and I think audiences were refreshed seeing that."

After *Pulp Fiction* played the New York Film Festival, it opened at 1200 theaters in the U.S. and simultaneously all around the world.

"We're going global!" crowed Harvey Weinstein as he mapped out the strategy, which included sending Quentin on the road—"And not only on the road in America, but worldwide."

Accompanied by publicist Bumble Ward, Quentin went everywhere. He sang karaoke in Japan and Korea; he did every TV show in Brazil.

"Why am I so popular in other countries? I did interviews with everybody, everywhere, and by the time the movie opened I had become a minor celebrity," says Quentin. "So regardless of how the film did there, they knew who I was when I left. And that just gave me tremendous power financially, because for future movies, the emphasis on the domestic market will be gone. Cause we know we have Europe and Asia."

CHAPTER 13
Four Rooms

Chester:	*First off, let me say that there's nothing homosexual about what we're going to ask you to do. There's nothing sexual at all about what we want. But I was thinkin' you might be thinkin' we want you to do some sex thing. Pee on us, suck us off, shit like that. Let me assure you nothing could be farther from what we want.*
Angela:	*Can I jump in here?*
Chester:	*No you can't jump in here. This is my story.*

—Four Rooms, Quentin Tarantino's segment

While Quentin was a houseguest at the downtown Manhattan apartment of Alex Rockwell and Jennifer Beals, he inspired the normally isolated Alex, who began thinking about the kinship among the new breed of independent filmmakers. "I had the feeling that there was a new wave of us. And I've always liked the French New Wave and German cinema at its emergence, or when the Italian cinema had its neorealist movement. And I thought maybe we would be a new wave of filmmakers and collaborate the way the French all got together—Godard, Truffaut—or the way Fellini would write for Rossellini. It would be kind of cool if we did something together."

Although there is some dispute as to who originated the idea—and there is a legal payoff involved somewhere along the line—it was decided to do an omnibus movie that takes place on one New Year's Eve at the Chateau Marmont hotel, "a bell-hop going from room to room." Each of the four stories would be written and directed by someone who had been at the 1992 Sundance festival.

"It was never thought of as a follow-up to *Pulp Fiction* or anything," says Quentin. "Alex and I talked about doing it a while ago, even before *Pulp Fiction*. And it just took us that long to kind of get serious about it and actually do it, and get the right four people. Then it just ended up happening. It was the perfect time. Allison [Anders] was finished with *Mi Vida Loca* and was getting ready to start her new movie, and Robert [Rodriguez] had just finished *Desperado*, and Alex had just got through the film festival circuit with *Somebody to Love*. So we were all just kind of finished with things before we started something else."

In 1992, Allison Anders went to the Sundance Film Festival with her first film, *Gas, Food, Lodging*. She didn't know all of the other filmmakers in competition, but she recalls that "it was a pretty amazing year." The world of independent filmmaking is relatively small, and Allison knew Greg Araki, (*The Living End*), Chris Munch (*The Hours and Times*, playing out of competition), Britta Sorgen (*Jojo at the Gates of the Lions*), Neal Jimenez and Mike Steinberg (*The Waterdance*). The only person she didn't really know was Quentin Tarantino.

"There was already a buzz about him, but I'm so clueless on shit like that, I never know what's happening," says Allison, a friendly, down-to-earth woman who would go on to win a New

York Film Critics Circle award for *Gas, Food, Lodging* and then make *Mi Vida Loca,* about Latina gang members. "I bought a ticket to *Reservoir Dogs* just 'cause I liked the title, and I wanted to see as many of the films in the competition as I could, because as independent filmmakers, we support each other's work."

But Allison didn't see the movie until nearly a year later, after her third date with Quentin. She hates violent movies because she has known violence firsthand in her life, "and nothing I know about movies helps, because I just go back into that space, and it's horrible for me, it's a nightmare."

She had heard of Quentin before; in fact, his name had monopolized a business meeting she was having with her ex-boyfriend Kurt Voss. Allison and Kurt had co-directed *Border Radio* in 1988, and they stayed friendly after the breakup. Kurt had known Quentin when they were both doing work for CineTel. "Kurt all of a sudden stops the pitch and starts talking for like half an hour about the script for *Reservoir Dogs,* and I couldn't believe it. Goddamn it, you know, this is *my* meeting, and I don't know who the hell they're talking about. Okay, so he's a great writer, can we get back to our meeting here?"

Later, Allison was at the Sundance screenwriters lab. Quentin had been there for the filmmakers lab six months earlier, and everyone was still talking about him. "They told me he's tall. So, okay, I'm expecting this really hard-edged, brilliant writer that's really macho and enormously tall. I was expecting, you know, Nick Ray, or John Sayles. Some very macho intimidating powerful monster."

At the film festival, Allison was having trouble meeting the other filmmakers, because there was no organized way to get them to socialize. "Eventually Quentin found me. But boy, I would never have known he was Quentin Tarantino if I hadn't looked at his name badge."

Like many of Quentin's friends, Allison does an excellent Quentin imitation, her voice high and rushed. *"Oh, hey, are you Allison Anders? Oh, hey, hey, I really like your movie."*

Allison thanked the fellow, but he wouldn't stop praising

her. *"Yeah, yeah, it was really neat. And you know, I really liked Border Radio too, I still have my ticket stub."*

Gee, this guy is such a film geek, thought Allison, "because it was very obscure to have seen *Border Radio.*"

At that point, Quentin pointed to his badge and announced with utter simplicity, "I'm Quentin!"

"I couldn't believe it!" says Allison. "That voice, I don't know how you describe it but it's so funny."

Quentin had noticed that in the background of a scene in Allison's movie, there was the *Charlie's Angels* board game, something that was in his home collection. He insisted she come over and play it with him, but it would be nearly a year before they met again. Allison was editing *Mi Vida Loca* and suffering from a broken heart. "I would edit in the morning, cry in the afternoon, edit in the morning, cry in the afternoon."

She called up her publicist, Bumble Ward, the take-charge Brit who also handled Quentin. Allison demanded that Bumble fix her up. "Well, lovely," chirped Bumble. "There's a party and a screening tonight."

It was a reception for Alexandre Rockwell's *In the Soup.* Alex had been at Sundance too but she hadn't met him there. "Anyway, I think I need a guy out of the business, a farmer or something," says Allison. Nevertheless, she went to the party and came away with Quentin.

At first she didn't realize it was a date. "Allison, we gotta go out! We gotta go out!" he said to her at the party.

"When are you free?" asked Allison.

"I'm free every night!"

They made a plan for Friday night. "I was joking about it, how it must be a date because it's on a Friday night, and when Friday came he was talking like really whispery on the phone, and I thought, damn, I guess this *is* a date. It kinda blew my mind."

Quentin and Allison had several things in common. Allison had been born in Ashland, Kentucky, in 1955, near enough to the kind of hillbilly sensibility Quentin was so fond of from the year he spent in Knoxville. She had father-figure problems; her father had deserted the family when she was five. Like Quentin, Allison left high school early, only she eventually returned to school and moved back to Kentucky, where she supported herself waitressing. After a traumatic childhood and difficult young adulthood, what saved her was attending UCLA film school and an enthusiastic correspondence with director Wim Wenders, who eventually gave her an assistant's job on *Paris, Texas*, thus launching her career.

On their first date, Quentin and Allison went out to dinner and, naturally, a movie—the Wesley Snipes action flick *Passenger 57*.

They returned to Quentin's apartment, where he gave Allison one of the strangest pick-up lines of all time: "Wanna come up and play the Mystery Date board game?"

Actually, Allison had wanted to play Mystery Date since she was seven years old. It's a game for girls, the object of which is to put together everything you need for a perfect date. There are cards for a date who will take you bowling, skiing, or to the beach, "and then there's, like, The Snazzy Guy is what I call him, he's going to take you to the prom, take you out for a really good time."

As you play the game, you collect the wardrobe for your date. So if you've collected the cards that make up an outfit for a beach date and you open the door in the middle of the board and find you have won a date with the Ski Guy, you have to keep playing, because the date isn't going to work out. "Now the big problem is if you get The Dud," says Allison. "He's the guy that's all disheveled, he looks all grunged out. Actually, he's the cutest guy, he's the one I would pick, a little like Lee Harvey Oswald. But if you open the middle door and you get The Dud, you have to forfeit your outfit and start all over."

Since the playing pieces are all female, Quentin chose The Blonde, and Allison was The Redhead. Quentin began putting together cards for his ski date. "And I was trying to get The Snazzy Guy. I've wanted The Snazzy Guy since I was a little girl, and I figured, tonight I'm going to get The Snazzy Guy. So I collected my evening wear, my little bag and gown and stuff, and then I opened the door and I got The Dud. And Quentin says, 'You know, Allison, I think this is telling you you've been going after the wrong type of guy.'"

They continued playing, only this time Allison put together the bowling outfit, and when she opened the door, there was The Bowling Guy. "I want you to take a good look at this guy, Allison," said Quentin in complete earnest. "'Cause he's nice, he's funny, and he's going to be there for you."

On another kind of date, maybe with The Snazzy Guy, this would have been the cue to hit the bedroom. Instead, Quentin and Allison played a round of the Mister T board game, and continued dating for another six weeks—without, Allison swears, ever having sex.

On the sixth week, Allison decided to get over her past heartbreak and make Quentin her boyfriend for real. She made elaborate plans to seduce him. "At dinner, I started realizing he could not be my boyfriend," she says. "We were sitting holding hands, and Quentin was talking about all the scenes that were no longer in *Reservoir Dogs*. And I had just been editing all day, and I was thinking, this guy could not be my boyfriend, because I'll never get away from my job. We'll be talking about film all the time. But, you know, a plan is a plan."

The meal ended, and Quentin asked Allison, "Do you want me to drive you home, or do you want to come back to my apartment and watch me alphabetize my videotapes?"

"No, I want to spend the night with you."

This led to the kind of elaborate discussion that kills off any possibility of romance. They never did sleep together, but remained good friends—such good friends that Quentin asked Allison to be one of four directors on a new project he had in mind after *Pulp Fiction*.

"I can tell you that he's a good kisser. A very good kisser," says Allison. "And that, yes, he talks about movies during the make-out session."

*   *   *

Asthmatics have a role model in the form of Martin Scorsese, who spent his asthmatic childhood in bed watching so many movies on television he just sort of inhaled cinema instead of air. When Alexandre Rockwell was a little boy—yes, his name is spelled the French way at his mother's insistence—his asthma made him weak. The weakness only fueled his desire to prove himself to the world through filmmaking.

Like many other filmmakers he knows, Alex is also dyslexic, another condition he secretly thanks. "I couldn't be a filmmaker if I weren't dyslexic," he says, only half joking. "It actually helps me to see things in a nonlinear way. It's one of life's little handicaps that make you develop a stronger muscle somewhere else."

Alex has a theory that many good filmmakers, Quentin included, turn inward to develop their imagination early in life when something externally isn't working for them—health, social skills, family situation, etc. "I wonder what it is in Quentin that drives him," says Alex. "He's gotten so much confidence in himself, he no longer needs what other people need—'computers, shmooters.' You should see his scripts, all chicken scratch. You can't read a damn word of them. His is literally the worst handwriting in the world."

Alex met Quentin at Sundance when Quentin was there with *Reservoir Dogs* and Alex was there with his second film, *In the Soup*, which starred Steve Buscemi, Seymour Cassell and Alex's wife, *Flashdance* actress Jennifer Beals. Alex had heard about Quentin earlier, because Steve Buscemi had told him about "this really weird guy, this hillbilly from Tennessee, and he's written this gangster movie with really great dialogue." Alex was intrigued by the name of the movie. "What the hell are reservoir dogs? I thought it was the coolest name."

They met at Quentin's very first Sundance screening, the one with the disastrous projection. "He was really nervous, and I thought he was an asshole because he was just this kind of arrogant puppy dog, if you can imagine it," says Alex. "But there was something weird about him that was very confident and kind of disturbing."

The jurors awarded Alex the Grand Jury Prize that year; Quentin went home empty-handed. "It was such a shock, because I thought that he should have won the Best Screenplay award for sure, because his movie was just so inventive." Instead, *The Waterdance* won for screenplay.

The shutout at Sundance was Quentin's first major career blow since his fortunes had changed, but instead of resenting Alex for taking home the big prize, he took him up on his offer to come stay at Alex's apartment in New York City. "There was this really touching moment, which shows the best of Quentin," says Alex. "We hardly knew each other and there was, you know, a competitive edge in the air over the prize. And I remember he was in the kitchen, and he came up to me and said, 'You know, Alex, about Sundance and everything, I'm really glad your film won the prize. I just want you to know I really dig you.' And then he dropped his head to the side, looked down, and wrapped his arms around me and hugged me. And he didn't just hug me quickly. We sat there in my kitchen—I think I had my underwear on, with a cup of coffee—and he held me in his arms for what seemed like minutes to me, but it was at least thirty seconds. And then I really got choked up, I got a lump in my throat. He was so vulnerable and so honest, and it was such a sweet thing for one filmmaker to say to another."

From that moment on, they were friends—which was a good thing, because Quentin stayed with Alex and Jenny for two weeks and drove them crazy. "He's the kind of guy who goes out and finds some retro store that sells old comic books and board games and then comes back with, like, four bags full of board games, and he drops them off in the back room. First of all, you don't want to go into the room he's staying in, cause it's like a pop/media bomb went off, with half-drunk Dr. Peppers, board games, full-sized John Travolta dolls. Quentin is intense."

Another aspect of Quentin to know before inviting him to live in your home is that he has boundless energy for staying up all night, talking to his hosts and making them watch movies. "About two in the morning he wants you to play the *Flintstones* board game, something like that, where Pebbles wipes out the car so you go back four steps to a rock jail or something. He's like that in his own apartment too; in that sense, he hasn't changed much except where he used to buy a few comic books, now he'll go down to Virgin Records and buy ten laserdiscs. If you go to his house now, it's like a college dorm, a total mess, with everything all over the floor, posters, things he's collected from all over the world. The more money he makes I think he'll just collect more and more stuff."

One of the ways Quentin has decorated his apartment is with a wall of wooden crates containing full Pepsi bottles. "He pulls one out every once in a while like a vintage wine. He'll watch you drink the thing, like you are appreciating this very rare Pepsi. That's what's so fun about him."

"You're the kind of audience that I'm going to get for this," Quentin said to fellow filmmaker Robert Rodriguez when he showed him the early stages of the script for *Pulp Fiction*. "This is a movie that a guy like you is going to think is really cool."

Robert and Quentin, who had met at the Toronto Film Festival in September 1992, had both graduated to the Sony Pictures lot—Robert to work on the sequel to his much-touted guerrilla action movie *El Mariachi*, Quentin to work on *Pulp Fiction* in the Jersey Films bungalow. "Anytime I walked around the lot I'd look through the window and I'd see Quentin there writing away, or looking at the ceiling, dreaming up more stuff. And I'd go in and he'd read scenes out—he wrote stuff that isn't even in the movie, the script was so thick—or we'd talk about movies and I'd show him storyboards, and I just hung out there with him and his producer Lawrence Bender. Sometimes it was late and we'd be the only ones on the lot, Quentin's light was the only one on. But it was a fun time. We'd go out to a movie or something. Then when TriStar passed on *Pulp Fiction* and he took it to Miramax, he was gone."

Robert visited the set of *Pulp Fiction* and told Quentin he'd like to work with him. "I was just kind of joking around, I knew they were way out of my league. And they called me and asked me to be the fourth 'room.' I thought, oh great, I'll be the one to fuck it up."

The project was *Four Rooms*, and there'd be four directors making individual segments. Originally, there were to be five directors, with Robert's colleague from Austin, Texas, Richard Linklater, as the possible fifth room. Eventually it was decided that five directors would make the film too long and unwieldy.

Robert felt insecure. He had made only one small feature for $7000, and it was in Spanish. He got right to work on his segment, but then he received an offer to do a piece for a Showtime series, so he cannibalized his *Four Rooms* script to make *Road Racers*, about two Mexicans, Dude and Donna, who are put up in a hotel room after something goes wrong with their apartment. They invite some friends over and wreck the place.

Now it was April 1994 and Robert's *Four Rooms* script was due, but the well was dry. "I was in the shower one day and I just decided, oh hell, I'll just do a kid's comedy like I did a long time ago with a short I made called *Bedhead*. I come from a family with ten kids, so we've got a million stories."

The four rooms of *Four Rooms* were to be directed by—in alphabetical order—Allison Anders, Alexandre Rockwell, Robert Rodriguez, and Quentin Tarantino. Each filmmaker would write and direct a segment, with linking material handled by Alex and Quentin, and it would all take place on New Year's Eve at the "Mon Signor Hotel," where in the good old days Tony Curtis "fucked a woman in every room."

The four filmmakers made a reservation at the Chateau Marmont, which was only appropriate. They would eat junk food all night while hashing out the continuity between their segments. "It was like a big pajama party or something," says Alex. "It was Quentin's fantasy night, you know, we all met in a room with videos and popcorn, whatever. We all sat and talked about the film and we all kinda told each other our basic outlines. And we concocted an order—we knew we had to do one after the other—and then we went off and wrote our stories and sent them to each other. And it was amazing when we got the script together, because it was remarkable how not one of the stories didn't fit, and how the sequences worked really perfectly."

Steve Buscemi was one of the first major actors Quentin had worked with; he had accompanied Quentin to the Sundance lab to work on scenes for *Reservoir Dogs*. Now Quentin had Steve in mind to play the bellhop Ted, the only character who would be a constant in each of the four "rooms." He tailored the role specifically to Steve's talents.

And therein lay the problem. Steve felt he had already done the ironic bellhop bit in the Coen brothers' *Barton Fink*. "I think Steve felt intimidated by it, and bothered a little bit by it because he felt that he'd done it before, and he was hesitant," says Alex. "With that hesitation, and with four directors, he sort of freaked out a bit. So we kinda switched to Tim Roth immediately and I think Steve may have some regrets about it. But we're all friends, I mean, we'll all work together again."

At first Quentin was miffed by the rejection, but he put that aside when he found a willing bellhop in Tim. "It was something I'd never done before, a very physical comedy," says Tim. "Because it has a bellboy's uniform I'm sure it will be compared to Jerry Lewis, but it's kinda different. It was weird and fun for me, the idea of getting up in the morning and trying to be funny. I wouldn't want to do it all my life. It's very risky. Although there are four different segments with four different directors, I have to remain consistent to a certain extent throughout the whole story so that it links them together and makes a complete film."

The casting change caused a minor problem for Allison, who had inserted references to Buscemi's Mr. Pink character of *Reservoir Dogs*. Alex rewrote some of his section to reflect Tim's British accent. "I think we all kind of incorporated that, although we didn't change the character's personality much," says Alex. "And then the wraparound came after we all got our four stories together. We were impressed by how they flowed pretty well together, but there were just a few little things that we needed to add. Quentin and I wrote the wraparound, I got like 50 percent of it, he got 50 percent of it. I think it's pretty obvious which parts he wrote and which parts I wrote. He put in one or two monologues that are pretty amazing." Producer Lawrence Bender has a cameo in one of the wraparound sections, in which he orders ice but winds up sending the bellhop to the wrong room.

As the movie opens, it's Ted the bellhop's first night on the job, and he's being broken in by an old-timer, played by Mark Lawrence. "We were actually going to get Lawrence Tierney," says Alex of the actor who played the ringleader in *Reservoir Dogs*, "but he's too impossible to work with. So Quentin found Mark down in Key Largo, he has this great old film noir face. Quentin's great at finding people like that. He'll go back to the annals of crime to find somebody to play a part."

Ted is left alone on the job his first night and gets sucked into Allison's segment, "Strange Brew," which takes place in room 309. This segment is about a meeting of witches who intend to restore their goddess Diana to life with a brew. The only ingredient missing is a man's fresh sperm, so the witches ring for the bellhop to provide this special service.

The witches are played by Valeria Golino, Lili Taylor, Sammi Davis, Ione Skye, Alicia Witt, Amanda de Cadenet, and Madonna.

In the old days of the studio system, each studio "owned" a stable of stars who they could mix and match on any of their pictures. The equivalent today is when several stars are handled by the same high-powered agent, who can negotiate a multiactor deal. Then there's Miramax, which has a paternalistic relationship with many of its actors. Harvey Weinstein had fought to get Daniel Day-Lewis, his *My Left Foot* star, into *Pulp Fiction* in the John Travolta role. He lost that round, but when it came time for *Four Rooms*, he hooked up Allison Anders with

Madonna, who cameos in Miramax's *Blue in the Face* delivering a singing telegram.

"I was completely thrilled, because I had wanted to work with her for years, before I was even a filmmaker," says Allison, who first bonded with Madonna at a Miramax party where they found out they shared the same intense dislike of a popular British actor. Allison was not daunted by Madonna's track record on film, where the only time she got unanimously good reviews was for her first major movie, *Desperately Seeking Susan*.

"I think she's best with women directors," says Allison. *Desperately Seeking Susan* had been directed by Susan Seidelman, and the only other movie where Madonna did relatively well was in the ensemble piece *A League of Their Own*, directed by Penny Marshall. "I think male directors are intimidated by her. Or intoxicated with her. Maybe she uses another part of her personality with them. I don't know what it is, but I think she does really well with women. Even my daughter was just knocked out by Madonna's performance, and she's such a cynical little shit that I raised. My daughter is twenty and hates everything, she's from that generation where everything sucks and everything's bad. But she was knocked out by Madonna."

Madonna plays the witch who is second in power to Valeria Golino, the high priestess (Ione Skye has the task of retrieving the bodily fluids). "She's funny and she's very clear, and she takes the piss out of her own image," says Allison. "And not only that, she was enormously professional."

In one scene, Madonna and Valeria have an argument over whether Madonna's friend can stay in the room, and Valeria has to suck in her cheeks and spit in Madonna's face. "It was just air that she was doing in the scene, with the understanding that I was going to add fire to it later in postproduction, but they were both so incredible. Madonna protects her face and I didn't direct any of that. It's a brilliant match that they did with all this energy."

Allison had rented *Dangerous Game* and *Body of Evidence* to see how Madonna had been in other movies. "I figured *Body of*

Evidence was probably as bad as it was going to get. But she wasn't lit well. A lot of cinematographers light for art and for men, they like shadows and they don't light for a woman's face or for a woman's body. They don't know how to light women. And don't seem to really care. Because they're afraid that it's going to look flat and uninteresting to enhance a woman's aura. I really think there's a different kind of aura that men and women have and that very few cinematographers are in touch with."

Each segment had its own crew; Allison used Rodrigo Garcia, who had shot *Mi Vida Loca*. "He will sacrifice arty lighting any time for warmth and for bringing out a woman's face."

Allison's script called for the women to take their shirts off, but in the end, only Sammi and Ione went topless for the camera. "The thing with me is that women's bodies have been so abused on the screen that I just can't justify making an actress take her clothes off, I can't do it," says Allison. "So when an actress said she didn't want to do it, I was fine. The trick was to see if it was still going to look natural with just a couple of them doing it."

It would certainly seem natural that Madonna, never one to be shy, would be topless as well. In fact, Madonna worried that it would look funny if only a few of them stayed buttoned up. Allison told her that Valeria was going to show her back for the first time on screen; Valeria had suffered as a child from scoliosis, curvature of the spine, and she has a scar.

"That's really cool, maybe I could show you something different," offered Madonna, to which Allison replied something along the lines of what Rosie O'Donnell told her in *A League of Their Own*: "You think there are men in this country who ain't seen your bosoms?"

When the time came to shoot, however, Madonna showed up in a black rubber dress and wouldn't remove it. "I just don't feel right about it, it's just not going to work," she told Allison. "It's not about you, it's about who I am, and what people expect of me."

Once Allison saw the dailies, she agreed. "If she had been topless I think it would have been a big deal, I think it would have been like, there's Madonna topless," says Allison. "It turned out looking just right, two of them topless, and Valeria with a tattoo on the scar down her back. And Lili is like a little cave child, so you never stop and wonder why she isn't taking her shirt off."

The second segment was originally called "Two Sides to a Plate," but when Alex dropped a line from the script, he changed the title to "There's No One Here but Us Chickens" for that Three Stooges feel: "You almost think you're going to hear Curly saying it."

In this segment, taking place in room 404, Ted walks into "this crazy beehive, where a husband mistakes him for the lover of his wife, and he's got his wife tied up in a chair," says Alex, who cast his real-life wife, Jennifer Beals, as the woman in ropes. "The bellhop comes bouncing in because he's got the wrong room, and the guy puts a gun to his head, turns on the light and he's held hostage for about twenty minutes. And they go through this entire crazy loop-de-loop. At the end of the story they're like embracing, looking out a window, talking about the nature of love."

The "nutty, crazy husband" is played by David Proval, the actor from *Mean Streets*. The man Ted is mistaken for, named Theodore, is played by a friend of Tim Roth's named Paul Skemp; he and Tim look remarkably alike, which is one of the jokes in the segment.

The third segment is Robert's "The Misbehavers," taking place in room 716. Spanish heartthrob Antonio Banderas and the Chinese-American Tamlyn Tomita (*The Joy Luck Club*) play parents who pay Ted $500 to babysit their two kids while they go out to a party. As soon as the parents leave and Ted goes back down to the reception desk, the kids tear the place apart, set it on fire and discover a dead body. Ted has just found the place in a shambles when the parents return.

"Everyone thought it was a really funny idea, but how was I going to shoot it because kids like these don't exist," says Robert. "You can't find child actors who can pull off this stuff. The kids would have had to be almost robots in order to do it.

But I found some really good kids, I told the casting department to just bring me ethnic kids. I have a little Asian girl, Lana McKissick, age nine, and a little Hispanic boy, Danny Verduzco, age six. He's actually the little brother of the boy I used in *Desperado*. And he was really funny."

Antonio Banderas had just finished starring in *Desperado*, and he and Robert were tired. "We had just spent seven weeks doing like sixty camera setups a day, he was all beat up, and we literally walked off that set and onto *Four Rooms*," says Robert. "He didn't want to do it because he was so tired, but I told him I'd cram all this shooting into three days, get them in and out, and then as soon as he put on the wardrobe and he was into it, he didn't want to leave after that. We were really in the groove. Alex before us had been doing a different pace, getting maybe five shots a day, and we came in and we got forty-five shots the first day. We had the kids, so we couldn't work long hours, so we'd shoot half the amount of time and get twenty times the number of shots done. We moved really fast, cause the movie's really fast and frenetic. So it was very frantic filmmaking. And with the kids, it was just a blast. We got it done on time, under schedule, under budget, and it came out really good."

Robert's section gets so frenetic that by the end of it, there's a cut every second. Then Quentin's section begins, and Quentin is known for dramatically long takes, giving actors time to perform whole monologues.

"His first take is seven minutes long," says Robert in wonderment. "His second cut is like an eight-minute take. There are no cuts at all, until the end when it gets really funny. But it's just cool seeing these segments back to back like that, because the styles are so completely different. He does stuff that would just drive me crazy. I tell him, man, you've got balls to shoot it this way. I'm such a pack rat, you know. I love being part of the actor's performance in a way, since I edit my own films, and the timing and stuff comes off through a lot of cuts. I can make a really good soup out of just cutting it all together. Whereas Quentin will do a whole five-minute sequence in one take and use only that one take, which means some lines were better in other takes. He says he goes for the overall performance in a take. He is more dependent on the actors creating their own timing and pace and rhythm, where I manipulate that quite a bit. I make movies for people like me who feel they don't have time to watch movies—just get me in and out as quick as you can. The editing gets so fast after a while it turns into subliminal moviemaking."

Quentin's segment, "The Thrill of the Bet," takes place in the penthouse. Quentin himself plays Chester Rush, who has only made one good movie, *The Wacky Detective*.

"It's interesting that Quentin plays the lead," says Alex. "It's about a guy who suddenly becomes famous with a hit movie and it's kind of autobiographical that way. And I think that's kind of moving. People who don't know Quentin will think it's just some big movie star who's kind of full of himself. But if you know him, you can see a vulnerability in it because it's about a guy who has the number-one movie in America and he's got all of his cronies hanging around him, and he's bossing them around."

Chester and the cronies order up a bucket of ice and some strange implements and then convince the bellhop to help settle a wager they've copied from a Peter Lorre–Steve McQueen episode of the old Alfred Hitchcock TV series. The wager stakes Quentin's beloved car against a portion of Paul Calderon's anatomy, bringing to mind the ear scene of *Reservoir Dogs*.

Bruce Willis joins the ensemble cast in Quentin's "room" to play Chester's manager. "It's a pretty weird film," says Bruce, who adds that he did this role as a favor to Quentin.

"All the segments turned out to be comedies," says Robert. "We didn't what know what we were doing when we first started. I was afraid we'd all do gangster things, and everyone would get blown up, and we'd tear the whole place down. I thought somebody's gotta get shot. And we ended up making like a Peter Sellers movie, it's really bizarre how it came together, a Jerry Lewis, Peter Sellers kinda flick. It's strange and it just happened as we were doing it, we didn't realize what we were making until it was done."

Four Rooms wrapped right before Christmas 1994, and was edited and tinkered with through March 1995. The segments were shot in the order in which they would appear, "which I think was very helpful for Tim Roth, because Tim was able to chart his arc as an actor," says Alex.

It's the first time Quentin has worked with creating a score from scratch instead of securing the rights to songs he likes; Allison convinced him of the logic of this and brought in the band Combustible Edison. "Lawrence Bender said Quentin would never use a score, because what if he wound up not liking it, or was unable to control it," says Allison. "But eventually he's going to need to work with scores. If he does a World War II picture, you know, which he's talked about doing, or a western, he's going to have to work with a score. So I told him here's a safe place to try it out. Quentin finally says, 'Okay, Anders, I'm going to say yes, but you know, I really think there's a boy involved somehow in this,' like that I was hot for one of the guys in the band."

Harvey Weinstein of Miramax remained a constant source of input, particularly in matters of casting. Certainly there were fights—Harvey was pushing Alec Baldwin for the David Probal role—but the screaming and cursing matches usually broke down into laughter at the end, because the heated tone couldn't sustain itself. "He'd tell me I was going to be an insignificant art film director for the rest of my life," says Alex, "and I'd tell him all he wants is to make commercial decisions and interfere, and then we'd start cracking up. It made me miss New York, because in Hollywood, no one is ever honest with what they have to say."

There was more to the success of the film than what was taking place on the set. At the William Morris Agency, Mike Simpson was finding new ways to construct Quentin's deal, which is an art unto itself. "In some cases we can make something rich on the front end," he says, meaning keeping preliminary costs down in anticipation of profits on the back end, after the movie is out there making money. "I can't tell you how risky it was to make this. Anthology films are tricky in the marketplace. So Quentin and I felt that the studio's exposure needed to be kept to a raw minimum. So I can't even tell you how cheap we made this"—he figures half of the $8 million it cost to make *Pulp Fiction*. "On the other hand, from the very first moment of earnings, everyone becomes a partner."

The plan was to ship out *Four Rooms* on the first gondola to the Venice Film Festival in September 1995, and based on how it played there, to open it either in the fall or even on New Year's Eve itself. Meanwhile, it was rejected by the selection committee of the New York Film Festival.

"People were saying we're supposed to be the new blood or something," says Robert. "So we thought we'd make this together. And we thought we'd hate each other afterwards, but we didn't. Everyone was different and we had to support each other's different styles, and it becomes less competitive when you're friends. I think it was kind of strange in that in the seventies, you had filmmakers who were coming from film school. And I look at Alex and Quentin and Allison and I'm sitting there, we couldn't afford film school. We couldn't get into film school. We were coming from different kinds of struggling families. I never thought I'd get into the business, simply because I lived in Texas and I didn't know anybody, I didn't have contacts. But it turns out you can get there if you just show people your film and they like it; that's what happened with all of us. We just concentrated on the work, and people found us. So it's kinda cool hanging out with people that just kinda made their own position in life through luck and perseverance and hard work. And we can offer stuff that you don't usually see coming out of film schools, cause we didn't learn how to do it by listening to someone else, but by watching movies and coming up with our own plans and ideas. And to see us get this kind of acceptance, even when your movie is bizarre and comes from left field, you can sleep good at night knowing that."

CHAPTER 14

Destiny

I think you're gonna find, when all this shit is over and done, I think you're gonna find yourself one smilin' motherfucker. Thing is, right now you got ability. But your days are about over. See, painful as it may be, ability don't last. Now that's a hard motherfuckin' fact of life, but it's a fact of life your ass is gonna hafta git realistic about. This business is filled to the brim with unrealistic motherfuckers who thought their ass aged like wine.

—Pulp Fiction, *1994*

After *Four Rooms*, Quentin announced he would be taking a year off—a smart move, considering that usually following so much hype comes a media backlash. As Tim Roth says of Quentin, "He deals with fame by being thrilled, a sort of glee, an innocent pleasure. I just hope he can stand it when the press starts looking for signs of weakness. They'll be looking to kill him."

The year off was to have consisted of lying on the couch watching videos, *Baywatch* and TV talk shows on his big-screen Panasonic, learning another language ("perhaps Japanese," says his assistant Victoria), and hanging out with friends.

Halfway into this "year off," Quentin had made an appearance satirizing *Pulp Fiction* (and doing a great Christopher Walken impersonation) on the TV show *All-American Girl,* directed the season finale of the popular medical drama *ER,* and starred in the quasi-mystical romantic comedy *Destiny Turns on the Radio* as Destiny himself, toasting marshmallows with space heaters around the pool for the cast and crew. He made cameos in Alex Rockwell's *Somebody to Love* as a bartender and in Robert Rodriguez's *Desperado* as a drug mule, agreed to produce *Button Man* for Alex, agreed to star in the romantic film noir *Hands Up!* as a low-life bootlegger who falls in love with a French woman involved in the S & M scene. He nearly executive-produced *Halloween 6* with his friend Scotty Spiegel as director, but the deal fell through. He did an uncredited rewrite on director Tony Scott's megabudget submarine drama *Crimson Tide,* what Tony calls "*The Caine Mutiny* on a nuclear sub," offsetting the technical gadgetry of the movie with his trademark dialogue and three-dimensional characterizations, adding what he calls "a human heart."

"You can tell which is my stuff," says Quentin. "It was the shit about the comic books and the *Star Trek* bathroom humor. Steve Zaillian rewrote a scene and his was the humanistic stuff, Robert Towne's was the political stuff, and Scott Rosenberg writes the best Guys Looking for Chicks dialogue."

He did another uncredited rewrite, as a favor to his *Saturday Night Live* pal Julia Sweeney, on *It's Pat,* which he courteously describes as "a cool movie, really funny, but there's nothing of me in it." The movie made the astonishingly low sum of $52,000 at the box office before going on to video hell; Quentin says only one of his jokes remains in the screenplay.

Also during this "year off," he embarked on a stint as a distributor of films through Miramax with the Hong Kong movie

Chungking Express. Like an indulgent parent, Harvey Weinstein has given Quentin his own distribution arm, tentatively titled "Rolling Thunder" (after the Vietnam vet movie where William Devane's hand is ground up in a kitchen sink's garbage disposal), through which he can choose four movies a year. Miramax will do the work, Quentin will lend his name and help with publicity, and some of the profits may go to film preservation, a subject Quentin cares deeply about. This arrangement seems less for profit than prestige, and as a handy tool for keeping Quentin happy with Miramax. "I don't think this is going to be a highly profitable venture, to say the least," says Harvey. "This is just a way of getting certain filmmakers across who would otherwise remain undiscovered."

Another thing Miramax did was to buy Quentin the rights to four novels he wanted. There is poetic justice in the fact that the books are by Elmore Leonard, the writer whose work led to Quentin being busted for shoplifting when he was fifteen.

Of the titles—*Killshot*, *Bandits*, *Rum Punch* and *Freaky Deaky*—it is most likely that Bruce Willis will produce *Bandits* for himself, and Quentin will direct and star in *Killshot*. He'll play one of two psychopaths who terrorize a couple, who will probably be played by Bruce and Holly Hunter.

"Quentin almost epitomizes the kind of thing that Miramax is," says Harvey with pride. "He's working class, we're working class. Yet he's got encyclopedic knowledge of films. I think his appeal is that people can see him, and they smell who's real and who's not. And what makes the difference between him and, say, Steven Spielberg or Bob Zemeckis, is that he's an actor, too. So people can say, 'There's the guy who wrote and directed the movie.' Quentin carries himself like an actor, he dresses the part with that skinny tie and the *Dogs* look. So the persona has grown. And he's so enthusiastic, there's the likability factor, it all combines and becomes this great personality."

Tony Scott calls him "the Michelangelo of the nineties," and *New York Times* critic Janet Maslin calls his work "the future, filmmaking reinvented from the ground up, with energy free of gimmicks and a bravado startlingly attuned to our dangerous world."

Quentin is so popular that his name has been banned from the computer chat lines of America Online. Tim Roth says he's tapped into "a sort of hipness which he's invented himself." What could be hipper than having been thanked in the liner notes for *In Utero* by the late Kurt Cobain?

Producer Pete McAlevey says Quentin has "the hippest take on black-white relations today, from the view of the white underclass." William Morris agent Mike Simpson says that his client's ability to have clear goals while maintaining flexibility has allowed Mike to make the most creative deals of his career.

If the backlash has begun, it's been minor so far. Quentin was hurt to the quick when emcee John Larroquette referred to him as "Jughead" at the Golden Globe awards. "It totally hurt my feelings," he says. "Am I a joke, am I just too goofy, you know? I thought people liked me."

Movieline magazine mentioned Quentin twice in their "100 dumbest things Hollywood's done lately" in May 1995, citing Quentin telling people at the Golden Globes that John Travolta's "was the best shooting-up scene in the history of motion pictures." Number 11 on their list: "Screenwriter-director Quentin Tarantino, who has proven he has almost no screen presence, is now devoting a large portion of his time to acting in films."

But Quentin is still treated as a rock god, especially in Europe and Japan. "Each of these countries has their own type of crime film," theorizes Quentin. "In Japan they have the yakuza movies, in Hong Kong they have the Triad gangster flicks, the French have the Jean-Pierre Melville *policiers,* and Italy has been doing these Mafia movies, with like Martin Balsam or Jack Palance. And I'm actually influenced by all of them. And I take those different styles and put them into my movies, so in Japan, you could totally watch *Reservoir Dogs* like a yakuza film. I mean, it could be a yakuza film tomorrow if they just did it in Japanese."

Allison Anders remembers going on LoveLines on

Valentine's Day with Quentin and with Simon Le Bon and Nick Rhodes of Duran Duran; it's a radio show where people ask celebrity couples love-life questions. Afterward, Simon and Nick were swamped by autograph hounds in the parking lot. "Simon had spaced out and looked off in the distance," says Allison, and Quentin asked him what he was doing.

"If I start getting overwhelmed, I look above the crowd and imagine that my body is being drenched in blue paint," said Simon.

"I saw Quentin storing that away for further use," says Allison. A year later in Japan when the girls were all screaming for him, "Quentin would do the same thing. I don't know if he imagines the blue paint, but the thing is, he knew he'd be famous, and he was preparing."

Even if the press turns on him, Quentin's movies seem to welcome the masses to come in and play with him. "He invites you in to hang out, to play board games and records and do the twist," says Allison. "He invites you into this world in a way that no other filmmaker does, in a way that is usually reserved completely for some rock subculture."

Epilogue

*There just ain't time to get tired. Big things are happenin'
tonight. I know 'cause I'm psychic about stuff like that. You
can't escape it. It's in the cards, and there's nothing you can do
about it . . . Hey, it's my best friend's birthday, and I promise
you before the sun rises, I'll show you a wild time.*
>—Clarence in My Best Friend's Birthday,
>screenplay by Quentin Tarantino and Craig
>Hamann, early draft

Before sunrise on the morning of Valentine's Day, 1995, Arthur
Hiller, president of the Motion Picture Academy of Arts and
Sciences, announced the year's Oscar candidates. In the film
world, this is known as the second most important day of the
year—the first being the actual night of the ceremony.

Miramax came away the morning's big winner, with
twenty-two nominations, far more than any of the major studios. Seven of those nominations were for *Pulp Fiction*.

The movie was nominated for Picture, Director, Actor (John Travolta), Supporting Actress (Uma Thurman), Supporting Actor (Samuel L. Jackson), Original Screenplay, and Editing (Sally Menke). Although Roger Avary had been shut out of some of the other critics' awards—Quentin had won for screenplay at the Golden Globes and not even mentioned Roger in his tipsy acceptance speech, leading Roger's wife, Gretchen, to curse him out in front of the revelers—the Academy had paired Roger and Quentin in that category.

Richard Gladstein pointed out that it was Quentin's special way of creating characters that accounted for Travolta's nomination. "He plays a guy who shoots up heroin, punches a knife through someone's heart, shoots someone's face off. He gets killed in the middle of the movie right after taking a shit, and he's able to get nominated for the best actor of the year."

Sam Jackson pretty much figured he'd be nominated, the way the buzz was going. "I'll be there, you know, sneering when they call Martin Landau's name," he said presciently.

The nominations were in accordance with a letter that producer Lawrence Bender had sent to the 1269 actors who voted for the acting nominations. The letter dictated the "correct placement of our ensemble of performers," using the reasoning that as Travolta's character links the story lines, he was eligible for Best Actor, while Jackson, Willis and Thurman were to be considered in the supporting categories. Of those pushed by Lawrence and Miramax for nominations, only Bruce Willis was left out in the cold.

For the next month and a half, the gears really started turning, because in a world populated by lobbyists, publicists and lawyers, winning an Oscar is not left to chance.

The chief rival to *Pulp Fiction* was *Forrest Gump*, an immensely popular movie by Robert Zemeckis that had grossed more than $300 million and touched a feel-good nerve in the heartland of America. *Pulp Fiction*, on the other hand, had a youthful exuberance and hipness that didn't always play to older, more conservative audiences, the kind that make up the voting membership of the Academy. "It seems like that old faction that everyone talks about is kind of dying off," said Quentin, perhaps a bit prematurely.

At first, there was a debate about whether to send out screener tapes to the voters; *Pulp* wouldn't necessarily shine under those circumstances. *The Hollywood Reporter* ran a story claiming it was Quentin's hubris that kept screeners from going out. Within days of that story, Miramax announced that screeners would indeed be shipped, although they neglected to mention that they had manually turned the volume down every time there was gunplay.

Then Miramax consigned Thomas Schatz, a professor at the University of Texas at Austin, to write an essay linking *Pulp* to its roots in forties film noir. The essay was to be the cornerstone of a slick black-and-white booklet sent to Academy voters, designed to help them plug *Pulp* into the grander tradition of cinema and assuage the sensitive among them about Quentin's use of violence and the vernacular. In short, it was a *Pulp* primer for those who just didn't get it, an attempt to make the movie seem more serious to those who saw the pop-culture references as artificial and gimmicky.

Harvey Weinstein of Miramax leaned on Quentin to go on the stump, as if he were running for office. "There's a hundred million things to do," said Harvey of the Oscar campaign. "I sent him to the Directors Guild Awards dinner, I sent him everywhere." The point was that Quentin would seem accessible, not dangerous, not like a Hollywood outsider. "Quentin is very good about that, he goes, he's active, he's proactive, he's a great cheerleader for his cast and for the movie. He goes to John's functions, Sam's functions, Uma's things, Sally's things; he's there for each of them."

An Oscar win in the Best Picture category would mean a lot to Harvey. "I've been a bridesmaid too long," he says, "from *My Left Foot* to *The Crying Game* to *The Piano*. I'm always going against the huge Hollywood establishment, and this time it's no different, you have Bob Zemeckis and Tom Hanks [of *Forrest*

Gump], who could both be mayor of Beverly Hills. I'm not deni-
grating their talents, 'cause I think they're great. But when
you're an outsider, you can't just show up and win, you have to
get to the inside, which means attending a lot of events, partici-
pating, just to show that there's a spirit, that we care about
movies, we care about the Academy."

Harvey figures the Oscar campaign on *Pulp Fiction* wound
up costing Miramax between $300,000 and $400,000, as compared
to perhaps the million dollars spent by Paramount for *Gump*.

"Believe me, I've always been Mr. Kick the Academy and
everything because I never agreed with a lot of the stuff that
they chose," said Quentin as he tried out his new team-player
image. "But lately it's actually been a little different. I mean, I
really loved *Unforgiven,* you know, and *Silence of the Lambs*."

To back him up, Miramax publicist Cynthia Swartz reeled
off a list of what she calls "edged" movies the Academy had
gone for in the past, including *In the Heat of the Night, Midnight
Cowboy* and *The French Connection*. "People forget this stuff, but
A Clockwork Orange was nominated for Best Picture. Z was nominated for Best Picture, and that's pretty amazing. *Pulp Fiction*
requires special handling, but my point is, it's not impossible. I
mean, it's certainly the best-reviewed film of the year and the
most honored film. It's doing something exciting for cinema. I
have this really eggheaded theory that it's like the ultimate
postmodern movie, because it takes fifty years of film and pop-
culture history and synthesizes it into something new."

The important thing was not to scare voters away. "We're
just presenting a case, reminding the voters about the movie's
themes of redemption, which is a real classic theme out of film
noir and gangster movies," says Cynthia. "It's not nihilistic."

There were hopeful signs along the way. Quentin and com-
pany had already swept the major critics' awards. He won best
picture, director, screenplay and actor (Travolta) from the L.A.
Film Critics. He won picture, director and screenplay from the
National Society of Film Critics. He won screenplay at the
Golden Globes. He sent Harvey Keitel to pick up his awards at

the National Board of Review, where *Pulp* and *Gump* tied. "Quentin asked me to do this for him," said Harvey at the podium, getting a laugh. "It wasn't so long ago I was asking him to do things for me."

The New York Film Critics Circle experienced the closest shave. Although Quentin handily won for director and screenplay, *Quiz Show* came up from behind after the first few ballots and edged out *Pulp Fiction* by a single point, which represents one-sixth of one critic's vote. The NYFCC was one of the few organizations to acknowledge Roger Avary's contribution as co-screenwriter, but the Golden Globes ceremony had taken place the night before in L.A., and Roger elected to stay behind, not realizing that the Golden Globes hadn't put his name on the ballot.

At the NYFCC Awards dinner, a private affair at the Rainbow Room overlooking midtown Manhattan, Uma practically wept as she handed Quentin his directing award. "Honor me like a dead man," he had told her before she got up to the podium.

"That would be deceitful," she said. "Because I think one of the reasons that we all love and respond to you like we do is because you offer so much life. And you certainly offered it back to me, things I thought I didn't have anymore. Trust and safety and care, and I appreciate it."

When accepting his screenplay award, Quentin flattered the critics, saying he reads all his reviews and would have been a film critic himself in a different life. He also pointedly repeated how he had incorporated Roger's material into *Pulp Fiction* to make it his own, since the Roger Avary Credit Thing had been picking up steam in the press.

On March 24, three nights before the Oscars, as *Pulp Fiction* was hitting the $94 million mark at box offices across the country, Quentin again cleaned up at the Independent Spirit Awards, where he won film, director, screenplay, and actor (Jackson). Finally, Roger Avary was invited to the podium to get his due in the screenplay category, and gave a hint of inappropriate acceptance speeches to come when he accepted his award by complaining that it was "too big to stick up my ass." This portion, naturally, was not broadcast on the Bravo Channel when it aired during the Oscar's commercial breaks the following Monday night.

The only setbacks were the Directors Guild Awards, which honored Robert Zemeckis for *Gump* and were usually a reliable indicator of how the Academy would vote, and the Writers Guild of America award to the screenplay of *Four Weddings and a Funeral*. Quentin is not a WGA signatory, so he was not eligible for that award anyway; nevertheless, it rocked the confidence of those around him, who all seemed to have more at stake in this Oscar than the casually noncommital Quentin.

On Oscar night, March 27, 1995, Connie Zastoupil was taken by limo to a special party in her honor at a salon in Georgetown, Washington, D.C., where celebrities and camera crews awaited. She wasn't happy about being so closely scrutinized by the media, just in case her son didn't win anything, but it was certainly a proud moment for her—not only because Quentin was a self-made man the way she was a self-made woman, but because tonight was her son's thirty-second birthday, and he had exceeded all her expectations in record time.

Meanwhile, in the Shrine Auditorium in Los Angeles, the three-and-a-half-hour ceremony had begun. The women were all clad in slinky gowns. The men were all in tuxes and either bow ties or band collars—except for Quentin, who wore a skinny black *Reservoir Dogs* tie.

That night, John Travolta lost to Tom Hanks for *Forrest Gump*, Uma Thurman lost to Dianne Wiest for *Bullets Over Broadway*, Samuel L. Jackson lost to Martin Landau for *Ed Wood*, Sally Menke lost the editing award to *Gump*, Quentin lost to director Robert Zemeckis, and *Pulp Fiction* lost, as expected, to *Forrest Gump*.

But Quentin and Roger Avary won the screenplay award, and when Anthony Hopkins announced their names, the two friends jumped up and ran to the stage from different sides of the auditorium, meeting halfway to the podium in a bear hug as the orchestra played "Misirlou," the energized opening theme of *Pulp Fiction*.

Quentin, naturally, took the mike first, with a nervous Roger clearly afraid that his former best friend would hog their acceptance-speech time limit. "Uh, thanks!" said Quentin, as if he'd been handed a fresh bowl of Cap'n Crunch. "Uh, this has been a very strange year. I can definitely say that. Uh, you know what? I was trying to think . . . I think this is the only award I'm going to win here tonight, so I was trying to think, maybe I should say a whole lot of stuff, *right here right now, just get it out of my system*, you know, all year long, everything roiling up, and everything, *just blow it all, just tonight, just say everything*!" He paused while Roger shook his long blond tresses in discouragement. "But I'm not," said Quentin. "Thanks."

It was perhaps Quentin's least effective monologue, but it was exuberant, and in any case wasn't as tasteless as what Roger had to say next. "I want to thank my beautiful wife, Gretchen, who I love more than anything in the world," said Roger, stumbling over the pronunciation of his wife's name. "And I really have to take a pee right now so I'm gonna go. Thank you."

Chasen's was a perfect choice for the Miramax post-Oscar bash. It marked the venerable Old Hollywood eating establishment's last night on earth before being razed for a shopping mall. Out with the old, in with the new.

The Chasen's party was hotter even than the one at Drai's for *Forrest Gump* or at Mortons, where *Vanity Fair* fed and watered the town's A-list. The place was so packed inside and out there were fire marshals guarding the entrance. The Oscar sitting on the table in the center of Quentin's circular red-leather booth was echoed at other tables, where other winners held forth. To make your way to where they were serving the last of the famous Chasen's chili you had to elbow aside Robert

De Niro, Christopher Walken, Hugh Grant, Gabriel Byrne, Ellen Barkin, Jodie Foster, Jessica Lange, Uma Thurman, and George Clooney, the heartthrob of TV's smash *ER* series, who was slated to co-star opposite Quentin in *From Dusk Till Dawn*. Even the most careful guest accidentally bumped into Sigourney Weaver's huge bustle or stepped on her train. A beaming Quentin no longer had to work so hard at masking his former video-geek persona; he was surrounded by gushing female admirers. "This place is a fucking feeding frenzy," one producer proclaimed as he surveyed the scene.

Perhaps the biggest loser of the night was John Travolta, although you'd never know it from the happy, expansive way he puffed on his stogie. His creative, incentive-oriented $5 million *Get Shorty* contract promised him an additional $750,000 if he won a *Pulp* Oscar. The blow was eased by the fact that he had already received $750,000 just for being nominated.

The night after the Oscars, Quentin invited a bunch of his old pals from Video Archives out to the movies to see *For a Few Dollars More*, the 1966 Clint Eastwood spaghetti western that is often on his All-Time Top 10 list. Grace Lovelace and her sister Laura were there, as were Jerry Martinez, Russ Vossler and the Two Reds. Lance Lawson, the mysterious proprietor of the failed Video Archives, couldn't make it because he claimed he had to stay home and dub a videotape.

Afterward, Quentin invited everyone back to the Beverly Hills hotel suite Miramax had reserved for him, a place where he could unwind in the days following the ceremony. They had provided him with a birthday cake and bottles of Dom Perignon. The golden statuette for Best Original Screenplay sat on the bureau. The discussion ranged from the minutiae of *For a Few Dollars More* to a possible future outing to the Indiana Jones ride at Disneyland.

The gang tried studiously not to discuss the Oscar and its implications, not wanting to seem like they were sucking up to the guy they had once worked with behind the video store counter, the guy they had to bail out of jail for parking tickets. Yet each one in turn picked up the statue and held it, feeling as if some small part of it was theirs. A warm glow suffused them. It was, after all, their best friend's birthday.